4.95

D1288589

Studies in Modern Chemistry

Advanced courses in chemistry are changing rapidly in both structure and content. The changes have led to a demand for up-to-date books that present recent developments clearly and concisely. This series is meant to provide advanced students with books that will bridge the gap between the standard textbook and the research paper. The books should also be useful to a chemist who requires a survey of current work outside his own field of research. Mathematical treatment has been kept as simple as is consistent with clear understanding of the subject.
Careful selection of authors actively engaged in research in each field, together with the guidance of four experienced editors, has ensured that each book ideally suits the needs of persons seeking a comprehensible and modern treatment of rapidly developing areas of chemistry.

William C. Agosta, The Rockefeller University
R. S. Nyholm, FRS, University College London

Consulting Editors

Academic editor for this volume

T. C. Waddington, University of Warwick

Studies in Modern Chemistry

Coordination compounds

S. F. A. Kettle
University of Sheffield

APPLETON-CENTURY-CROFTS
EDUCATIONAL DIVISION
New York   MEREDITH CORPORATION

Appleton-Century-Crofts
Educational Division
Meredith Corporation
440 Park Avenue South
New York, N.Y. 10016

Printed in Great Britain

Contents

41609

Appendices

Preface

This book is largely devoted to the chemistry of coordination compounds formed by the transition metal ions. However, there are many points at which the discussion applies equally to complexes formed by non-transition elements and so these are also included. Organometallic compounds and complexes in which the central atom exhibits a low valence state are excluded, as they will be dealt with elsewhere in this series.

Although no knowledge of coordination compounds is assumed, some acquaintance with such topics as atomic orbital theory and elementary kinetics and thermodynamics is. As far as possible, the discussion is non-mathematical. A few mathematical proofs are, however, included; almost invariably these are at points where a vital relationship is presented and for which a simple proof would otherwise probably not be available to the student. In these cases I have given the proof in detail. My hope is that this book will take the reader to the point at which he will be able to understand most research papers in coordination chemistry.

I should like to thank Drs. E. D. McKenzie and I. Paul and the editor of this volume, Professor T. C. Waddington, for reading the first draft of the manuscript and making comments which enabled me to improve both the content and presentation of the book. Defects which remain are, of course, my own responsibility.

S. F. A. Kettle

1 Introduction

Since the subject of this book is coordination compounds (or, as they are often called, *complexes*), our first task is to define the term 'coordination compound'. This is not straightforward, for the use of the term is determined as much by history and tradition as by chemistry. In practice, however, confusion seldom arises. Let us consider an example.

When boron trifluoride, a gas, is passed into trimethylamine, a liquid, a highly exothermic reaction occurs and a creamy-white solid separates. This solid has been shown to be a 1:1 adduct of the two reactants, in which the molecules have the structure shown in Fig. 1-1, the boron atom of boron trifluoride being bonded to the nitrogen atom of trimethylamine. The adduct is an example of a coordination compound. An electron count shows that the boron atom in boron trifluoride possesses an empty valence shell orbital, whilst the nitrogen of the trimethylamine has two valence shell electrons not involved in bonding. It is believed that the bond between the boron and nitrogen atoms in the complex results from the donation of these 'nitrogen' electrons into the empty boron orbital, so that they are shared by both atoms. Coordination compounds in which such electron transfer appears to be largely responsible for the bonding are called donor–acceptor complexes (it is to be emphasized that, once formed, there is no difference in kind between these and ordinary covalent bonds). In the boron trifluoride–trimethylamine adduct, the nitrogen atom of the trimethylamine molecule is said to be coordinated to the boron atom. That is, the

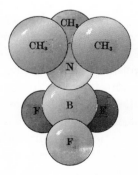

Fig. 1-1 The structure of the coordination compound formed between boron trifluoride and trimethylamine.

electron donor is said to be coordinated to the electron acceptor. A coordinating group (usually called a *ligand*) need not be a molecule and need not be uncharged. For example, boron trifluoride reacts with ammonium fluoride to give the salt $NH_4[BF_4]$ which contains the complex anion $[BF_4]^-$, where we adopt the convention of placing the complex species within square brackets. In the $[BF_4]^-$ anion the boron atom is tetrahedrally surrounded by ligands, just as it is to a first approximation in $[BF_3 \cdot NMe_3]$ (Fig. 1-1). Notice that, for non-transition metals and metalloids, complex formation is associated with a change (usually an increase) in the number of groups to which the central atom is attached. Boron trifluoride, BF_3, is not normally thought of as a complex, but its adduct with trimethylamine certainly is. Most workers regard both trimethylamine and the fluoride anions as ligands in the adduct (as we have just done). Further, the criterion of change in number of bonded atoms outweighs all others for these elements. Thus, phosphorus pentachloride exists in the gas phase as discrete PCl_5 molecules. The solid, however, is an ionic lattice, containing $[PCl_4]^+$ and $[PCl_6]^-$ ions. These species are usually classed as complex ions, although the molecule in the gas phase is not.

The detailed geometry of a complex molecule is not simply a combination of those of its components. In the trimethylamine–boron trifluoride adduct, for instance, the B—F bond length is 1·39 Å and the F—B—F bond angles 107° compared with 1·30 Å and 120° in the isolated BF_3 molecule. Similarly, the geometry of the trimethylamine fragment differs from that of the free amine. Information about the bonding within a complex may, in favourable cases, be obtained by a detailed consideration of these bond and angle changes.

Complexes are formed by both transition metal and non-transition elements; indeed, at the present time all compounds of transition-metal ions, with very few exceptions, are regarded as complexes. However, the simple donor–acceptor bond approach does not seem immediately applicable to coordination complexes of the transition metals, since the molecular geometry does not depend greatly on the number of valence shell electrons. As we shall see in Chapter 5, in the simplest model of transition metal complexes no electron donation is involved, a molecule being regarded as held together by electrostatic attraction between a central transition metal cation and the surrounding anions or dipolar ligands. In more sophisticated discussions of the bonding (Chapter 6) the donor–acceptor concept is to some extent reinstated for these compounds and we may conveniently (but not always correctly) regard a coordination compound as composed of (a) an electron donor (ligand or Lewis base) of which an individual atom or molecule possesses non-bonding lone-pair electrons but no low-lying empty orbitals; (b) an electron acceptor ('metal atom', 'cation', or Lewis acid) which possesses a low-lying empty orbital. The donor atom of a ligand is usually of high electronegativity and the acceptor an atom of either a metal or metalloid element. However, a compound containing a metal or metalloid element bonded to a methyl group is not usually viewed as a complex in which CH_3^- functions as a ligand, although the CH_3^- group is isoelectronic with ammonia, a molecule which is frequently a ligand. Similarly, although the manganate ion MnO_4^{2-} might well be considered a complex (of Mn^{6+} and O^{2-}), the sulphate anion SO_4^{2-} would not. Evidently, we have reached the point at which history and tradition enter the definition of a coordination compound.

The father of modern coordination chemistry is Alfred Werner, who was born in France in 1866 but lived most of his life in Zürich. It was known that the oxidation of cobalt(II) ('cobaltous') salts made alkaline with aqueous ammonia led to the formation of cobalt(III) ('cobaltic') salts containing up to six ammonia molecules per cobalt atom. These ammonia molecules were evidently strongly bonded because very extreme conditions—boiling sulphuric acid, for example—were needed to separate them from the cobalt. There had been considerable speculation about this bonding and structures such as

$$\begin{array}{c} NH_3\!-\!Cl \\ \diagup \\ Co\!-\!NH_3\!\cdot\!NH_3\!\cdot\!NH_3\!\cdot\!NH_3Cl \\ \diagdown \\ NH_3\!-\!Cl \end{array}$$

had been proposed for the cobalt(III) salt which we would today write as $[Co(NH_3)_6]Cl_3$. Werner's greatest contribution to coordination chemistry came in a flash of inspiration (at two o'clock in the morning) when he recognized that the number of groups attached to an atom (its 'secondary valency') need not equal its oxidation number (he called it 'primary valency'). Further, for any element, primary and secondary valencies could vary independently of each other. The chemistry of the cobalt(III)–ammonia adducts could be rationalized if in them cobalt had a primary valency of three, as in $CoCl_3$, but a secondary valency of six, as in $[Co(NH_3)_6]Cl_3$.

Subsequently, Werner and his students obtained a vast body of experimental evidence, all supporting this idea. They further showed that the six coordinated ligands were arranged octahedrally about the central atom (Fig. 1-2). Werner was awarded the Nobel prize for chemistry in 1913 and died six years later. Some measure

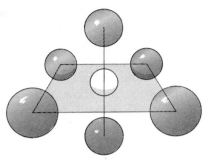

Fig. 1-2   An octahedral complex ML_6. M is represented by the central white atom. A regular octahedron has eight faces (each an equilateral triangle) and six equivalent vertices. In an octahedral complex the ligands are placed at the vertices. In Fig. 1-2, and in similar diagrams throughout this book, the perspective is exaggerated (the central four ligands lie at the corners of a square).

of his stature and work is provided by the fact that in one field (that of polynuclear cobalt complexes) there has, to this day, been scarcely any addition to the list of compounds he prepared.

Following Werner, manganese is recognized as a transition element which forms coordination complexes. Thus, as we have seen, the $[MnO_4]^{2-}$ anion is regarded as a complex. Sulphur is not noted for the complexes it forms and so the SO_4^{2-} anion is not regarded as one. Similarly, there is a well-founded tradition that the ammonia molecule functions as a ligand, but there is no such tradition for the CH_3^- anion and most people prefer to regard compounds containing the methyl group as involving the methyl radical $CH_3\cdot$.

Most textbooks discuss transition metal complexes separately from those of the main group elements. There is, in fact, much in common between the two classes and, whenever possible, we shall treat them as one. However, complexes of the transition metal ions may possess an incomplete shell of d electrons. This makes it particularly useful to determine the magnetic and spectral characteristics of members of this class of complexes.

The water-soluble ionic species of transition elements such as chromium, manganese, iron, and copper seem to exist in aqueous solution as, for example, $[Cr(H_2O)_6]^{3+}$, $[Mn(H_2O)_6]^{2+}$, and $[Fe(H_2O)_6]^{2+}$. That is, it is more accurate to talk of the aqueous chemistry of the $[Cr(H_2O)_6]^{3+}$ ion than of 'the aqueous chemistry of the Cr^{3+} ion'. Similarly, in solid $FeCl_3$, the iron atoms are not attached to three chlorines but to six, arranged octahedrally (each chlorine is bonded to two iron atoms). We have already encountered the fact that solid PCl_5 is really $[PCl_4]^+[PCl_6]^-$. The lesson to be learnt from all this is that coordination compounds are much more common than one might at first think. Many more examples of coordination compounds of both transition and non-transition elements are given in the next chapter, where we discuss their names, constituents, shape, and isomerism.

In summary, there is no precise definition of a coordination compound—at one extreme methane could be regarded as one—and the usage of the term is extended to all compounds to which some of the concepts developed in the following chapters can usefully be applied.

2 Nomenclature and geometrical structure of coordination compounds

2-1 Nomenclature

In order to facilitate communication between chemists it is desirable that a generally accepted convention for naming coordination compounds be followed. In this section we give an outline of the system suggested by a Nomenclature Committee of the International Union of Pure and Applied Chemistry (IUPAC). Although this convention is commonly adopted—the Russian literature contains some variants—it is often simpler to give a structural formula, e.g. $[Co(NH_3)_4(NO_2)Cl]^+$, than to write the name in full, and we shall do this frequently in the following chapters.

Trivial names also persist so, although one should talk of the hexacyanoferrate(II) and hexacyanoferrate(III) anions, most workers bow to common usage and continue to refer to them as the ferrocyanide and ferricyanide ions. The practice of naming a coordination compound after the person who first prepared it is also still encountered, thus: $NH_4[Cr(NH_3)_2(NCS)_4]$, Reinecke's salt; $[Pt(NH_3)_4][PtCl_4]$, Magnus's green salt; and $K[Pt(C_2H_4)Cl_3]$, Zeiss's salt. A system which has mercifully disappeared, but which will be found in the older literature, is that of naming a compound according to the colour of the corresponding cobalt(III) complex (no matter what the colour of the complex itself). Thus, *purpureo* salts meant $[M(NH_3)_5Cl]^{n+}$.

The following rules summarize the more important decisions of the IUPAC committee.

Although in writing the formula of a complex, the central atom is given first, in the corresponding name it is given last, thus: $[Fe(CN)_6]^{3-}$, hexacyanoferrate(III). For anionic complexes the characteristic ending is -ate (as in hexacyanoferrate(III)), but for neutral or cationic complexes the name of the central element is not modified: $[Fe(H_2O)_6]^{2+}$, hexaaquoiron(II). A distinction is made for anionic complexes so that the corresponding acids can be systematically named, the characteristic ending for the acid being -ic:

$H_4[Fe(CN)_6]$, hexacyanoferric(II) acid. As indicated in these examples, the formal oxidation state of the central atom (Werner's 'primary valency') is indicated by a Roman numeral in parentheses after the name of the complex, but with no space between them. A formal oxidation state of zero is indicated by (0) and a negative state by a minus sign, e.g. (−I).

The name of the complex species is written as one word, the negatively charged ligands (all of which end in -o) preceding uncharged ligands. Within each class, ligands are listed in order of increasing complexity: $[Co(NH_3)_4(NO_2)Br]^+$, bromonitrotetraamminecobalt(III). Note that NH_3 is written 'ammine' although neutral ligands are generally named as the molecule. Other exceptions are H_2O (aquo), CO (carbonyl), and NO (nitrosyl). When a ligand may complex in more than one way, the coordinated atom(s) (if known) are given after the name of the ligand. If two identical ligands are present, but are differently attached, they are included separately in the name. Thus, the complex

$$\left[\begin{array}{cccc} S & O & S & O \\ & Pt & & \\ O & O & O & O \end{array}\right]^{2-}$$

is called thiosulphato-*O,O*-thiosulphato-*O,S*-platinate(II). For $-NO_2^-$ and $-ONO^-$, nitro and nitrito, respectively, may be used, as may thiocyanato and isothiocyanato for $-SCN^-$ and $-NCS^-$.

When several identical ligands are coordinated to the same central atom, two cases arise. If the ligand is simple, the number is indicated by the prefix di-, tri-, tetra-, penta-, or hexa-. Several examples have already been given. When the ligand is complicated, so that it has a polysyllabic name, the name is enclosed in parentheses and the number of the ligands present indicated by the prefix bis-, tris-, tetrakis-, pentakis-, or hexakis-. Examples are ethylenediamine, $NH_2 \cdot CH_2 \cdot CH_2 \cdot NH_2$, which gives rise to the complex tris-(ethylenediamine)nickel(II), $[Ni(en)_3]^{2+}$ (en is the usual abbreviation for ethylenediamine), and triphenylphosphine, $P(C_6H_5)_3$, in the complex $[Ni(P(C_6H_5)_3)_2Cl_2]$, dichlorobis(triphenylphosphine)nickel(II).

Bridging groups attached to two coordination centres are indicated by the prefix μ:

$$\left[\begin{array}{c} NH_2 \\ (NH_3)_4Co \qquad Co(NH_3)_4 \\ NO_2 \end{array}\right]^{4+}$$

μ-amido-μ-nitrooctaamminedicobalt(III).

These names give the ligands attached to the central atom but do not indicate the positions of the ligands relative to one another. If we wish to convey this information, an extension of the nomenclature is necessary. It often happens that the prefixes *cis-* or *trans-* are adequate, as in *cis*-dichlorodipyridineplatinum(II)

$(py = pyridine)$

or even *trans*-chlorobromo-*trans*-amminepyridineplatinum(II)

Note that the name *cis*-bromoammine-*cis*-chloropyridineplatinum(II) could not be used as it would fail to distinguish between the above structure and

There would be no ambiguity if the *trans-* and *cis-* prefixes occurred only once in the last two names. The duplication is tolerated for the sake of clarity. An alternative, and more general, system is to number the coordination positions. The numbering system for square planar complexes is

$$
\begin{array}{c}
1 \\
| \\
4\text{---M---}2 \\
| \\
3
\end{array}
$$

so that an alternative to *trans*-chlorobromo-*trans*-amminepyridine-platinum(II) is 1-chloro-3-bromoamminepyridineplatinum(II). The numbers -2- and -4- before ammine and pyridine are superfluous and are omitted.

For octahedral complexes the *cis-* and *trans-* nomenclature is often simplest, but for complicated cases the numbering system shown in Fig. 2-1 is adopted, the ligands at the corners of the 'front' face of the octahedron being cyclically numbered 1 → 3 and those on the 'back' face numbered 4 → 6.

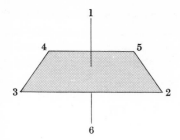

Fig. 2-1

Since no system of naming optically active complexes has yet been generally adopted, we shall not discuss these complexes here. One final point must be made, however. This is that the name of a cationic species, complex or not, always precedes the name of an anionic species, complex or not.

In the above examples we encountered one in which two atoms of the thiosulphate anion were coordinated to a single platinum atom, leading to the formation of a ring structure. The formation of such rings by coordination is termed *chelation* (from the Greek word for a crab's claw, $\chi\eta\lambda\acute{\eta}$) and the ligand a *chelating* ligand. Ligands in which more than one atom may be coordinated are termed bidentate ('two teeth'), tridentate, quadridentate, quinquidentate, sexadentate, and so on. (Some people prefer to use tetradentate, pentadentate, and hexadentate, and to refer to the whole class as polydentate, rather than multidentate, ligands. However, a multidentate ligand is not necessarily a chelating ligand—the coordinating atoms of the ligand may be so arranged that they cannot be coordinated to the same metal atom.)

Ligands, and multidentate ligands in particular, can be rather complicated. To simplify the description of complexes involving such ligands, abbreviated forms of the ligands' names are used—we have already used 'py' as a shorthand for 'pyridine'. With but a few exceptions, there is no system of standard abbreviations. Fortunately it is common practice for authors of papers to define the abbreviations they use, so little confusion arises. A representative selection of ligands is given in Table 2-1, together with commonly used abbreviations. Points of potential bonding between ligand atoms and a metal are indicated by arrows.

2-2 Coordination numbers

Werner was the first to recognize that one characteristic of a coordination compound is the number of ligands bonded to the central atom. He called this number the 'secondary valency' of the central

Table 2-1   Some common multidentate ligands (charges on anions are omitted)

Name	Abbreviation	Formula
Bidentate ligands		
Acetylacetonato (or 2,4-Pentanedionato)	acac	
2,2′-Dipyridyl (or 2,2′-Bipyridyl)	dipy (or bipy)	
Oxalato	ox	
Ethylenediamine	en	
o-Phenylenebisdimethylarsine	diars	
Tridentate ligands		
2,2′,2″-Terpyridine	terpy	
Diethylenetriamine	dien	
Quadridentate ligands		
Triethylenetetramine	trien	

Table 2-1   (*contd.*)

Name	Abbreviation	Formula
Quadridentate ligands		
Tris-(*o*-diphenylarsineophenyl)-arsine	QAS	(structure) $(Ph = C_6H_5)$
Sexadentate ligand		
Ethylenediaminetetraacetato	EDTA	$\leftarrow N - CH_2 - CH_2 - N \rightarrow$ with $CO_2\rightarrow$ groups

atom, but this usage has not persisted and it is now called the 'coordination number'. The coordination number need not have a unique value—for example, in pink cobalt(II) chloride it is six and in the blue form it is four. In particular, when a coordination compound is participating in a reaction in which one ligand is being replaced by another, there is evidence that the coordination number in the reaction intermediate is different from that in either the initial or product coordination complex.

Coordination number is not only a convenient method of classifying coordination compounds—all complexes of a given transition metal ion with the same coordination number also have closely related magnetic properties and electronic spectra. In later chapters this feature is discussed in some detail. In the present section we describe some of the geometrical arrangements of ligands which have been found and give examples of each.

2-2-1   Complexes with coordination numbers two or three

Coordination numbers of two and three are rare. The best-known example of coordination number two is the complex ion formed when silver salts dissolve in aqueous ammonia, $[Ag(NH_3)_2]^+$. This, like all other known cases of this coordination number, is linear, $H_3N{-}Ag{-}NH_3$. Other complexes of this coordination number, which is almost entirely confined to copper(I), silver(I), gold(I), and mercury(II), are $[CuCl_2]^-$ and $[Hg(CN)_2]$.

Examples of coordination number three are few, the $[HgI_3]^-$ anion perhaps being the best characterized. In this anion the iodide ions are arranged at the corners of a slightly distorted equilateral triangle which has the mercury atom at its centre. A recently reported example of three-coordination in transition metal chemistry is the iron(III) complex $[Fe(N(SiMe_3)_2)_3]$.

2-2-2 Complexes with coordination number four

A tetrahedral arrangement of ligands is commonly exhibited by complexes with coordination number four. It is found for both transition metal and non-transition elements. We have already encountered $[BF_3 \cdot NMe_3]$ and $[BF_4]^-$, in both of which the boron is tetrahedrally coordinated, and other examples amongst main group elements are the $[BeF_4]^{2-}$, $[ZnCl_4]^{2-}$, and $[Cd(CN)_4]^{2-}$ anions. Complexes of transition metals in their higher oxidation states are often tetrahedral—$TiCl_4$, $[CrO_4]^{2-}$, and $[MnO_4]^{2-}$ are examples—but the same geometry is found for other valence states also. Transition metal chlorides, for instance, quite often give tetrahedral anionic species when dissolved in concentrated hydrochloric acid: copper(II) chloride gives $[CuCl_4]^{2-}$, iron(III) chloride gives $[FeCl_4]^-$, and cobalt(II) chloride gives $[CoCl_4]^{2-}$.

The four-coordinate arrangement in which the ligands lie at the corners of a square ('square planar complexes') is almost entirely confined to transition metal complexes (XeF_4 also has this structure), where it is common for those ions having d^8 configurations—rhodium(I), iridium(I), palladium(II), platinum(II), and gold(III). Examples are the $[PtCl_4]^{2-}$, $[PdCl_4]^{2-}$, and $[AuF_4]^-$ anions. Nickel(II), also a d^8 ion, is interesting in that it forms both tetrahedral and square planar complexes (the red precipitate obtained by adding dimethylglyoxime to nickel(II) solutions is a square planar complex).

As Fig. 2-2 shows, it is possible in principle, if not in practice, to distort a tetrahedral arrangement of ligands so that they eventually

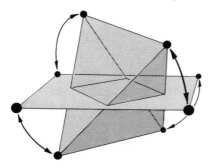

Fig. 2-2 Both a tetrahedral and a square planar complex are drawn in this diagram. By distorting one structure as indicated by the arrows it may be converted into the other.

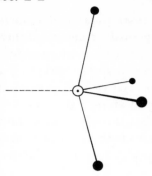

Fig. 2-3   A mode of four-coordination found for main group elements.

assume the square planar structure, and vice versa. This suggests that complexes may exist with structures which are neither tetrahedral nor square planar, but intermediate between the two. Indeed, such is the case with, for example, the $[CuCl_4]^{2-}$ anion.

A related, but rather different, structure (Fig. 2-3) is found for some main group compounds, for example $[SbCl_4]^-$ and $[AsCl_4]^-$. The coordination geometry here may be regarded as derived from trigonal bipyramidal five-coordination (Fig. 2-4 and Section 2-2-3) by omitting one of the three 'equatorial' ligands. It is believed that the 'empty' coordination position of the trigonal bipyramid is occupied by a non-bonding lone pair of electrons of the central atom (Sb, As).

2-2-3   Complexes with coordination number five

A number of examples of five-coordination have been found recently and it appears that this coordination number is much more common than was once supposed. There are two idealized five-coordinate

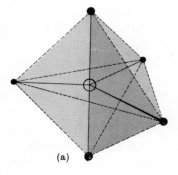

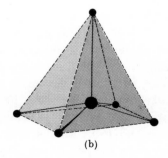

(a)   (b)

Fig. 2-4   (a) The trigonal bipyramidal and (b) square pyramidal modes of five-coordination.

structures, the trigonal bipyramidal and square pyramidal arrangements (Fig. 2-4). These structures are energetically similar and there seems to be no general way of anticipating which is adopted by a particular complex.* Indeed, it is possible that the structure is determined by intermolecular forces within the crystal (almost all structures have been determined in the solid state). In some five-coordinate compounds it has been shown that there is a facile interchange of ligands between the non-equivalent sites in either structure. The probable mechanism for this is shown in Fig. 2-5; only relatively

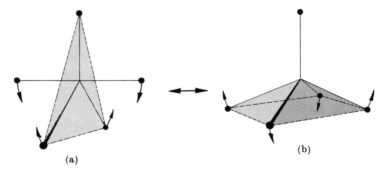

(a)   (b)

Fig. 2-5   (a) The ligand displacements needed to change a trigonal bipyramidal complex into one of square pyramidal geometry and (b) vice versa.

small angular displacements are needed to interconvert the square pyramid and the trigonal bipyramid, and alternation between the two would lead to the observed interchange of ligand position. Moreover, geometries between the two extremes are possible and are, in fact, those commonly observed, particularly for complexes containing chelating ligands.

Examples of trigonal bipyramidal structures are the $[Co(NC \cdot CH_3)_5]^+$ and $[Cudipy_2I]^+$ cations. In the latter, one nitrogen of each dipyridyl is in an axial position. Anionic examples are $[CuCl_5]^{3-}$, $[SnCl_5]^-$, and $[Pt(SnCl_3)_5]^{3-}$ (the latter, with Pt—Sn bonds, is formed when acidic tin(II) chloride solution is added to many platinum salts).

The best-known example of square pyramidal coordination is vanadylbisacetylacetonate, $[VOacac_2]$, in which the oxygen atom occupies the unique position. In the $[Cu_2Cl_6]^{2-}$ anion, bridges between adjacent anions lead to a square pyramidal configuration about each copper atom (Fig. 2-6); compare this example with

---

* One exception should be noted. Complexes containing strongly π-bonding ligands adopt the trigonal bipyramidal configuration.

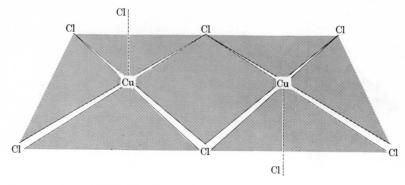

Fig. 2-6   The structure of the $[Cu_2Cl_6]^{2-}$ anion.

$[CuCl_5]^{3-}$, mentioned above. Amongst the main group elements, the $[SbCl_5]^{2-}$ anion provides an example of square pyramidal coordination.

A feature of square pyramidal structures is that there is the possibility of an additional ligand occupying the vacant axial site to produce a six-coordinate complex. The small variations that have been observed in the electronic spectrum of $[VOacac_2]$ in different solvents are believed to be caused by a solvent molecule being weakly bonded at the sixth coordination position.

2-2-4 Complexes with coordination number six

The majority of coordination compounds are six-coordinate, the structure adopted being that of a regular or distorted octahedron (Fig. 1-2). It is important to recognize that the octahedral geometry is found for complexes of *both* main group and transition metal elements; the emphasis which we shall place on transition metal complexes in some of the following chapters may tend to obscure this fact. Examples of octahedral complexes of main group elements are $[Alacac_3]$, $[InCl_6]^{3-}$, and $[PCl_6]^-$. We shall also have to consider distortions from the regular octahedral arrangement, both static (i.e., permanent) and transient (resulting from vibrations of the complex).

An octahedron is highly symmetrical. In particular, it has two-fold, three-fold, and four-fold rotation axes (denoted C_2, C_3, and C_4 respectively in Fig. 2-7). A distortion (compression or elongation) of the regular octahedron along a two-fold axis is called a *digonal* distortion, along a three-fold axis it is called a *trigonal* distortion, and a distortion along a four-fold axis is called a *tetragonal* distortion.

An alternative but rare form of six-coordination is the trigonal pyramidal arrangement which has recently been observed in the

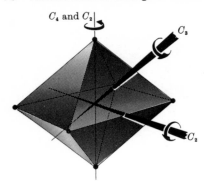

Fig. 2-7   The symmetry axes of an octahedron. There are four C_3 axes, passing through the mid-points of pairs of opposite faces. There are three C_4 axes, passing through pairs of opposite apices. There are two sorts of C_2 axes. One set is coincident with the C_4 axes and the others, six in number, pass through the mid-points of opposite edges of the octahedron. Note that the structure also has a centre of symmetry.

complex $[Re(S_2C_2Ph_2)_3]$ (Fig. 2-8); this is also the configuration about the metal atoms in MoS_2 and WS_2 (the crystals of these compounds contain layer lattices and not discrete molecules). Another possible six-coordinate arrangement is that of six ligands at the corners of a regular hexagon with the metal atom at the centre. This has never been found, but there is a related structure in which the coordination number of the central atom is eight (*vide infra*).

2-2-5   Complexes with coordination number seven

There are three main structures adopted by complexes with co-ordination number seven; as is commonly the case with the higher coordination numbers there appears to be no great energy difference

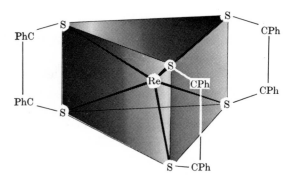

Fig. 2-8   The trigonal prismatic mode of six-coordination.

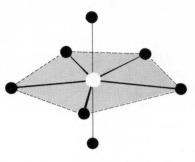

(*Left*) **Fig. 2-9**   The pentagonal bipyramidal (1:5:1) mode of seven-coordination.
(*Right*) **Fig. 2-10**   The one-face centred trigonal prismatic (1:4:2) mode of
seven-coordination.   In the $[NbOF_6]^{3-}$ anion the oxygen occupies the unique
position.

between them.   In the salt $Na_3[ZrF_7]$, the anion has the structure
of a pentagonal bipyramid (Fig. 2-9), but in $(NH_4)_3[ZrF_7]$ it has the
structure shown in Fig. 2-10.   No doubt the hydrogen-bonding in the
ammonium salt is a factor contributing to the difference in geometry.*
The anion $[NbOF_6]^{3-}$, which is isoelectronic with $[ZrF_7]^{3-}$, adopts the
third mode of seven-coordination, shown in Fig. 2-11.

A nomenclature which is sometimes used to distinguish these
three forms of seven-coordination is to proceed down the axes
indicated by arrows in Figs. 2-9–2-11 (these are the axes of highest
symmetry) and to list the number of ligands lying in planes perpendicular to those axes.   In this nomenclature the geometries are called

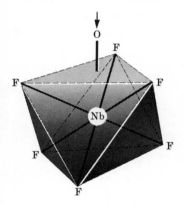

Fig. 2-11   The one-face centred octahedral (1:3:3) mode
of seven-coordination.

* It is interesting that the salt $(NH_4)_3(HfF_7)$ is actually $(NH_4)_2[HfF_6] + NH_4F$; this
is one of the few clear-cut distinctions between the chemistries of zirconium and
hafnium.

the $1:5:1$ (Fig. 2-9), $1:4:2$ (Fig. 2-10), and $1:3:3$ (Fig. 2-11) modes of seven-coordination.

The arrangements shown in Figs. 2-10 and 2-11 may be regarded as formed, respectively, by adding a ligand to the centre of a rectangular face of a trigonal prismatic arrangement of ligands or to the centre of a (triangular) face of an octahedron of ligands. The former arrangement has a two-fold rotation axis, but no three-fold, whilst the latter has a three-fold axis, but no two-fold. That is, the arrow shown in Fig. 2-10 indicates a two-fold rotation axis and that in Fig. 2-11 a three-fold rotation axis (the arrow in Fig. 2-9 indicates a five-fold rotation axis).

2-2-6   Complexes with coordination number eight

There are only two common arrangements of eight ligands about a central atom, the square antiprismatic and the dodecahedral. Consider an array of eight ligands at the corners of a square-based box (not necessarily a cube). If the top set is rotated by 45° about the four-fold rotation axis a square antiprism results (Fig. 2-12). Dodecahedral coordination is more difficult to describe and to envisage. Consider two pieces of cardboard cut and marked as shown in Fig. 2-13a. If these are interleaved as shown in Fig. 2-13b, the eight points lie at the corners of a dodecahedron (Fig. 2-13c) (a dodecahedron has twelve faces—count them). There appears to be little difference between the two structures energetically so, whilst $[Zracac_4]$ is square antiprismatic, $[Zrox_4]^{4-}$ is dodecahedral. Similarly, whilst the $[Mo(CN)_8]^{4-}$ anion has a dodecahedral geometry in the solid state, controversy still exists as to its structure in solution. Other examples of square antiprismatic coordination are the $[TaF_8]^{3-}$ and $[ReF_8]^{2-}$ anions.

Both the dodecahedron and square antiprism may be regarded as distortions of a cubic arrangement of ligands (Fig. 2-14). They

Fig. 2-12 The square antiprismatic mode of eight-coordination.

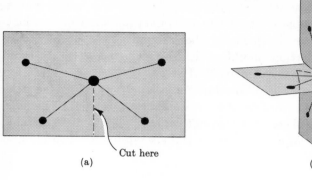

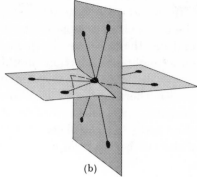

(a)   (b)

Fig. 2-13a
Fig. 2-13b Construction of a dodecahedral
arrangement of ligands.
Fig. 2-13c The dodecahedral mode of eight-
coordination. This diagram shows almost
the same perspective view as Fig. 2-13b.

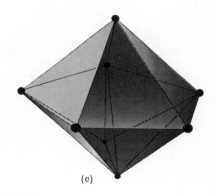

(c)

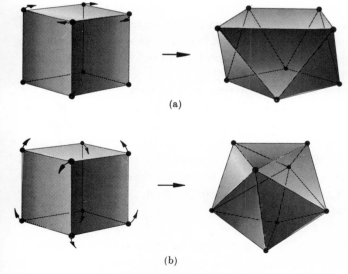

(a)

(b)

Fig. 2-14 Distortion of a cubic arrangement of ligands to
give (a) the antiprismatic and (b) dodecahedral structures.

are favoured because a cubic configuration would involve greater interligand steric interactions. However, a similar argument favours the octahedron as opposed to a trigonal prism (for six-coordination) and yet the latter arrangement has been found. This suggests that cubic eight-coordination should exist. In fact, it has recently been found for the $[PaF_8]^{3-}$ anion in Na_3PaF_8.

Another form of eight-coordination, largely confined to the actinide series, is the hexagonal bipyramidal arrangement of ligands (Fig. 2-15). The ideal geometry has not yet been observed. When the distances between adjacent pairs of the six equivalent ligands are

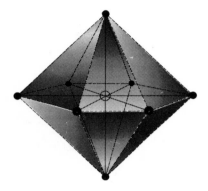

Fig. 2-15   The hexagonal bipyramidal arrangement of eight-coordination.

equal then the hexagon is found to be puckered. If the hexagon is planar then these distances are alternately long and short. The two axial ligands are usually oxygen atoms which are strongly bonded to the central metal, as in the uranylacetate anion, $[UO_2(acetate)_3]^-$.

2-2-7   Complexes with coordination number nine

A spectacular example of nine-coordination is that of the $[ReH_9]^{2-}$ anion. This has the structure commonly found for nine-coordination, a trigonal prismatic arrangement of six ligands, each of the three rectangular faces of the prism being centred by an additional ligand (Fig. 2-16). Many hydrated salts of the lanthanide elements (for example, $[Nd(H_2O)_9]^{3+}$) adopt this coordination. It is also found for salts such as $PbCl_2$ and UCl_3.

2-3   The Gillespie–Nyholm approach to molecular structure

The best of the simple approaches to molecular structure is that based on the concept of repulsion between electron pairs, a model refined and popularized by Gillespie and Nyholm. It is postulated

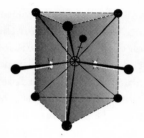

Fig. 2-16 The three-face centred mode of nine-coordination.

that the repulsions between valence electron pairs surrounding an atom lead to a structure in which these electron pairs are as far apart as possible. That is, it is postulated that bonding forces are *not* the vital factor in determining molecular geometry. This rather un-orthodox view finds support in some theoretical calculations and in the observation that rather little energy is required to excite those molecular vibrations which correspond to bond angle changes (these, of course, change the geometry around the central atom).

The simplest way of looking at the Gillespie–Nyholm approach is to regard each valence electron pair as being represented by a point, the points being constrained to move over the surface of a sphere drawn around the atom. As the points (i.e. valence electron pairs) repel each other, the most stable molecular arrangement will be that in which the points are as far apart as possible. If we represent each valence-electron pair as P, then we at once predict the following geometries of the Ps around the central atom M

MP_2 linear

MP_3 equilateral triangular

MP_4 tetrahedral

MP_6 octahedral

Comparison with the geometries which we have discussed earlier in this chapter will show that, for main group elements these predictions are rather good. So $[BF_3 \cdot NMe_3]$, in which there are four valence electron pairs around the boron, is approximately tetrahedral, the distortion being consistent with the fact that one of the valence electron pairs (that involved in the B—N bond) would not be expected to have exactly the same spatial distribution as the other three, so that (B—N)–(B—F) bond repulsions will be slightly different to (B—F)–(B—F) repulsions. Similarly, extending the discussion to a compound which would not normally be regarded as a complex, the oxygen atom in water is surrounded by four electron pairs (two from the O—H bonds and two from the lone pairs on the oxygen atom). Repulsion between these electron pairs leads to a tetrahedral distribution and, in accord with this, the H—O—H bond angle in water has roughly the tetrahedral value, the deviation from regularity being in accord with the suggestion that the centre of gravity of the electron density in the O—H bonds is further away from the oxygen atom than is the case for the lone pair electrons. This leads to the prediction that the relative magnitude of the electron repulsion is in the order

lone pair–lone pair $>$ lone pair–bonding pair

$>$ bonding pair–bonding pair

an order which almost invariably explains distortions from totally symmetric structures. At this point the reader might find it useful to return to the discussion of the $[SbCl_4]^-$ structure and try to understand why Fig. 2-3 does not show exactly the trigonal bipyramidal arrangement discussed in the text.

So far, we have not discussed coordination numbers five, seven, eight, and nine. The last of these is simple, for the predicted geometry which we discussed in Section 2-2-7 is the one commonly observed. The others are not so clear-cut, because the valence electron pair arrangements which involve minimum electron repulsion are not intuitively obvious. This difficulty can be removed by assuming some form for the repulsive energy between the points constrained to move over the surface of a sphere (representing the valence electron pairs), for example, that the energy varies as $1/r^n$, where r is the interpoint distance and thus determining the arrangement of lowest energy. Unfortunately, the results depend to some extent on the value of n chosen (which is usually between six and twelve) and, in any case, it is not certain that the energy varies in this simple way. It seems safest to conclude for coordination numbers five, seven, and eight that other factors besides valence shell electron repulsions may play a part in determining the molecular geometry. Bonding forces (of both σ- and π-types) and lattice forces, for instance, may play a vital part. These cases are those for which, as we have mentioned earlier, experimentally there seems little energetic difference between several possible geometries.

There appear to be four main classes of compound which do not follow the Gillespie–Nyholm predictions.

1. Molecules with very polar bonds. Thus, Li_2O (gaseous) does not have the same structure as water but is linear. If we regard this

molecule as an ion triplet, then the valence-electron distribution of the oxygen is in essence spherically symmetrical and the structure will be that in which the Li^+—Li^+ repulsion (and not electron repulsion) is a minimum. That is, the molecule will be linear, as observed.

2. Molecules with extensive delocalized π-electron systems. The anion $C(CN)_3^-$, predicted to be of the same shape as ammonia, is planar. For such molecules a correct prediction of molecular geometry is obtained if the π-electrons are assumed not to influence the molecular geometry. That is, they are assumed to be so delocalized that their contribution to the electron repulsion forces is negligible. Thus, in the above example, if the π-electrons are omitted, there are three valence electron pairs around the central carbon atom which will lie in a plane, at 120° to each other, in agreement with the observed structure.

3. Some compounds formed by elements with an 'inert pair' of electrons. Many of the heavier non-transition elements exhibit two valencies which differ by two, e.g. Sn(II) and Sn(IV). This led to the idea that two of the valence electrons—the 'inert pair'—of these elements are chemically less available than the others. Although most molecules containing these elements in their low valence states follow the Gillespie–Nyholm predictions, in others the inert pair seems sterically inactive. For example, some anions of the group five elements such as $[SbCl_6]^{3-}$ and $[BiCl_6]^{3-}$ are octahedral although they have seven valence shell electron pairs. The correct geometry is predicted if it is assumed that the inert pair of electrons is confined to an s-orbital ($4s$ for arsenic, $5s$ for antimony, and $6s$ for bismuth) and excluded from the valence set.*

These are all retrospective rationalizations and one would have to rely on intuition to predict the structure of, say, the $C(NO_2)_3^-$ anion. Is it like ammonia or is it planar?† However, they do indicate points at which caution is needed in using the Gillespie–Nyholm approach. Nonetheless, this approach is usually reliable for the prediction of the structure of complexes of the main-group elements.

4. Compounds of the transition metals. Although they are in the valence shell, d electrons do not usually have the predicted effect on molecular structure. For instance, $[TiF_6]^{3-}$, with a single unpaired d electron, is a regular octahedron. Similarly, as we have seen, complexes in which the transition-metal ion has a d^8 configuration

---

* This explanation seems to be inconsistent with the observed steric activity of the inert pair in related compounds.
† It is planar.

are often square planar. This cannot be explained readily by the simple Gillespie–Nyholm theory.

Experimentally, it appears that the frequency of occurrence of coordination numbers for some ions of the first transition series is roughly as follows:

chromium(III)	6(oct.) $\gg$ 5, others very rare
iron(III)	6(oct.) $>$ 5 $>$ 4(tet.) $\simeq$ 7
cobalt(II)	6(oct.) $>$ 4(tet.) $>$ 5 $>$ 4(planar)
cobalt(III)	6(oct.) $\ggg$ 5, others not known
nickel(II)	6(oct.) $>$ 4(planar) $>$ 4(tet.) $\simeq$ 5
copper(II)	6(oct.)† $\simeq$ 5† $\simeq$ 4(planar) $\simeq$ 4(tet.)†

† usually distorted

Although not exhaustive, this series emphasizes that there is no fixed coordination number for any given ion.

There is at present no complete rationalization of the stereo-chemical behaviour of transition metal ions. Some of the more important factors have been recognized and are discussed later in this book (particularly in Chapter 10). For the present it is sufficient to note that the majority of complexes of transition metal ions are octahedral.

2-4 Isomerism in coordination compounds

The evidence used by Werner to conclude that six-coordinate complexes are almost invariably octahedral was obtained from a study of the isomerism of these compounds. Although there are few studies in inorganic chemistry nowadays of isomerism *per se* (except optical isomerism), it remains an important aspect of the chemistry of coordination compounds because ligand interchange often occurs readily in solution; that is, when a pure complex is dissolved, the solution may contain a variety of compounds, including isomers of the original solid-state structure. In this section the various forms of isomerism which have been recognized for octahedral complexes are outlined. It should be remembered that the categories are not mutually exclusive and that two or more of the classes we define may have to be invoked to describe the isomerism between two compounds.

2-4-1 Conformation isomerism

This is a simple form of isomerism in which the isomers have different stereochemistries but are otherwise identical, e.g. *trans* planar and tetrahedral $NiCl_2(Ph_2PCH_2Ph)_2$ (cf. Fig. 2-2). Its occurrence is confined to relatively few metal ions.

2-4-2 Geometrical isomerism

We have already encountered this when discussing nomenclature; *cis* and *trans* isomers are examples of geometrical isomerism, e.g.

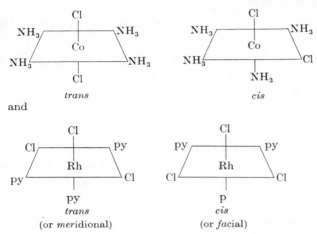

trans

and

cis

trans
(or *meri*dional)

cis
(or *fac*ial)

2-4-3 Coordination position isomerism

In this form of isomerism the distribution of ligands between two coordination centres differs, e.g.

$$\left[(NH_3)_4Co \begin{matrix} OH \\ \diagup \quad \diagdown \\ \diagdown \quad \diagup \\ OH \end{matrix} Co(NH_3)_2Cl_2 \right]^{2+} \quad \text{and} \quad \left[Cl(NH_3)_3Co \begin{matrix} OH \\ \diagup \quad \diagdown \\ \diagdown \quad \diagup \\ OH \end{matrix} Co(NH_3)_3Cl \right]^{2+}$$

Note that each of these two cations exists in a number of isomeric forms. The reader may find it a useful exercise to draw pictures of all of the forms and to enquire into the isomeric relationship between pairs.

2-4-4 Coordination isomerism

This may occur only when the cation and anion of a salt are both complex, the two isomers differing in the distribution of ligands between the cation and anion, e.g.

$[Co(NH_3)_6][Crox_3]$ and $[Cr(NH_3)_6][Coox_3]$

The same atom may be the coordination centre in both cation and anion, e.g.

$[Cr(NH_3)_6][Cr(SCN)_6]$ and $[Cr(NH_3)_4(SCN)_2][Cr(NH_3)_2(SCN)_4]$

2-4-5 Ionization isomerism

Two coordination compounds which differ in the distribution of ions between those directly coordinated and counter-ions present in the crystal lattice are called ionization isomers, e.g.

$$[Co(NH_3)_5Br]SO_4 \quad \text{and} \quad [Co(NH_3)_5SO_4]Br$$

2-4-6 Hydrate isomerism

Hydrate isomerism is similar to ionization isomerism except that an uncharged ligand changes from being coordinated to a free-lattice position whilst another ligand moves in the opposite sense. Although the uncharged ligand need not be a water molecule in practice it almost always is (hence the term 'hydrate' isomerism), e.g.

$$[Cr(H_2O)_6]Cl_3, \quad [Cr(H_2O)_5Cl]Cl_2{\cdot}H_2O \quad \text{and} \quad [Cr(H_2O)_4Cl_2]Cl{\cdot}2H_2O.$$

2-4-7 Linkage isomerism

In our discussion on nomenclature we encountered the problem that some ligands may coordinate in two or more ways. This phenomenon gives rise to linkage isomerism, e.g.

$$[Cr(H_2O)_5SCN]^{2+} \quad \text{and} \quad [Cr(H_2O)_5NCS]^{2+}$$
$$[Co(NH_3)_5NO_2]^{2+} \quad \text{and} \quad [Co(NH_3)_5ONO]^{2+}$$
$$[Co(NH_3)_5SSO_3]^+ \quad \text{and} \quad [Co(NH_3)_5OSO_2S]^+$$

2-4-8 Polymerization isomerism

Strictly speaking, polymerization isomerism, in which n varies in the complex $[ML_m]_n$ (the Ls are not all identical), is not isomerism. It is included in this list because it represents an additional way in which an empirical formula may give incomplete information about the nature of a complex. For example, all members of the following series are polymerization isomers

$$[Co(NH_3)_3(NO_2)_3] \qquad\qquad n = 1$$
$$[Co(NH_3)_6][Co(NO_2)_6] \qquad\qquad n = 2$$
$$[Co(NH_3)_4(NO_2)_2][Co(NH_3)_2(NO_2)_4] \qquad n = 2$$
$$[Co(NH_3)_5(NO_2)][Co(NH_3)_2(NO_2)_4]_2 \qquad n = 3$$
$$[Co(NH_3)_6][Co(NH_3)_2(NO_2)_4]_3 \qquad n = 4$$
$$[Co(NH_3)_4(NO_2)_2]_3[Co(NO_2)_6] \qquad n = 4$$
$$[Co(NH_3)_5(NO_2)]_3[Co(NO_2)_6]_2 \qquad n = 5$$

2-4-9 Ligand isomerism

If two ligands are isomers the corresponding complexes are isomers also, e.g. the ligands

CH₂—CH—CH₃ and CH₂—CH₂—CH₂
NH₂ NH₂   NH₂   NH₂
1,2-diaminopropane   1,3-diaminopropane
(pn)   (tn)

are isomers both of which form complexes of the type

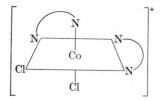

(Here we have adopted a convenient representation for the two isomeric ligands which shows only the coordinated atoms.)

A special case of ligand isomerism arises when the ligands are optical isomers—enantiomorphs—of each other. One interesting problem is the extent to which electronic absorption bands, which, as a first approximation, are supposed to be localized on a transition-metal ion, acquire optical activity because of the activity of a coordinated ligand. An example of this is provided by the ligand mentioned above, 1,2-diaminopropane (pn), which exists in optically isomeric forms.

2-4-10   Optical isomerism

A molecule is optically active when it cannot be superimposed on its mirror image. Although this condition is met by an octahedral complex $ML_aL_bL_cL_dL_eL_f$ no such complex has been resolved. In practice, optical activity is only observed for octahedral complexes of chelating ligands. (Optical activity has been observed for chelated tetrahedral and square planar complexes but only rarely.) It is further necessary for the chelated complex to be stable kinetically; to permit resolution, it must retain its configuration for at least a matter of minutes. This confines our attention to complexes of a few ions, of which cobalt(III), chromium(III), and rhodium(III) are examples. Although the optical activity of complexes of many polydentate chelating ligands has been studied, for simplicity we shall confine our discussion to the bidentate case.

Two classes of optically active complexes formed by bidentate chelating ligands which have been extensively studied are $[M(L_2)_3]$ and $cis[M(L_2)_2L_2']$, where (L_2) is a bidentate ligand. Fig. 2-17 shows the pairs of isomers for $M = Co$ and $L_2 =$ ethylenediamine (en). It should be noted that $trans[M(L_2)_2L_2']$ might be superimposable on its mirror image and thus not optically active. However, the spatial arrangement of atoms within the bidentate ligands, L_2, may destroy this mirror symmetry, in which case the $trans$ species, like the cis, is optically active.

The determination of the *absolute* configuration of an optically active molecule is not easy. Normal X-ray diffraction techniques cannot distinguish between a structure and its mirror image. However, if the wavelength of the X-rays is chosen to correspond to an

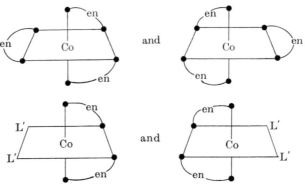

Fig. 2-17 Enantiomeric forms of $[Co(en)_3]^{3+}$ and $[Co(en)_2L_2']^+$ (charges are omitted from the diagrams).

electronic transition of the atom at the coordination centre, additional effects arise which allow the determination of absolute configuration ('anomalous dispersion' occurs). Optical activity in coordination compounds is further discussed in Section 9-3.

Problems

2-1 Give systematic names for the following:

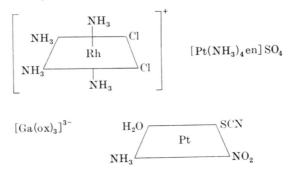

$[Pt(NH_3)_4en]SO_4$

$[Ga(ox)_3]^{3-}$

2-2 List the isomers which may exist for the following:

$Co(NH_3)_4(NO_2)(SO_4)$
$[Co(en)_2(NH_3)Cl]^{2+}$
$[Cr(NCS)_6]^{3-}$
$[Ni(en)_3]^{2+}$
$[Pt(py)(NH_3)BrCl]$

Preparation of coordination compounds

3-1 Introduction

This chapter reviews the most common methods by which coordination compounds are prepared. In the reactions involved, there are two important variables—coordination number and oxidation number (often called valence state). In principle, either may increase, decrease, or remain unchanged in a reaction, and the reader may find it helpful to classify the preparative methods described according to changes in these two numbers. In practice, however, it is not always possible to be certain of either. A ligand which is potentially tridentate may, for example, act as a bidentate ligand and so the coordination number differs from that expected. Similarly, is the complex ion $[Co(NH_3)_5NO]^{2+}$ a complex of cobalt(II) or cobalt-(III)? It depends on whether you believe that the NO is better represented as NO· (where the odd electron is paired with a 'cobalt' electron) or as NO⁻. We shall return to this matter of formal valence states later in this chapter and again in Chapter 6.

Complications apart, reactions in which the coordination number of an electron acceptor is increased are called *addition* reactions, and when it is unchanged they are called *substitution* reactions. The coordination number decreases for *dissociation* reactions. Reactions involving valence-state changes are called *oxidation* or *reduction* reactions, as appropriate.

An important classification of complexes depends on the speed with which they undergo substitution reactions. When excess of aqueous ammonia is added to a solution of copper(II) sulphate in water the change in colour from pale to deep blue is almost instantaneous, because an ammine complex is formed very rapidly (in this reaction ammonia replaces the water molecules coordinated to the copper(II) ion). That is, copper(II) forms kinetically *labile* complexes. On the other hand, it takes hours (or even days at room temperature) to replace the water molecules coordinated to the chromium(III) ion by other ligands. The chromium(III) ion forms kinetically *inert* complexes. It is important to recognize the distinction between kinetic and thermodynamic stability at this point. The thermodynamic stability of a complex (which will be discussed at length in the next chapter) refers to the concentrations of complex species and ligands *at equilibrium*. Kinetic stability refers to the speed at which equilibrium conditions are reached. As one would expect, the preparations of kinetically inert and labile complexes present quite different problems. In general, the second- and third-row transition elements form inert complexes. With the exception of chromium(III) and cobalt(III), first-row transition elements form labile complexes. Main group elements usually form labile complexes.

3-2   Preparative methods

3-2-1   Simple addition reactions

The most direct method of preparing $[BF_3 \cdot NH_3]$ is by gas-phase addition, in which a carefully controlled flow of each of the gaseous reactants is led into a large evacuated flask, where the product deposits as a white powder:

$$BF_3 + NH_3 \rightarrow [BF_3 \cdot NH_3]$$

When one reactant is a liquid and the other a gas at room temperature, a different technique is usually followed. In the preparation of $[BF_3 \cdot OEt_2]$ the ether and boron trifluoride are condensed separately into an evacuated flask cooled in liquid nitrogen. When the flask is warmed slowly, a controlled reaction takes place:

$$BF_3 + Et_2O \rightarrow [BF_3 \cdot OEt_2]$$

Reactions between two liquids are best carried out by mixing solutions of them in a readily removable inert solvent, e.g.:

$$SnCl_4 + 2NMe_3 \xrightarrow[\substack{\text{petroleum} \\ \text{ether}}]{40-60^\circ \text{b.p.}} trans[SnCl_4(NMe_3)_2]$$

If at all possible, the presence of a solid reactant should be avoided. For example, the complex anion $[BF_4]^-$ is more conveniently made by reaction between boric acid and hydrofluoric acid, the latter conveniently generated *in situ*:

$$8NH_4F + 2H_3BO_3 + 3H_2SO_4 \rightarrow 3(NH_4)_2SO_4 + 2NH_4[BF_4] + 6H_2O$$

than by the solid–gas reaction:

$$NH_4F + BF_3 \rightarrow NH_4[BF_4]$$

When a solid reactant is unavoidable, purification of the product may be difficult; however, a large number of anionic complexes of formula $[MX_n]^{m-}$, where X is a halogen (usually F or Cl), have been made in this way, e.g.:

$$2KCl + TiCl_4 \rightarrow K_2[TiCl_6]$$

As one would expect, good examples of simple addition reactions of transition metal complexes are confined to those ions which readily change their coordination number. Copper(II) provides many examples, for instance the addition of pyridine to $[Cuacac_2]$:

$$[Cuacac_2] + py \rightarrow [Cuacac_2py]$$

3-2-2   Substitution reactions

The majority of complexes, both of transition and non-transition elements, may be prepared by substitution reactions. The mechanisms of some of these reactions have been extensively investigated and will be discussed in Chapter 11. Although the coordination number of the atom at the coordination centre in both reactant and product species is the same in these reactions, it must be emphasized that little can be inferred about reaction mechanism from a study of the products of a reaction and, in particular, that phrases such as 'the ligand A displaces ligand B' should be avoided. However, for the non-transition elements in particular, where substitution reactions usually proceed if thermodynamically favourable, a study of substitution reactions enables both qualitative and quantitative assessments to be made of the relative strength of donor–acceptor bonds. Thus, because ammonia displaces ether from $[BF_3 \cdot OEt_2]$, even in ether solution, to give crystals of $[BF_3 \cdot NH_3]$ it has been concluded that the B—N bond is stronger than the B—O.

As noted earlier, there is an experimental distinction between the substitution reactions of labile and inert complexes. The formation of labile complexes is virtually instantaneous upon mixing of the reactants, so that there are few practical difficulties in their preparation, but three points must be remembered. First, it is found in practice that it is difficult to prepare such complexes with several different non-ionic ligands bonded to the same metal atom, although an anionic species may be coordinated together with a neutral ligand. Second, although it may be possible to isolate and characterize a solid complex, quite a different complex may be the predominant species in solution. The third point, that some complex ions display incongruent solubility (*vide infra*), is related to the second.

If an aqueous solution containing iron(II) sulphate and ammonium sulphate in a 1:1 ratio is allowed to crystallize then Mohr's salt, $[Fe(H_2O)_6]SO_4(NH_4)_2SO_4$, is obtained. The ferrous ammonium sulphate is said to show congruent solubility. On the other hand, if an aqueous solution containing a $2:1$ ratio of potassium chloride and copper(II) chloride crystallizes, crystals of potassium chloride are obtained at first. Only later does the complex $K_2[Cu(H_2O)_2Cl_4]$ crystallize. Similarly, attempts to recrystallize the salt will lead to the initial deposition of potassium chloride. The complex is said to display incongruent solubility; it can only be obtained from solutions containing excess of copper(II) chloride. A system which displays incongruent solubility at one temperature may display congruent solubility at another.

Examples of the formation of complex ions by substitution reactions of labile complexes are:

1. The action of excess of ammonia on aqueous solutions of copper(II) salts:

$$[Cu(H_2O)_4]^{2+} + 3NH_4(aq) \rightarrow [Cu(NH_3)_4]^{2+} + 4H_2O$$

Although this equation shows the complete substitution of coordinated water by ammonia all such reactions occur in steps and the species $[Cu(H_2O)_4]^{2+}$, $[Cu(H_2O)_3NH_3]^{2+}$, $[Cu(H_2O)_2(NH_3)_2]^{2+}$, $[Cu(H_2O)(NH_3)_3]^{2+}$, and $[Cu(NH_3)_4]^{2+}$ will all be present in the solution, although the concentration of some will be low. By a suitable choice of concentrations (using stability-constant data of the sort discussed in the next chapter) it is possible to ensure that the concentration of one particular component, $[Cu(H_2O)_2(NH_3)_2]^{2+}$ say, is a maximum in the solution. However, it does not follow that if crystallization is induced (for example, by adding ethyl alcohol to the solution and so decreasing the solubility of the complex species) the complex which crystallizes will contain the $[Cu(H_2O)_2(NH_3)_2]^{2+}$ cation. There are many labile complexes which may be studied readily in solution but which are very difficult to obtain in the solid state.*

2. The reaction between aqueous solutions of thiourea and lead nitrate:

$$[Pb(H_2O)_6]^{2+} + 6SC(NH_2)_2 \rightarrow [Pb(SC(NH_2)_2)_6]^{2+} + 6H_2O$$

The nature of the lead(II) ion in aqueous lead nitrate solutions is not known. The solution is probably a mixture containing polymeric species and the reaction given above is, therefore, oversimplified both for this reason and because it makes no mention of species intermediate between $[Pb(H_2O)_6]^{2+}$ and $[Pb(SC(NH_2)_2)_6]^{2+}$.

---

* A common coordination geometry for the copper(II) ion is to be surrounded by four ligands in a plane which, together with two ligands one above and one below this plane but further from the copper atom, form a tetragonally distorted octahedron. In this discussion we have neglected these two, more weakly bonded, ligands.

3. If an uncharged complex is prepared it is precipitated from aqueous solution and, unless highly polymeric, may be recrystallized from organic solvents, e.g.:

$$[Fe(H_2O)_6]^{3+} + 3acac^- \rightarrow \underset{\substack{\text{insoluble} \\ \text{in water}}}{[Fe(acac)_3]} + 6H_2O$$

Rather more is known about the substitution of inert, as opposed to labile, complexes because more kinetic data are available for the former class (Chapter 11). Some examples of preparations involving substitution reactions of inert complexes are given below.

1. The oxidation of cobalt(II) salts in aqueous solutions containing both ammonia and ammonium carbonate leads to the formation of the $[Co(NH_3)_5CO_3]^+$ cation. On heating with aqueous ammonium bifluoride solution (90°, 1 hour) this is converted into the $[Co(NH_3)_5F]^{3+}$ cation. The species $[Co(NH_3)_5H_2O]^{3+}$ is almost certainly an intermediate in the reaction (see Section 11-5):

$$[Co(NH_3)_5CO_3]^+ + 2HF \rightarrow [Co(NH_3)_5F]^{2+} + F^- + CO_2 + H_2O$$

2. Potassium cobaltinitrite reacts with an aqueous solution of ethylenediamine fairly rapidly at *ca* 70° to give *cis*-dinitrobis (ethylenediamine)cobalt(III):

$$[Co(NO_2)_6]^{3-} + 2en \rightarrow cis[Coen_2(NO_2)_2]^+ + 4NO_2^-$$

In this reaction the complex $[Coen(NO_2)_4]^-$ is presumably an intermediate. However, the solid obtained by removing the solvent from a solution in which the major component is $cis[Coen_2(NO_2)_2]^+$ will also consist largely of this complex ion, because it is kinetically inert.

In the preparation of some complexes the presence of water must be avoided. For example, the action of ammonia on hydrated chromium(III) salts—those commercially available—leads to the precipitation of insoluble hydroxy complexes and not to the formation of $[Cr(NH_3)_6]^{3+}$. This complex is readily prepared, however, by reaction between liquid ammonia and anhydrous chromium(III) chloride:

Other preparations requiring the use of non-aqueous solvents are those in which the ligand is insoluble in water. Thus, alcoholic solvents are often used for the preparation of complexes in which an organic phosphine is a ligand. Aliphatic ethers and acetals such as tetrahydrofuran or 1,1-dimethoxyethane, in which many ligands and anhydrous metal halides have an appreciable solubility, are widely used as solvents. It is unusual to find hydrated reactants used in non-aqueous systems, anhydrous metal halides, in particular, being commonly employed. An exception is when the aliphatic acetal 2,2-dimethoxypropane is used as solvent. Under reflux this removes water from hydrated species, evolving methanol and acetone:

$$[Ni(H_2O)_6]Cl_2 + 6(MeO)_2CMe_2 \rightarrow 6MeOH + 6Me_2CO + NiCl_2$$

The reaction product may not be an anhydrous salt (as indicated by the above equation) but a complex containing coordinated methanol or acetone. However, these ligands usually bond rather weakly and are readily replaced by other ligands present in the solution.

Examples of the preparation of complexes by substitution reactions in non-aqueous media are:

1. Potassium thiocyanate melts at 173°C and may be used as a solvent at temperatures above this. For example, in this medium water is readily displaced from the $[Cr(H_2O)_6]^{3+}$ ion:

$$[Cr(H_2O)_6]^{3+} + 6NCS^- \xrightarrow[\text{molten KNCS}]{180°} [Cr(NCS)_6]^{3-} + 6H_2O$$

2. Refluxing thionyl chloride reacts with water to give sulphur dioxide and hydrogen chloride and may be used to prepare anhydrous metal chlorides from the hydrated chlorides. Additionally, it is a suitable, if somewhat unpleasant, solvent for the preparation of the chloro-anions of metals:

$$2NEt_4Cl + NiCl_2 \xrightarrow[\text{reflux}]{SOCl_2} (NEt_4)_2[NiCl_4]$$

At high temperatures thionyl chloride slowly decomposes to give chlorine and this reduces its usefulness as a solvent.

3. Most salts are converted by bromine trifluoride into the highest fluoride of the element, or, if an alkali metal salt is present, into a fluoro-anion. It is so powerful a fluorinating agent that it will even react with metals and alloys. For example, with a 1:1 alloy of silver and gold:

$$AgAu(alloy) \xrightarrow{BrF_3} Ag[AuF_4]$$

3-2-3 Oxidation–reduction reactions

As we have seen, inert complexes of the transition metals may be interconverted by substitution reactions, but such methods cannot generally be relied upon and it is preferable to prepare inert complexes by a different method. The chosen method is to take a compound containing the metal in a different oxidation state and oxidize or reduce it, as appropriate, in the presence of the coordinating ligand. This technique is used extensively in the preparation of complexes of cobalt(III). Cobalt(II) salts are the precursors and either air or hydrogen peroxide is the usual oxidizing agent. Many chromium(III) complexes are prepared from chromium(VI) (i.e. chromates or dichromates); a wide variety of reducing agents may be used but, where suitable, the ligand itself is used. Other chromium(III) complexes are prepared by the oxidation of chromium(II) salts.

The success of this preparative method rests on two factors. First, although the product is an inert complex, the starting material is relatively labile. Concentrations used in the preparation are usually those which maximize the concentration of a complex species identical in composition with the desired product but differing from it in charge. Electron addition or removal (i.e. reduction or oxidation) then gives the product. Second, as we have seen earlier, there will be several labile complexes in equilibria, each of which can undergo oxidation (or reduction) to give an inert product. In general, the product will be derived from that labile complex which is the most readily oxidized (or reduced).

Examples of complexes prepared by oxidation–reduction reactions are:

1. The preparation of hexamminocobalt(III) chloride by oxidation of an aqueous solution of cobalt(II) chloride made alkaline with ammonia in the presence of ammonium chloride:

$$2CoCl_2 + 2NH_4Cl + 10NH_3 + H_2O_2 \xrightarrow{\text{charcoal}} 2[Co(NH_3)_6]Cl_3 + 2H_2O$$

This reaction is catalysed by the presence of charcoal; in its absence the product consists largely of pentamminocobalt(III) complexes, the sixth coordination site being occupied by either H_2O or Cl^-. The function of the charcoal is not known with certainty but it is believed that it may act by donating an electron to a pentamminocobalt(III) ion, converting it momentarily into a (labile) pentamminocobalt(II) species into which a further ammonia molecule substitutes.

2. An aqueous solution of oxalic acid and potassium oxalate reduces potassium dichromate to the trisoxalatochromium(III) anion:

$$K_2Cr_2O_7 + 7H_2C_2O_4 + 2K_2C_2O_4 \rightarrow 2K_3[Cr(C_2O_4)_3] + 6CO_2 + 7H_2O$$

3. Complexes containing manganese in less-common formal valence states may be made either by reduction of the permanganate anion, $[MnO_4]^-$, or by oxidation of the hexaquomanganese(II) cation. Sometimes, as in the preparation of the $[MnF_5(H_2O)]^{2-}$ anion, containing manganese(III), the two are combined:

$$8[Mn(H_2O)_6]^{2+} + 2[MnO_4]^- + 25HF_2^- \rightarrow 10[MnF_5(H_2O)]^{2-} + 9H^+ + 46H_2O$$

In this example we see another reason for using an oxidation–reduction reaction for the preparation of a complex—the non-availability of suitable precursors in which a metal is in the desired valence state.

Recently, systems in which a series of complex ions of identical stoichiometry are interrelated by a series of one-electron oxidations or reductions have been extensively studied. The existence of such a related series is conveniently investigated polarographically,* the half-wave potentials obtained suggesting suitable chemical oxidizing or reducing agents for the bulk preparation of the related species. An alternative technique is to carry out the oxidation or reduction electrolytically, preferably at a potential which is held constant despite fluctuations in current. This technique is called 'controlled potential electrolysis'.

For example, it has been shown polarographically that a square planar complex of nickel, $[Ni(S_2C_2(C_6H_5)_2)_2]$, in which the ligand is

$$C_6H_5—C—S^-$$
$$\|$$
$$C_6H_5—C—S^-$$

(the dianion derived from stilbenedithiol) undergoes reduction to give the species $[Ni(S_2C_2(C_6H_5)_2)_2]^-$ and $[Ni(S_2C_2(C_6H_5)_2)_2]^{2-}$. There has been considerable discussion of the valence state of the metal atom in these and similar complexes. Is it the metal or ligand which is being reduced, or is it both? It seems that the added electrons are delocalized over the whole complex (the stilbenedithiolate ligand is planar and has a delocalized π-system) and so it becomes difficult to define the valency state of either the metal or ligand. We shall return to this problem in Chapter 6.

3-2-4   Thermal dissociation reactions

By controlled heating, some complexes can be degraded to others, a volatile compound being expelled. For example, when it is heated, ordinary blue copper(II) sulphate loses water in a stepwise manner until above *ca* 220° the anhydrous sulphate is left:

$$CuSO_4 \cdot 5H_2O \xrightarrow{96 \cdot 5°} CuSO_4 \cdot 4H_2O \xrightarrow{102°} CuSO_4 \cdot 3H_2O \xrightarrow{115°} CuSO_4 \cdot H_2O$$
$$\downarrow 220°$$
$$CuSO_4$$

Many other complexes behave similarly and heating (usually under vacuum) to a carefully controlled temperature is a useful preparative

---

* In polarography the potential between two electrodes in a solution is continuously varied and the consequent variation in current recorded. At certain potentials electrolytic reduction of species in solution occurs and the current rises. Because the cathode is very small (a mercury drop or platinum wire) the increase in current is diffusion-limited and a characteristic step-like plot of current *vs* voltage results, one step for each reduction process. The voltage corresponding to the mid-point of the 'riser' part of a step is a characteristic of the reduction process and is termed the half-wave potential.

method. Hydrogen halide elimination, for example, is a reaction which occurs readily for almost any complex which has the electron-donor atom attached to a hydrogen (e.g. H_2O, ROH, NH_3, R_2NH) and the electron acceptor attached to a halogen (e.g. BF_3, $SnBr_4$, $FeCl_3$). Another very common thermal reaction is the expulsion of one or more neutral ligands (as in the case of copper(II) sulphate), with a consequent reduction in the apparent coordination number of the central atom. Often some monodentate ligand (generally an anion) becomes either bidentate or a group bridging two metal atoms (the acetate and halide anions, respectively, exemplify these two cases). Another possibility is that an anion, initially non-coordinated, becomes attached to the metal. The actual coordination number of the central atom is seldom reduced.

Heating to a relatively high temperature can lead to the complete dissociation of the complex species. For example:

$$K[BF_4] \rightarrow BF_3 + KF$$

and

$$BrF_2[RuF_6] \rightarrow BrF_3 + RuF_5$$

In the absence of some other suitable cationic species, complex fluorides containing the BrF_2^+ cation are formed when transition-metal salts are dissolved in BrF_3. Thermal decomposition of these salts is a convenient way of making small quantities of many fluorides.

Examples of complexes prepared by thermal dissociation reactions are:

1. The preparation of $cis[Cr(en)_2Cl_2]^+$ by heating $[Cr(en)_3]Cl_3$:

$$[Cr(en)_3]Cl_3 \xrightarrow{210°} cis[Cr(en)_2Cl_2]Cl + en$$

The temperature of this reaction has to be carefully controlled to achieve maximum yields; the reaction is complete in 2–3 hours. In an analogous reaction $trans[Cr(en)_2(SCN)_2]SCN$ is prepared by heating $[Cr(en)_3](SCN)_3$ to 130°.

2. Anhydrous nickel(II) chloride reacts with excess pyridine in non-aqueous solvents to give $trans[Nipy_4Cl_2]$. On heating this complex to 180° in $vacuo$ a compound of empirical formula $Nipy_2Cl_2$ is formed. The structure of this complex is not known with certainty but it appears to be polymeric with each chlorine bridging two nickel atoms to give an octahedral arrangement of ligands around each metal atom. At 220° a material of empirical formula $NipyCl_2$ is formed in which the nickel still seems to be octahedrally coordinated (presumably some of the chlorines bridge three nickel atoms). At 350° anhydrous nickel chloride is the product.

Two experimental techniques have recently been used to study the preparation of new complexes by the thermal dissociation reactions. These are:

Differential Thermal Analysis (D.T.A.). Two cells, one containing the complex under study and the other a similar amount of a thermally stable material, are slowly warmed, each receiving an identical amount of thermal energy. The temperature difference between the two cells is measured and remains zero until thermal dissociation of the complex occurs. Both the temperature (at a particular pressure) and enthalpy of dissociation may be obtained by this technique.

Thermo-Gravimetric Analysis (T.G.A.). The weight of a complex is measured as its temperature is raised. When thermal dissociation occurs the weight of any volatile ligand expelled is measured and the empirical formula of the product may usually be deduced. Both dissociation pressure and temperature are recorded as they are, of course, interrelated.

3-2-5   Reactions of coordinated ligands

We noted earlier that substitution reactions of inert complexes proceed slowly at room temperature; however, there are exceptions. For example, addition of acid to the $[Co(NH_3)_5CO_3]^+$ cation leads to the rapid evolution of carbon dioxide and formation of the complex ion $[Co(NH_3)_5OH_2]^{3+}$. Indeed, a whole series of facile interconversions exists between species containing $Co—OH_2$, $Co—OH$, $Co—CO_3$, $Co—SO_3$, $Co—NO_2$, and similar bonds. The explanation for this non-typical behaviour is that in none of these reactions is a $Co—O$ bond broken (although, because they are commonly written as above, it is not immediately obvious that all of them contain $Co—O$ bonds. (Note that the NO_2^- anion may also bond through the nitrogen—see Section 2-4-7.)

Using isotopically labelled oxygen it can be shown, for example, that in the reaction:

$$[(NH_3)_5Co—O—CO_2]^+ \xrightarrow{\text{acid}} [(NH_3)_5Co—O—H_2]^{3+}$$

it is the O—C bond that is broken. Other reactions of the same type are:

$$[Cr(NH_3)_5(H_2O)]^{3+} \xrightarrow{\text{HNO}_2} [Cr(NH_3)_5(ONO)]^{2+}$$

and a rather unusual reaction which proceeds in aqueous solution:

$$[Co(NH_3)_5NCS]^{2+} \xrightarrow{\text{H}_2\text{O}_2} [Co(NH_3)_6]^{3+}$$

(The mechanism of this reaction is not known.)

So far we have considered only reactions of an atom directly bonded to a transition metal. Recently there has been much work on the more remote modification of a ligand. One relatively simple complex which has been the subject of extensive study is tris-acetylacetonatochromium(III). The action of bromine in acetic acid leads to bromination of the acetylacetone ring:

$$
\left[\ \underset{\substack{\displaystyle \\ \text{CH}_3}}{\overset{\substack{\text{CH}_3}}{\text{Cr}\!\!\!\bigcirc\!\!\!\!-\text{C}\!-\!\text{H}}}\ \right]_3 \xrightarrow{\text{Br}_2} \left[\ \underset{\substack{\displaystyle \\ \text{CH}_3}}{\overset{\substack{\text{CH}_3}}{\text{Cr}\!\!\!\bigcirc\!\!\!\!-\text{C}\!-\!\text{Br}}}\ \right]_3
$$

It is reported that the N-halosuccinimides are the best agents for halogenating coordinated acetylacetonate rings. All the available evidence indicates that it is the coordinated ligand which reacts, and not any free ligand in equilibrium with it. Examples of other groups which have been used to replace the active hydrogen atoms in metal acetylacetonates are $-NO_2$, $-NH_2$, $-N_3^+$, $-CHO$, $-COCH_3$, and $-SCl$.

Many reactions are known in which the presence of a metal ion influences the products of a reaction and the explanation for this may well lie in the different reactions of free and coordinated ligands. Peptide chemistry is one field in which this may prove to be of great importance.

3-2-6   The *trans* effect

The ligand arrangement around an atom after a substitution reaction may or may not be similar to that of the starting material, even for inert complexes. An example of this is provided by the formation of $trans[Cr(en)_2(NCS)_2]^+$ on heating $[Cr(en)_3](NCS)_3$ with solid ammonium thiocyanate at 130°. Similarly, $cis[Co(NH_3)_4(H_2O)Cl]SO_4$ is converted into $trans[Co(NH_3)_4Cl_2]HSO_4$ by the action of a mixture of concentrated hydrochloric acid and sulphuric acid at room temperature.

The chemistry of platinum(II) is exceptional in this respect in that the product of a substitution reaction can be predicted with confidence. This is because the lability of a ligand bonded to platinum(II) is largely determined by the group which is *trans* to it (virtually all platinum(II) complexes are square planar) and *not* by the nature of the ligand itself. Although this *trans effect* is not fully understood, its operation is reliable and renders the synthesis of platinum(II) complexes a class on its own. It follows that the stereochemistry of the products of reactions of platinum (II) complexes can often be varied by altering the order of reagent addition. An example of this is provided by the synthesis of *cis* and *trans*[Pt(NH₃)(NO₂)Cl₂]⁻ (for simplicity we have omitted the charges on the complex species):

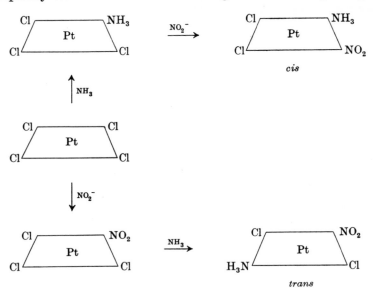

cis

trans

Ligands can be arranged in a series depending on the relative magnitude of the *trans* effect which they exert. It is left as an exercise for the reader to show that the above reactions indicate that the relative magnitude of the *trans* effect for the three ligands Cl⁻, NH₃, and NO₂⁻ is:

$$NO_2^- > Cl^- > NH_3$$

A more extended series is:

CN⁻, CO, C₂H₄, NO₂⁻ > thiourea, PR₃, SR₂ > I⁻, SCN⁻
(S-bonded) > Br⁻ > Cl⁻ > NH₃, py > OH⁻ > H₂O

We shall discuss the *trans* effect again in Chapter 11.

Problems

3-1   Suggest preparative methods for the following coordination compounds using the starting material indicated

[AlCl₃py] from Al (commercial AlCl₃ contains FeCl₃ as impurity)
[SnCl₃]⁻ from SnCl₂ (the choice of cation is left to you)
[Pt(SnCl₃)₅]³⁻ from K₂PtCl₄
[Coen₃]³⁺ from [Co(H₂O)₆]²⁺
[Co(NH₃)₆]²⁺ from [Co(H₂O)₆]²⁺
[Cr(ox)₂(H₂O)₂]⁻ from KCrO₄ (the isomeric form of the product does not matter)

3-2   Use the abbreviated *trans* effect series NO₂⁻ > Cl⁻ > NH₃ to plan the synthesis of *cis*- and *trans*-[Pt(NH₃)(NO₂)Cl₂]. What ambiguity arises?

Stability of coordination compounds

4-1 Introduction

The statement that a compound is 'stable' is rather loose, for several different interpretations may be placed upon it. Used without qualification it means that the compound exists and, under suitable conditions, may be stored for a long period of time. However, a statement such as 'a compound is stable in water' may mean one of two things, either that there is no reaction with water which would lead to a lower free energy of the system (thermodynamic stability) or that, although a reaction would lead to a more stable system, there is no available mechanism by which the reaction can occur (kinetic stability). For example, there may not be enough energy available to break a strong bond, although once broken it could be replaced by an even stronger one. As we have seen, boron trifluoride forms a stable complex with trimethylamine, $[BF_3 \cdot N(CH_3)_3]$. A similar complex is formed with trisilylamine, $[BF_3 \cdot N(SiH_3)_3]$, which is thermodynamically unstable with respect to the reaction:

$$[BF_3 \cdot N(SiH_3)_3] \rightarrow BF_2 \cdot N(SiH_3)_2 + SiH_3F$$

The complex can be prepared and stored at low temperatures ($ca\ -80°$) since the decomposition then proceeds very slowly—the complex is kinetically fairly stable. At room temperature the complex is kinetically unstable and the rate of decomposition is much greater.

We have already seen that the species which crystallizes from a solution of a mixture of related labile complexes depends not only on the cation and ligand concentrations but also on the solvent and crystallization temperature. Although it may be a relatively minor component in the solution, the least soluble complex is the one which crystallizes. In the solution there is a series of equilibria such that, if one component crystallizes, the concentrations of the others also change. In this chapter we discuss the stability constants which characterize such equilibria.

4-2 Stability constants

When a complex is formed by the reaction:*

$$M + L \rightleftharpoons ML$$

the equilibrium constant, K_1, will be $K_1 = [ML]/[M][L]$ where, for the moment, we have assumed activity coefficients of unity. If ML adds a further molecule of L:

$$ML + L \rightleftharpoons ML_2$$

then $K_2 = [ML_2]/[ML][L]$. In general, the equilibrium constant for the formation of the complex ML_n from ML_{n-1} will be $K_n = [ML_n]/[ML_{n-1}][L]$. The equilibrium constants $K_1, K_2 \ldots K_n$ are known as *stepwise* formation constants. Alternatively, one may consider the equilibrium $M + nL \rightleftharpoons ML_n$ which is characterized by an equilibrium constant, $\beta_n = [ML_n]/[M][L]^n$. β_n is known as the nth *overall* formation constant. β_n is related to the stepwise formation constants:

$$\beta_n = \frac{[ML]}{[M][L]} \cdot \frac{[ML_2]}{[ML][L]} \cdots \frac{[ML_n]}{[ML_{n-1}][L]} = \frac{[ML_n]}{[M][L]^n}$$

$$= K_1 . K_2 \ldots . . K_n$$

That is:

$$\beta_n = \prod_{l=1}^{n} K_l$$

There is the same number of overall formation constants as stepwise formation constants: $\beta_1 = K_1$; $\beta_2 = K_1 . K_2$; $\beta_3 = K_1 . K_2 . K_3$ etc.

4-3 Determination of stability constants

In order to determine the values of n formation constants, $n + 2$ independent concentration measurements are needed. These can then be used to obtain the concentrations of the n species ML, $ML_2 \ldots ML_n$, and also those of M and L. Two pieces of information are at once available; we (should!) know the quantities of M and L (or alternative starting materials) used in the experiment. This means that n additional pieces of information are needed. If it is certain that only one complex, of known empirical formula, is formed, then a measurement of the concentration of the uncomplexed M or L is sufficient to determine the formation constant. This measurement

---

* Throughout this chapter we shall not specify the charges on the species in reactions or equilibria. Further, square brackets are used to indicate concentrations of complex species and sometimes the species themselves as well. It will be clear from the context which is intended.

can be made in many ways: by polarographic or e.m.f. measurements (if a suitable reversible electrode exists), by pH measurements (if the acid dissociation constant of HL is known) and by many other techniques.

For the more general case where more than one formation constant is to be determined, the problem is usually more difficult. For inert complexes it may be possible to separate, and separately estimate, the various complex species. In this way Bjerrum was able to determine the six stability constants within the $[Cr(H_2O)_6]^{3+}$, $[Cr(H_2O)_5SCN]^{2+}$ ... $[Cr(SCN)_6]^{3-}$ series. However, this is a potentially unreliable method and has been little used. Some methods of tackling the general problem will now be indicated. The variants are many for this is a field in which considerable ingenuity has been used in the design of experiments and in the analysis of experimental data.

From the composition of the original mixture the average number of ligand molecules complexed with each metal atom, $\bar{n}$, is known. $\bar{n}$ is related to the composition of the mixture of complex ions by the equation

$$\bar{n} = \frac{1[ML] + 2[ML_2] + \ldots N[ML_N]}{[M] + [ML] + [ML_2] + \ldots [ML_N]} = \frac{\sum\limits_{n=1}^{N} n[ML_n]}{[M]_t}$$

where the complex species are $ML, ML_2 \ldots ML_N$, and $[M]_t$ is the total concentration of metal ion, complexed and uncomplexed, in the solution.

Now,

$$[M]_t = \sum_{n=0}^{N} [ML_n] = [M] + \sum_{n=1}^{N} [ML_n]$$

and

$$[ML_n] = \beta_n[M][L]^n$$

so

$$\bar{n} = \frac{\sum\limits_{n=1}^{N} n\beta_n[M][L]^n}{[M] + \sum\limits_{n=1}^{N} \beta_n[M][L]^n} = \frac{\sum\limits_{n=1}^{N} n\beta_n[L]^n}{1 + \sum\limits_{n=1}^{N} \beta_n[L]^n}$$

If a series of solutions, with varying $\bar{n}$, is prepared and $[L]$ measured in each, then values of β_n, $n = 1, 2 \ldots N$, must be chosen so that the above equality holds. This may be done, for example, by plotting $\bar{n}$ against $[L]$ and determining the βs by a curve-fitting procedure.

If it is easier to measure [M] than [L], a different but related relationship is used. We know that

$$\frac{[M]_t}{[M]} = \frac{[M] + [ML] + [ML_2] + \ldots [ML_n]}{[M]}$$

$$= \frac{1}{[M]} \{[M] + \beta_1[M][L] + \beta_2[M][L]^2 + \ldots \beta_N[M][L]^N\}$$

$$= 1 + \beta_1[L] + \beta_2[L]^2 + \ldots \beta_N[L]^N$$

That is,

$$\frac{[M]_t}{[M]} = 1 + \sum_{n=1}^{N} \beta_n[L]^n$$

If both [M] and [L] can be measured, keeping $[M]_t$ constant, this relationship leads to a set of simultaneous equations in the βs (one equation for each measurement) which provide a quick way of determining βs. Alternatively, if [L] is made large, so that $[L] \gg [M]$, it is essentially constant. By varying $[M]_t$ and measuring [M], the βs may similarly be found.

A variety of optical methods is used to determine both complex formation and stability constants. Job's method of continuous variations is the best known. A wavelength is chosen at which the complex in question absorbs (usually in the visible or near ultraviolet region). Several solutions are examined, for all of which $[M]_t + [L]_t$ is a constant, although each has different values for $[M]_t$ and $[L]_t$. Here, $[L]_t$ is the total concentration of ligand, free and complexed. Some measure of the intensity of absorption (usually optical density) is plotted against composition (usually against the ratio $[M]_t/([M]_t + [L]_t)$; that is, against $[M]_t$/constant). If *a single* complex is formed then we have an equilibrium:

	M	$+$ nL	$\rightleftharpoons$	ML_n
Initial concentration	$(1 - \alpha)C$	αC		0
Final concentration	$(1 - \alpha - \gamma)C$	$(\alpha - n\gamma)C$		γC

where the sum of concentrations $[M]_t + [L]_t$ is set equal to C, αC is the initial concentration of the ligand L and γC is the final concentration of the complex species ML_n. Remembering that $\beta_n = [ML_n]/[M][L]^n$ (where the concentrations are those in the final solution), substituting the above values for these concentrations, and differentiating to obtain $d\gamma/d\alpha$, it is readily shown that γ is a maximum when $(n - 1)\gamma_{max} - 2\alpha_{max} + 1 = 0$. At this point the concentration of M will be very small; if we assume that it is zero, then $(1 - \alpha_{max} - \gamma_{max})C = 0$. Combining the last two relationships gives $\alpha_{max} = n/(n + 1)$.* If the absorption is primarily due to ML_n at the wavelength being studied, then this absorption will be a maximum at

$$\frac{[M]_t}{[M]_t + [L]_t} = \frac{(1 - \alpha_{max})C}{(1 - \alpha_{max})C + \alpha_{max}C} = \frac{1 - \alpha_{max}}{1} = \frac{1}{n + 1}$$

so n, and hence α_{max}, may be determined from the position of the maximum (we assume that optical density, say, is being plotted against $[M]_t/([M]_t + [L]_t)$). Conversely, if the absorption is primarily

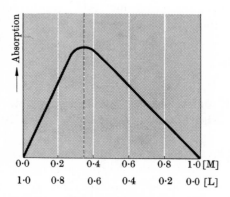

| 0·0 | 0·2 | 0·4 | 0·6 | 0·8 | 1·0 [M] |
| 1·0 | 0·8 | 0·6 | 0·4 | 0·2 | 0·0 [L] |

Fig. 4-1   The Job's plot obtained when only one complex species, ML_2, is formed between M and L.

due to either M or L, it will reach a minimum at this value. Fig. 4-1 shows a typical Job's plot for a ML_2 complex ($\alpha_{max} = \frac{2}{3}$). The rounding at the peak is due to the inaccuracy of the assumption that $1 - \alpha_{max} - \gamma_{max} = 0$. The more stable the complex the less rounded the peak; indeed, in favourable cases the peak shape may be used to determine β_n.

When more than one complex is formed there will usually be a corresponding number of peaks in a Job's plot, but stability constants may only be determined from such a plot under very special circumstances.

There is another method for the determination of stability constants which, although not much used for this purpose, is of some value in reaction kinetics as a method of estimating rate constants which cannot be measured readily (see Chapter 11). Suppose the

* A simpler but less rigorous derivation of this relationship is as follows. When the complex concentration is a maximum, both [M] and [L] $\simeq 0$. That is, $1 - \alpha_{max} - \gamma_{max} = 0$ and $\alpha_{max} - n\gamma_{max} = 0$. Combining these two gives $\alpha_{max} = n/(n + 1)$.

reaction:

$$ML_n + L \rightarrow ML_{n+1}$$

proceeds by a one-step process. The rate of the formation of ML_{n+1} is $k_f[ML_n][L]$, where k_f is the rate constant of this 'forward' reaction. The corresponding 'backward' reaction is:

$$ML_{n+1} \rightarrow ML_n + L$$

and the rate of disappearance of ML_{n+1} is $k_b[ML_{n+1}]$, where k_b is the rate constant of the backward reaction. At equilibrium, $k_f[ML_n][L] = k_b[ML_{n+1}]$. Therefore:

$$\frac{[ML_{n+1}]}{[ML_n][L]} = K_{n+1} = \frac{k_f}{k_b}$$

That is, if the rate constants k_f and k_b can be independently determined, the corresponding stepwise stability constant is given by their quotient.

So far we have assumed activity coefficients of unity, but they seldom have this value. Consequently, the 'stability constants' determined above are not constants at all, but are a function of concentration. The simplest way out of this difficulty is to determine the 'stability constants' over a range of reactant concentrations and then extrapolate to zero concentration (where activity coefficients are unity). K_n and β_n at zero concentration are true thermodynamic equilibrium constants and are distinguished by the prefix T, thus, $^T K_n$ and $^T \beta_n$. More commonly, activity coefficients are kept essentially constant by carrying out measurements in the presence of a backing electrolyte which keeps the ionic strength of the medium constant. Stability constants obtained in this way are proportional to the thermodynamic stability constants, the constant of proportionality being a function of the activity coefficients of the species involved in the complex. Such stability constants are referred to as 'stoichiometric stability constants'. Strictly, it is these which we have discussed—they are given the symbols K_n and β_n which we have been using.

The most useful source of stability constant data is *Stability Constants*, Special Publication number 17 of The Chemical Society (London, 1964). Reference to this volume will show that stepwise stability constants cover a range of $\sim 10^{35}$ and so values of $\log K_n$ and $\log \beta_n$ are given. Generalizations based on these data are given in the next section.

4-4 Stability correlations

Two schemes have been proposed which systematize the available stability constant data. In addition to these data more qualitative evidence, based, for example, on the results of displacement reactions, has also been included.

Chatt and Ahrland have pointed out that electron acceptors may be placed in one of three classes. 'Class a' forms more stable complexes with ligands in which the coordinating atom is a first-row element (N, O, F) than those of an analogous ligand in which the donor is a second-row element (P, S, Cl). 'Class b' has the relative stabilities reversed. It is possible to extend the stability relationships to include heavier donor atoms. Class a behaviour is then typified by a stability order:

$$F^- > Cl^- > Br^- > I^-$$
$$O \gg S > Se > Te$$

and

$$N \gg P > As > Sb > Bi$$

Class b behaviour is rather more complicated and is typified by relative stability constants in the order:

$$F^- < Cl^- < Br^- < I^-$$
$$O \ll S \simeq Se \simeq Te$$

and

$$N \ll P > As > Sb > Bi$$

In addition, there is a third class of electron acceptor for which the stability constants do not display either class a or b behaviour uniquely.

The classification of some electron acceptors is given in Table 4-1 (normal valence states are assumed). The 'a' and 'b' classification is based on a comparison of the relative stabilities of complexes formed by closely related ligands with a wide range of metal ions. When the metal is kept constant and the ligands varied it is more difficult to generalize, but it is roughly true that the stabilities of class

Table 4-1   Classification of cationic species (after Ahrland, Chatt, and Davies)

Class a behaviour
   H, the alkali and alkaline earth metals, the elements Sc → Cr, Al → Cl, Zn → Br, In, Sn, Sb, and I, the lanthanides and actinides
Class b behaviour
   Rh, Pd, Ag, Ir, Pt, Au, Hg
Borderline behaviour
   the elements Mn → Cu, Tl → Po, Mo, Te, Ru, W, Re, Os, Cd

---

b metal complexes decrease with change in coordinated atom in the order:

$$S \simeq C > I > Br > Cl > N > O > F$$

For class a metal complexes this order is reversed.

Although not included within the above classification, there are some other useful gradations which have been noted and are conveniently included at this point. For a given ligand, corresponding stability constants of complexes of bivalent ions of the first transition series are usually in the 'natural order' (sometimes called the Irving–Williams order):

$$Mn(II) < Fe(II) < Co(II) < Ni(II) < Cu(II) > Zn(II)$$

Copper(II) does not coordinate a fifth and sixth ligand particularly strongly, and this order is incorrect for stability constants relating to CuL_5 and CuL_6 complexes. Complexes of chelating ligands also tend not to follow this order.

For non-transition metal ions complex stability decreases roughly in the order of 'ionic potential' (or 'polarizing power'), which is defined as formal charge/ionic radius. Thus, corresponding stability constants decrease in the order:

$$Li^+ > Na^+ > K^+ > Rb^+ > Cs^+$$
$$Mg^{2+} > Ca^{2+} > Sr^{2+} > Ba^{2+} > Ra^{2+}$$

and

$$Al^{3+} > Sc^{3+} > Y^{3+} > La^{3+}$$

provided that the ligand is not changed from one ion to the next. Similarly, for approximately constant ionic radius, the stability constants are in the order:

$$Th^{4+} > Y^{3+} > Ca^{2+} > Na^+$$

and

$$La^{3+} > Sr^{2+} > K^+$$

An alternative approach which has been used to classify metal ion–ligand interactions is based on the concept of hard and soft acids and bases. 'Hard' metal ions are those which parallel the proton in their attachment to ligands, are small, often of high charge and have no valence shell electrons that are easily distorted or removed. 'Soft' metal ions are large, of low charge or have valence shell electrons which are easily distorted or removed. They bond strongly to highly polarizable ligands—which often have a very small proton affinity. Similarly, ligands are divided into those that are non-polarizable ('hard') and those that are polarizable ('soft'). Remembering the Lewis definition of acids and bases as electron acceptors and donors respectively, the cations are classified as either soft or hard acids, whilst the ligands are classified as either soft or hard bases. An important empirical generalization is that the most stable complexes are those of soft acids with soft bases and of hard acids with hard bases.

This approach has the advantage that it is not restricted to complexes of the transition metal ions. Indeed, it may be applied to a wide range of chemical equilibria and systematizes a great deal of chemical 'intuition'. Also, a semi-quantitative interpretation of the phenomenon is emerging which, when fully developed, may prove a useful bridge between theory and experiment. At the moment, however, it appears that many transition metal ions in particular cannot be classified as either hard or soft and the approach cannot be usefully applied to them. Further, it lacks the detailed inequalities which are part of the class a and b system. One concept which is particularly useful, however, is that of 'symbiosis'. A cation which is classified as a relatively 'hard' acid (or, indeed, one which is regarded as 'borderline') is made softer by the coordination of a soft ligand (or harder by the coordination of a hard ligand) and so more likely to add further soft (or hard) ligands. For the non-transition elements the principle of hard and soft acids and bases systematizes stability data in a useful way. In Table 4-2 some metal ions and ligands are classified as hard or soft. Generally, ligands in which the coordinating

Table 4-2   Classification of some (formally) ionic species as hard and soft acids and bases (after Pearson)

Hard acids	H^+ Li^+ Na^+ K^+
	Be^{2+} Mg^{2+} Ca^{2+} Sr^{2+} Mn^{2+}
	Al^{3+} Sc^{3+} Ga^{3+} In^{3+} La^{3+}
	Cr^{3+} Co^{3+} Fe^{3+} Ce^{3+}
	Si^{4+} Ti^{4+} Zr^{4+} Th^{4+}
	VO_2^+ VO^{2+} MoO^{3+}
Soft acids	Cu^+ Ag^+ Au^+ Tl^+ Hg^+
	Cd^{2+} Hg^{2+} Pd^{2+} Pt^{2+}
	Tl^{3+}
	Pt^{4+}
Borderline	Zn^{2+} Sn^{2+} Pb^{2+}
	Fe^{2+} Co^{2+} Ni^{2+} Cu^{2+} Ru^{2+} Os^{2+}
	Sb^{3+} Bi^{3+} Rh^{3+} Ir^{3+}
Hard bases	H_2O R_2O ROH NH_3 RNH_2
	OH^- OR^- Cl^- ClO_4^- NO_3^- $CH_3 \cdot CO_2^-$
	SO_4^{2-} CO_3^{2-}
	PO_4^{3-}
Soft bases	R_2S RSH R_3P R_3As
	RS^- I^- SCN^- CN^- H^- R^-
	$S_2O_3^{2-}$
Borderline	py
	Br^- N_3^- NO_2^-
	SO_3^{2-}

atom has a high electronegativity are hard bases, those in which it has a low electronegativity are soft.

4-5   Statistical and chelate effects

The variations in stability constants which we have discussed so far in this chapter are rather large. Superimposed on them are some smaller but systematic variations which also merit attention.

Most stability constant measurements are made in aqueous solutions at a constant ionic strength. The species we have called M must, in reality, be a complex mixture of species. The majority will probably be $[M(H_2O)_n]^{x+}$, where n may well be four or six. Other species present will include 'foreign' anions—ones not involved in the reaction, but arising from the salt used to maintain a constant ionic strength—coordinated to M. The addition reaction:

$$ML_n + L \rightarrow ML_{n+1}$$

should more properly be written as a substitution reaction (L' is usually H_2O):

$$ML'_m L_n + L \rightarrow ML'_{m-1} L_{n+1} + L'$$

In this reaction we have assumed that the number of ligands around M is constant, and equal to $m + n$. If we let this number (usually four or six) be N, then the reaction may be written:

$$ML'_{N-n} L_n + L \rightarrow ML'_{N-n-1} L_{n+1} + L'$$

It is almost always found that for a given M and L there is a decrease in successive formation constants $K_1, K_2 \ldots$ or $\beta_1, \beta_2 \ldots$. This is largely a statistical effect. It is easier to attach L to ML'_N than to $ML'_{N-1}L$ because there are N reaction 'sites' on the former but only $N - 1$ on the latter (replacement of L in $ML'_{N-1}L$ by L gives an identical molecule). Consider the equilibrium:

$$ML'_{N-n} L_n + L \rightleftharpoons ML'_{N-n-1} L_{n+1} + L'$$

The rate of formation of $ML'_{N-n-1}L_{n+1}$ is, for a simple one-step reaction, $k_f[ML'_{N-n}L_n][L]$. If the statistical effect is the only one which varies as n changes, the forward rate constant will vary with n in proportion to the number of 'reaction sites', that is, the number of L' ligands in $ML'_{N-n}L_n$. We therefore rewrite the above rate as $k'_f(N - n)[ML'_{N-n}][L']$. Similarly, for the rate of disappearance of $ML'_{N-n-1}L_{n+1}$, $k_b[ML'_{N-n-1}L_{n+1}][L]$, k_b will vary with n in proportion to the number of L ligands in $ML'_{N-n-1}L_{n+1}$. Hence, in the above case $k_b = k'_b(n + 1)$. It follows that:

$$K_{n+1} = \frac{k_f}{k_b} = \frac{k'_f(N - n)}{k'_b(n + 1)}$$

(Section 4-3). In a precisely similar way one finds that:

$$K_n = \frac{k'_f(N - n + 1)}{k'_b \cdot n}$$

The ratio between successive formation constants:

$$\frac{K_{n+1}}{K_n} \quad \text{is} \quad \frac{n(N - n)}{(n + 1)(N - n + 1)}$$

The values of this expression for $N = 6$ and $n = 1 \rightarrow 6$ are compared with the experimental data for the Ni^{2+}/NH_3 system

Table 4-3   Statistical predictions and experimental ratios for the equilibrium constants in the system
$[Ni(H_2O)_{6-n}(NH_3)_n]^{2+} + NH_3 \rightleftharpoons$
$\qquad\qquad [Ni(H_2O)_{5-n}(NH_3)_{n+1}]^{2+} + H_2O$

	Experimental ratio	Statistical prediction*
K_2/K_1	0·28	0·42
K_3/K_2	0·31	0·53
K_4/K_3	0·29	0·56
K_5/K_4	0·36	0·53
K_6/K_5	0·2	0·42

$$\text{* using} \quad \frac{K_{n+1}}{K_n} = \frac{n(6 - n)}{(n + 1)(7 - n)}$$

(where L' is H_2O) in Table 4-3. The agreement is not exact, but the predictions are certainly of the correct order of magnitude. The experimental ratios are, as is commonly the case, rather smaller than those predicted statistically.

When a hydrogen atom in a ligand such as ammonia is replaced by an alkyl group, the stability constants of complexes of the ligand are usually lowered. This may be due partly to increased steric interaction in complexes of the substituted ligand, but the observation that the stability constants of complexes with sulphur-containing ligands are usually $H_2S < RSH < R_2S$ suggests that other factors also operate (for example, both the energy and the shape of the lone-pair-containing orbital(s) of the coordinating atom will change slightly on substitution). It might be expected on this basis that complexes of a bidentate ligand such as ethylenediamine $(NH_2 \cdot CH_2 \cdot CH_2 \cdot NH_2)$ are less stable than the corresponding complex with two ammonia molecules. Quite the opposite is true. Complexes containing chelate rings are usually more stable than similar complexes without rings. This is termed the chelate effect, and is illustrated in Table 4-4. The origin of this effect can be determined by a more detailed analysis of stability constant data. To do this, we note the relationships:

$$-RT \ln K = \Delta G^0 = \Delta H^0 - T \Delta S^0$$

which shows that the chelate effect could originate in either the heat term, ΔH^0, or the entropy term, ΔS^0.

To proceed further, we must analyse the equilibrium constants in Table 4-4, in pairs, using these thermodynamic relationships. We can simplify matters by considering, instead, the equilibrium:

$$[M(NH_3)_4]^{2+} + en \rightleftharpoons [M(NH_3)_2 en]^{2+} + 2NH_3$$

Table 4-4   **Comparative stability of the Ni^{2+}/NH_3 and Ni^{2+}/en systems**

	*Equilibrium**	log K
Non-chelated complex	$Ni^{2+} + 2NH_3 \rightleftharpoons [Ni(NH_3)_2]^{2+}$	5·00
	$[Ni(NH_3)_2]^{2+} + 2NH_3 \rightleftharpoons [Ni(NH_3)_4]^{2+}$	2·87
	$[Ni(NH_3)_4]^{2+} + 2NH_3 \rightleftharpoons [Ni(NH_3)_6]^{2+}$	0·74
Chelated complex		
	$Ni^{2+} + en \rightleftharpoons [Nien]^{2+}$	7·51
	$[Nien]^{2+} + en \rightleftharpoons [Nien_2]^{2+}$	6·35
	$[Nien_2]^{2+} + en \rightleftharpoons [Nien_3]^{2+}$	4·32

* Coordinated water is omitted for simplicity

Available data for $M = Ni(\text{II})$ and $Zn(\text{II})$ (remembering that ΔS^0 is quoted in terms of cal/degree, whilst ΔH^0 is given in kcal) are:

	ΔG^0	ΔH^0	ΔS^0	$-T\Delta S^0$(kcal)
$Ni(\text{II})$	-3.4	-2.0	-4.8	-1.4
$Zn(\text{II})$	-1.5	0.1	-5.3	-1.6

These results are qualitatively general: the chelate effect is largely an entropy effect; for non-transition metal ions the heat term is particularly small.

There are two important contributions to the ΔH^0 term. First, when two monodentate anionic ligands are brought together to occupy adjacent coordination sites in a complex, there will be an electrostatic repulsion between them against which work has to be done. The same is true for uncharged monodentate ligands because such ligands are always dipolar. For chelating ligands the coordinating centres do not have to be brought together and most of this repulsive energy is 'built in' (it makes a contribution to the enthalpy of formation of the ligand). That is, in the above equilibrium this contribution to the heat term would be expected to favour the chelated species because the two ammonia molecules repel each other. The second, more variable, contribution to the ΔH^0

term comes from solvation energies. Each of the species in the equilibrium will be solvated (by hydrogen bonding, for example). Further, there will be anions closely associated with the cationic species. We shall see in Chapter 11 that there is kinetic evidence that counter-ions, although not directly bonded to the coordination centre—they are not in the first coordination sphere—are often present in an outer sphere (the so-called 'second coordination sphere'). It does not seem possible to predict, in general, whether this term makes a positive or negative contribution to ΔH^0, but it appears to make a positive contribution when the coordination centre is a main group element.

The entropy effect is readily understood. An increase of randomness is associated with a concomitant increase in entropy. A complex molecule has a lower entropy than its separated and therefore independent components. In the equilibrium above there is a 50 per cent increase in the number of independent molecules on the right-hand side compared with the left. Another aspect of the entropy effect is the following. When one end, and only one end, of an ethylenediamine molecule is coordinated, the effective concentration of the other end in the system, and the probability that it will coordinate, is high, because it is constrained to stay close to the cation. This means that it is easier to form a chelate ring than to coordinate two independent molecules since the two acts of coordination are related for the former, whilst for the latter they are entirely independent of each other.

The chelate effect varies with the size of ring formed on coordination. It is usually a maximum for five-membered rings and only slightly smaller for six-membered rings. Although complexes with rings of other sizes have been synthesized they show little sign of the chelate effect. This is partly because of the reduced effective concentration of the 'other end' of the ligand for larger chelating molecules and because of the increase in work against electrostatic forces needed to bring the coordinating atoms together. Another potentially destabilizing influence for larger-membered rings is the relative difficulty of finding a sterically non-crowded ring configuration. The relationship between the geometry of free and coordinated multidentate ligands is currently the subject of research but it is already clear that ligand geometry is an important factor in determining the relative stabilities of complexes formed by such ligands.

4-6 Solid complexes

In this chapter we have been concerned with equilibria in solution. As we have already noted, it is sometimes possible to study a complex in solution but not to obtain it in the solid state. This is because an additional energy factor is involved, the relative lattice energies of the crystals formed from each of the components in solution. Usually, the crystal form with the highest lattice energy will be obtained (this will be the least soluble complex). For an ionic complex species the lattice energy of a crystal will depend on the counter-ion with which it crystallizes. Lattice energies are a maximum when the cation and anion are of similar charge and size (and, usually, of the same hardness or softness). This suggests a method by which crystals containing an elusive complex may be obtained and accounts for the widespread use in preparative complex chemistry of such species as $[PF_6]^-$, $[B(C_6H_5)_4]^-$, $[NEt_4]^+$, and $[As(C_6H_5)_4]^+$.

4-7   Conclusions

Although several aspects of the stability of coordination compounds have been discussed in this chapter we have avoided the most fundamental question of all: why is one particular complex more stable than another? What is the fundamental explanation for class a and b behaviour (or for the hard and soft distinction)? It is now generally accepted that the interaction of the orbitals of the two uniting atoms is the most important factor. This interaction depends on the matching of the orbitals—orbitals of similar energies also have similar sizes—but it is not a simple matter because several orbitals or sets of orbitals of different energies and sizes on each atom are involved. We shall consider this in more detail in Chapter 6. However, at the present time it does not seem possible to give more than a semi-quantitative answer to such questions.

Problems

4-1   Give, in your own words, detailed accounts of
    (a) Job's method
    (b) The chelate effect
4-2   Use the following data to show that, under the experimental conditions, the highest complex formed between silver(I) and ammonia is $[Ag(NH_3)_2]^+$. All solutions contained a total silver ion concentration of 0.020 M.

Total ammonia concentration	pH of the resulting solution
0.0050 M	4.97
0.0150 M	5.37
0.0300 M	5.79
0.0500 M	6.34

(The answer to this problem is given by F. Basolo and R. Johnson in *Coordination Chemistry*. Benjamin, New York, 1964, p. 136).

Crystal field theory of transition metal complexes

5-1 Introduction

In this chapter we shall discuss transition metal complexes exclusively. Transition metals have their d orbitals incompletely filled. Consequently their complexes have properties not shared by complexes of the main group elements.

In 1928 Bethe published a paper in which he considered the effect of taking an isolated cation, such as K^+, and placing it in the lattice of an ionic crystal, such as KCl. In particular, he was interested in what happened to the energy levels of the free ion when it was placed in the electrostatic field existing within the crystal (the so-called *crystal field*). The energy levels of a free ion show a considerable degeneracy, particularly if one is prepared to ignore effects which cause only small splittings. That is, there exist sets of wavefunctions, each member of any set being quite independent of all other wavefunctions (i.e. orthogonal to them), yet all members of any one set correspond to the same energy. What happens to these ions when placed in an ionic crystal? Do their different wave functions still correspond to the same energy? Bethe showed that in some cases the free ion degeneracy was retained and in others it was lost, the crucial factors being the geometry of the crystalline environment and the term (^1S, ^3P, ^2D, ^1F, etc.) to which the wavefunction of the free ion corresponded.

In 1931 Garrick demonstrated that an ionic model gave heats of formation for transition metal complexes which were in remarkably good agreement with the experimental values. That is, these complexes behaved as if the bonding between the central metal ion and the surrounding ligands were purely electrostatic. If this is so, then Bethe's work may be applied to complexes as well as to ionic crystals and the energy levels of the central ion related to those of the same ion in the gaseous state. All that is needed is a suitable quantitative calculation to obtain the energy level splittings due to the crystal field. This approach to the electronic structure of transition metal complexes is known as *crystal field theory*. Before discussing this theory in detail, however, we must familiarize ourselves with its language.

5-2   Group theoretical symbols

It is convenient for the moment to confine our discussion to octahedral complexes. These are molecules with high symmetry, possessing, for example, fourfold rotation axes, threefold rotation axes, twofold rotation axes, mirror planes, and a centre of symmetry (Fig. 2-7). In the following account certain symbols will be used which are symmetry labels, used to describe the behaviour of wavefunctions when subjected to these symmetry operations. The symbols A_{1g}, A_{2g}, E_g, T_{1g}, T_{2g}, T_{1u}, and T_{2u} will be encountered, often with a spin state designated, for example, ^2E_g and $^3T_{1g}$. Similar lower-case symbols will also be used, for example, a_{1g}, e_g, t_{1g}, etc. These symbols may also have superscripts. We shall refer to t_{2g}^2, for example (other works may refer to this as $(t_{2g})^2$). These symbols are not very difficult to understand. For example, an s orbital on the central metal atom is rotated into itself by a twofold rotation operation (Fig. 5-1) but under the same operation a p_y orbital is turned into minus itself (i.e. the phases of its lobes change sign) (Fig. 5-2). This difference in behaviour is reflected in the different symmetry labels associated with the s and the three p orbitals on the central atom of the complex (a_{1g} and t_{1u}, respectively).

Besides the one-electron wavefunctions associated with s and p orbitals there will be a many-electron wavefunction which describes the total electronic composition of the central ion. Each of the possible many-electron wavefunctions may be distinguished by symmetry labels which also indicate degeneracies. The symbols A (or a) and B (or b), with any suffixes, indicate wavefunctions which are singly degenerate. Similarly E (or e) indicates double degeneracy and T (or t) indicates triple degeneracy. Lower-case symbols (a_{1g}, a_{2u}, e_g, etc.) are used to indicate one-electron wavefunctions

Rotate the orbital by 180°

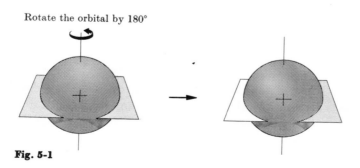

Fig. 5-1

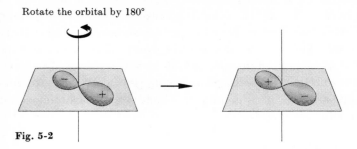

Rotate the orbital by 180°

Fig. 5-2

('orbitals'). The symbol t_{2g} indicates, for example, a set of three degenerate orbitals. The symbol t_{2g}^3 (or $(t_{2g})^3$) indicates that these orbitals are occupied by three electrons. Upper-case symbols are used to describe electronic energy levels and when so used also contain a spin designation. Thus, $^2T_{2g}$ means an energy level which is orbitally triply degenerate. That is, there are three orbital wavefunctions which are degenerate. In addition *each* of these wavefunctions is doubly degenerate in spin space (i.e. may be associated with either of two spin wavefunctions). We may say that a metal ion is in a $^2T_{2g}$ state, and we shall talk of the energy of the ion in terms of 'the energy of $^2T_{2g}$ state'. Upper-case symbols may also be used without any spin designation and they then refer to symmetry alone. We may say that something 'is of A_{1g} symmetry' or 'transforms as A_{1g}', these two expressions being synonymous. The subscripts g and u indicate behaviour under the operation of inversion in the centre of symmetry. An a_{1g} orbital is turned into itself under this operation, hence g (*gerade* = even), but each member of a t_{1u} set is turned into the negative of itself, hence u (*ungerade* = odd). Other subscripts (and/or primes, where these appear) serve only to distinguish general symmetry properties. So the symbols t_{1g} and t_{2g} represent two sets of triply degenerate orbitals, all centrosymmetric, but the members of one set behave differently from the members of the other under some symmetry operations, just as s and p orbitals behave differently under a twofold rotation operation.

Two points should be emphasized here. First, although the same symbols may be applied to molecules of different symmetries there need be no obvious logical connection between them. Symmetry symbols and symmetry, reasonably enough, go together. A change of symmetry probably means a change of symbol. For example, although the metal s and three p orbitals are labelled a_{1g} and t_{1u} in an octahedral complex, in a tetrahedral complex the labels are a_1 and t_2.

Secondly, the distinctions which we have made between the various uses of the symbols are strictly valid only for discussions of the type given in this and the following chapters. If we were talking about molecular vibrations, for example, we should have to slightly redefine them. The symbols are group theoretical in origin and for a discussion of their fundamental significance the reader is referred to one of the excellent texts on group theory now available. An outline account is given in Appendix 1, which also contains material needed later in this chapter.

5-3   Crystal field splittings

In the crystal field theory a complex is regarded as consisting of a central metal cation surrounded by ionic or dipolar ligands which are electrostatically attracted to the cation. The bonding within the complex arises from the electrostatic attraction between the nucleus of the metal cation and the electrons of the ligands. The interaction between the electrons of the cation and those of the ligands is entirely repulsive. We now consider the effect of these repulsive forces in more detail, for they largely cause the splittings which were the subject of Bethe's paper.

Consider the octahedral complex shown in Fig. 5-3. What will be the effect of the crystal field on a single s electron of the central metal ion (or, an equivalent question, what is the effect of the field on the central metal ion in a free ion S state?)? The crystal field will raise the energy of the s electron (or S state), but, as there is no orbital degeneracy, no orbital splittings can result. Next, what will be the effect of the crystal field on a single p electron (or P state) of the metal ion? As is evident from Fig. 5-4, all the p orbitals are equally affected by the crystal field and so, no matter which of them the p electron occupies, the repulsion is the same. That is, the p orbitals (or a P state) remain triply degenerate in an octahedral

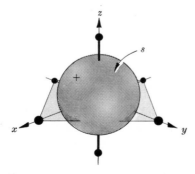

Fig. 5-3

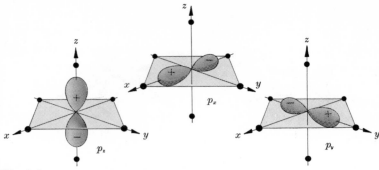

Fig. 5-4

crystalline field. The case of a single d electron (or a D state) is both more difficult and more interesting. All five d orbitals are not spatially equivalent. Three, d_{xy}, d_{yz}, and d_{zx}, are evidently equivalent for they are equivalently situated with respect to the ligands (Fig. 5-5) and may be interchanged by simply interchanging the labelling of the Cartesian coordinate system. The other two d orbitals, $d_{x^2-y^2}$ and d_{z^2}, are not equivalent, although they both have their maximum amplitudes along the Cartesian coordinate axes (Fig. 5-6). Interchange of the labels associated with each of these axes has the effect not of interchanging the orbitals but of generating new orbitals. So, starting with the coordinate system of Fig. 5-6, the interchange $x \to y \to z \to x$ gives us Fig. 5-7, in which these same d orbitals are now labelled d_{x^2} and $d_{y^2-z^2}$. We show in Appendix 2 that the new d orbitals are simply mixtures of the old ones, d_{z^2} and $d_{x^2-y^2}$. The fact that it is possible to mix two orbitals by such a trivial operation as re-labelling the axes shows that the two orbitals are degenerate. If they were not, the mixed orbitals would have different energies from those of the starting pair, and it is obviously ridiculous that the

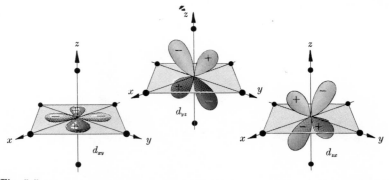

Fig. 5-5

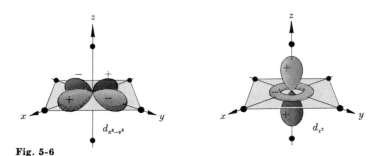

Fig. 5-6

energies should be a function of the labelling of the axis system. We conclude that the d orbitals (or a D state) split into two sets, a set of three degenerate orbitals and a set of two degenerate orbitals. We shall discuss the relative energies of these two sets shortly. Finally, we consider the effect of an octahedral crystal field on a single f electron (or an F state). Fig. 5-8 shows that the seven-fold degeneracy is lost to give two sets of triply degenerate and one singly degenerate orbital.

The analogy which we have noted between orbitals and states arises because, for example, the seven mathematical expressions which define the f orbitals either are the same as the seven used to define the components of an F state or are in some way related to them.

So far we have shown that sets of d and f orbitals, and D and F states, split into sub-sets in an octahedral crystal field but have said nothing about the relative energies of these sub-sets. For the moment, we shall restrict the discussion to orbitals only. In subsequent sections we shall assume that the reader is familiar with the Russell–Saunders coupling scheme encountered in the theory of atomic structure. (Appendix 3 gives an outline of this scheme.)

Consider the d orbitals shown in Figs 5-5 and 5-6. The more stable set is that in which an electron experiences least repulsion—

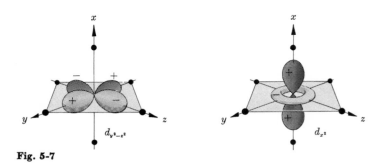

Fig. 5-7

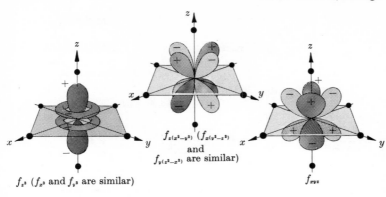

$f_{z(x^2-y^2)}$ $(f_{x(y^2-z^2)}$
and
$f_{y(z^2-x^2)}$ are similar)

f_{z^3} $(f_{x^3}$ and f_{y^3} are similar)

f_{xyz}

Fig. 5-8

destabilization—from the electrons on the ligands. Evidently, this set is that composed of d_{xy}, d_{yz}, and d_{zx}, because this set keeps the d electrons away from the ligand electrons, at least when the ligands are represented as point charges. This set has T_{2g} symmetry and we shall refer to these orbitals as 'the t_{2g} orbitals' or 'the t_{2g} set.' The less stable set, the 'e_g orbitals' or 'e_g set,' consists of d_{z^2} and $d_{x^2-y^2}$.

In a similar way it can be seen that the relative stabilities of the f orbitals (Fig. 5-8) is f_{xyz} (a_{2u}), most stable; $f_{x(y^2-z^2)}$, $f_{y(z^2-x^2)}$ and $f_{z(x^2-y^2)}$ (t_{2u}), intermediate stability; and f_{x^3}, f_{y^3}, and f_{z^3} (t_{1u}), least stable. The splitting patterns for d and f orbitals are shown in Fig. 5-9a. The vast majority of experimental data on transition metal complexes gives information on the splitting between the orbitals but not on their absolute displacements from the free ion energy. It is therefore convenient to delete this unknown quantity from the diagrams and to regard the free ion energy as lying at the centre of gravity of the energies of the split orbitals (Fig. 5-9b). The splitting between the t_{2g} and e_g sets of d electrons we shall call Δ (some authors prefer to call it $10Dq$). Δ has a value of ca 10,000 cm^{-1}; for dipositive transition metal ions its value is usually 5,000–15,000 cm^{-1} and for tripositive ions 10,000–30,000 cm^{-1}. Its value increases roughly in proportion to the cationic charge, depends markedly on the ligands and, to a smaller extent, on the metal (within any one transition series). A complex of the second or third transition series has a value of Δ which is up to twice that of the corresponding first row complex.

A modified d-orbital splitting pattern showing only the crystal field splitting is given in Fig. 5-10.

The argument to derive these splittings used plausibility in place of mathematics so one cannot be absolutely confident of the results.

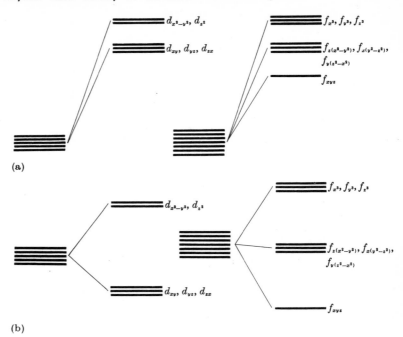

Fig. 5-9

Similarly, almost all of the detailed calculations that have been carried out make the approximation of replacing the ligands by point charges, so one still cannot be absolutely certain that they lead to the correct answer, although they agree with our conclusions. Ultimately, the justification for the splittings in Fig. 5-10 is experimental so that Δ is to be regarded as an experimental quantity.

One immediate consequence of the splitting of d orbitals into t_{2g} and e_g sets must be recognized. When there are between four and seven d electrons present there exist two quite different ways of allocating these electrons to the t_{2g} and e_g orbitals. These are shown

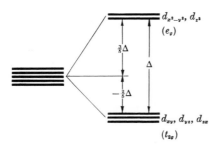

Fig. 5-10   The splitting of a set of d orbitals by an octahedral crystal field.

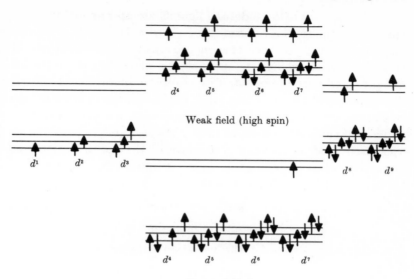

Weak field (high spin)

Strong field (low spin)

Fig. 5-11   Weak and strong field arrangements of d electrons.

in Fig. 5-11. The *weak field* arrangement is the one in which the (destabilizing) inter-electron repulsions between the d electrons are smallest—the electrons are spatially less concentrated—and the inter-electron exchange stabilization is greatest (which is also why the maximum number of spins parallel arrangement is of lowest energy). There also exists the *strong field* arrangement which differs from the weak field in that one or more electrons have been trans-ferred from the less stable e_g to the more stable t_{2g} orbitals. Each electron so transferred contributes a crystal field stabilization of Δ to the system, but only at the cost of an increase in the electron repulsion destabilization and a decrease in the exchange stabiliza-tion (the latter, together, are often called the *pairing energy*). For any one transition metal ion with from four to seven d electrons the vital factor determining whether a particular complex is of the weak or strong field type is the magnitude of Δ. The change from one type to the other is discontinuous; for other d^n configurations there may be related, but less dramatic, continuous changes associated with the transition from weak to strong field type. We may note at this point that the two types of complex display quite different spectral and magnetic properties. For example, the $[Fe(CN)_6]^{4-}$ ion, which is a strong field complex of Fe(II), is yellow and has no unpaired elec-trons. The $[Fe(H_2O)_6]^{2+}$ ion, a weak field complex of Fe(II), is very pale green and is paramagnetic, with four unpaired electrons (cf. Fig. 5-11).

In the crystal field model the ligands are approximated by point charges or dipoles, the value of Δ for a particular complex depending on the magnitude of both this charge and that on the metal. This suggests that it should be possible to place ligands in order of increasing effective charge and, therefore, of increasing Δ. Further, this order should be the same for all metals. Such an order of ligands was discovered by Tschida before the advent of crystal field theory, and called the *spectrochemical series*. As its name implies the series was discovered as a result of a study of the spectra of transition metal complexes. We shall meet it again in Chapter 7. An abbreviated spectrochemical series, in order of increasing Δ, is:

$$\text{I}^- < \text{Br}^- < \text{SCN}^- \text{ (S-bonded)} < \text{F}^- < \text{OH}^- < \text{H}_2\text{O} < \text{SCN}^- \text{ (N-bonded)}$$
$$< \text{NH}_3 \simeq \text{py} < \text{SO}_3^{2-} < \text{dipy} < \text{NO}_2^- \text{ (N-bonded)} < \text{CN}^-$$

A similar series exists for the variation with metal ion:

$$\text{Mn}^{2+} < \text{Ni}^{2+} < \text{Co}^{2+} < \text{Fe}^{2+} < \text{V}^{2+} < \text{Fe}^{3+} < \text{Cr}^{3+} < \text{V}^{3+}$$
$$< \text{Co}^{3+} < \text{Mn}^{4+} < \text{Rh}^{3+} < \text{Pd}^{4+} < \text{Ir}^{3+} < \text{Pt}^{4+}$$

Despite the above argument, the former series should not be regarded as a series in which the charge on the ligand increases from left to right. Other factors are involved, as we shall see in Chapter 6.

We now return to the problem we met at the beginning of this chapter. What are the energy levels of a transition metal ion in an octahedral crystal field? There are alternative approaches to this problem depending on whether one is interested in a weak or a strong field complex. We shall discuss the cases separately and then consider complexes in which the crystal field is of intermediate strength.

5-4 Weak field complexes

Weak field complexes are those for which the crystal field splitting, Δ, is smaller than the electron-repulsion and exchange energies. This at once indicates a suitable theoretical approach to a discussion of their structure. In a discussion of the energy levels of a free atom or ion one considers the various interactions in order of importance. The most important is the attraction between an electron and the nucleus. Next, the effects of inter-electron repulsion (this includes the exchange energy) are considered, then the coupling between the spin and orbital motion of the electron (spin–orbit coupling) and so on.

There would be no need to preserve this pecking order if each step in the calculation were carried out exactly for both the ground and all excited states of the atom. However, each step usually involves approximations and is only carried out for the ground and a few low-lying excited states. Consequently, the step-wise procedure becomes necessary to ensure that the properties of the ground state and states immediately above it in energy are described with fair accuracy.

In crystal-field theory the central atom of a complex is regarded as a free ion subject to an additional perturbation due to its environment. Evidently, this perturbation must be introduced at the correct point in a calculation and, for weak field complexes, this point is after the effects of electron repulsion have been dealt with, that is, when the calculation has reached the stage of the classification of states, such as ^2D, ^3F, ^1S, and so on. What we must now do is to determine how the 21 wavefunctions of a ^3F state, for example, are going to split under the influence of the crystal field. (This, of course, is where we came in at the beginning of this chapter.) As we have pointed out, the splitting of an F state parallels the splitting of f orbitals. That is, we ignore the spin degeneracy (because the effects of a crystal field are the same whether an electron spin is 'up' or 'down'; the crystal field may only have a small indirect effect on the spin degeneracy via the coupling which exists between the spin and orbital motions of an electron), the F state being split into three sub-states, two of which are triply degenerate. We have seen that a set of f orbitals split up into t_{1u}, t_{2u}, and a_{2u} sub-sets. Similarly, an F state splits up into either T_{1u}, T_{2u}, and A_{2u} or T_{1g}, T_{2g}, and A_{2g} sub-sets. Which of these is correct is determined by the g or u nature of the configuration from which the F state is derived. Because f orbitals are u in character the ^2F state corresponding to an f^1 configuration splits up into $^2T_{1u}$, $^2T_{2u}$, and $^2A_{2u}$ components. Similarly, the ^3F state derived from the d^2 configuration splits into $^3T_{1g}$, $^3T_{2g}$, and $^3A_{2g}$ components because the d orbitals are g in character. In this chapter we are concerned only with the crystal field splitting of states derived from d^n configurations, so we shall encounter only g suffixes. Table 5-1 gives the splittings for all of the transition metal ions (d^1–d^9 configurations); it lists ground states and, where we shall need the information later, the splitting of the lowest excited state. Two points should be noted in connection with this table. First, that only S, P, D, and F states occur; for each the splitting is similar to that of the corresponding orbitals. Second, the table has some symmetry. Apart from the first column, the bottom half is the mirror image of the top half. These two features combine to simplify the remainder of our discussion of weak field complexes.

We turn now to the problem of the relative energies of the crystal-field components listed in Table 5-1. Consider the D states,

Table 5-1   Crystal field components of the ground and some excited states of d^n ($n = 1 \rightarrow 9$) configurations

Configuration	Free ion ground state	Crystal field sub-states	Important excited state	Crystal field state
d^1	^2D	$^2T_{2g} + {}^2E_g$		
d^2	^3F	$^3T_{1g} + {}^3T_{2g} + {}^3A_{2g}$	^3P	$^3T_{1g}$
d^3	^4F	$^4T_{1g} + {}^4T_{2g} + {}^4A_{2g}$	^4P	$^4T_{1g}$
d^4	^5D	$^5T_{1g} + {}^5E_g$		
d^5	^6S	$^6A_{1g}$		
d^6	^5D	$^5T_{2g} + {}^5E_g$		
d^7	^4F	$^4T_{1g} + {}^4T_{2g} + {}^4A_{2g}$	^4P	$^4T_{1g}$
d^8	^3F	$^3T_{1g} + {}^3T_{2g} + {}^3A_{2g}$	^3P	$^3T_{1g}$
d^9	^2D	$^2T_{2g} + {}^2E_g$		

which give T_{2g} and E_g components. Which component is the more stable and by how much? We shall take for granted that it is an experimental fact that the five d orbitals split as shown in Fig. 5-10, the splitting being denoted by Δ. Consider the d^1 case (Fig. 5-12). Here the ground state will be that in which the electron occupies the lowest, t_{2g}, orbital. Just as a d^1 configuration gives rise to a ^2D term so, too, a t_{2g}^1 configuration (which is what we have here) gives rise to a $^2T_{2g}$ term. Similarly, the (excited) e_g^1 configuration gives rise to a ^2E_g term. We conclude that, for the d^1 case, the $^2T_{2g}$ level is the more stable. The (excited) ^2E_g level is generated from it by excitation of an electron from the t_{2g} orbitals to the e_g orbitals. This, by definition, requires an energy Δ, so we conclude that the $^2T_{2g}$ and ^2E_g states are also separated by the energy Δ.

Two points should be noted. First, a detailed argument is required to relate the splitting of orbital energies to the splitting of term energies. This caution is necessary because, as we shall see in the following paragraph, the fact that t_{2g} orbitals are more stable than e_g does not imply that T_{2g} states are necessarily more stable than E_g. Second, nine more electrons could be accommodated in the orbitals of Fig. 5-12. The other positions are vacant or, as it is more usually put, occupied by *holes*. A filled shell of electrons has spherical

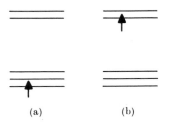

(a)   (b)

Fig. 5-12   (a) Ground and (b) excited states derived from the d^1 configuration.

symmetry; so too does a half-filled shell, provided that no orbital of the shell is doubly occupied. The complement of a half-filled shell is a half shell of holes which, therefore, also has spherical symmetry. It follows that when we have a half shell of holes this half shell may be neglected.

There are two ways of describing the situation in which the t_{2g} orbitals are occupied by a single electron. We may say that the situation differs from spherical symmetry *either* by the presence of a t_{2g} electron *or* by the presence of two holes in the e_g set and two holes

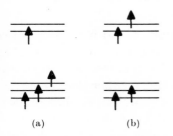

(a)   (b)

Fig. 5-13   (a) Ground and (b) excited states derived from the d^4 configuration.

in the t_{2g} set—that is, a hole is *missing* in the t_{2g} set! Obviously no one would use the hole description in the case described, but for some cases it is useful to do so. Such a case is provided by the ground state ^5D term of the d^4 configuration. The quintet spin state means that all of the d electrons have parallel spin, as shown in Fig. 5-13. The electron distribution differs from spherical symmetry by the presence of four electrons or, what is equivalent, by the presence of one hole, in terms of which this case is best discussed. The most stable situation is that in which the hole is in the e_g orbital. The ground state is therefore ^5E_g. At an energy Δ above the ground state is the $^5T_{2g}$ state, in which the hole is present in the t_{2g} orbitals. In the d^4 case, therefore, the splitting of the E_g and T_{2g} levels is the inverse of that in the d^1 case. In the ^5D state arising from the d^6 configuration the orbital occupation is as shown in Fig. 5-14. It differs from spherical symmetry by the presence of a single electron, which is most stable when in the t_{2g} orbitals. The splitting therefore follows the d^1 case, the $^5T_{2g}$ state being more stable than the ^5E_g state by an energy Δ. Similarly, the ^2D state arising from the d^9 configuration differs from spherical symmetry by the presence of a hole in the e_g orbitals in the ground state (Fig. 5-15). The ground state is therefore of ^2E_g symmetry and the excited state, at an energy of Δ above, is of $^2T_{2g}$ symmetry.

Why is the hole formalism so useful? When a set of t_{2g} orbitals

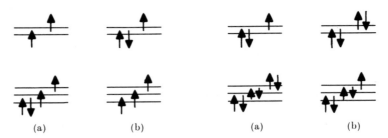

(Left) **Fig. 5-14** (a) Ground and (b) excited states derived from the d^6 configuration. *(Right)* **Fig. 5-15** (a) Ground and (b) excited states derived from the d^9 configuration.

contains a single electron a T_{2g} state results. What if it contains two electrons; does this also result in a T_{2g} state? The answer, as we shall see later, is that it may, but other possible symmetries exist (in the same way that a d^2 configuration gives rise to other than D states). Similarly, if we evaluate the terms arising from the $t_{2g}{}^3 e_g$ configuration (using methods to be described later) we find a multitude of them. Some terms correspond to singlet spin states, others to triplets and one to a quintuplet. If we are interested in the splitting of the ^5D state (of the d^4 configuration) we are only interested in the spin quintuplet, and work is obviously involved in sorting it out from the others. The hole formalism does this work for us. Similarly, if we wish to write down an explicit expression for the wavefunctions of the ^5D term arising from the d^4 configuration it is much easier to write down a wavefunction appropriate to the single hole, than to write down a (product) wavefunction appropriate to the four electrons. However, care is needed in the use of these pseudo-wavefunctions because holes behave differently to electrons. For example, we have argued that metal electrons are repelled by the ligand field. Holes, however, behave as if they are *attracted* by a ligand field. It is left to the reader to convince himself of this.

The lowest term arising from the d^2 configuration of a free metal ion is ^3F. We have already shown that this gives $^3T_{1g}$, $^3T_{2g}$, and $^3A_{2g}$ components in a ligand field. What is their relative ordering? Following our discussion of the splitting of f orbitals in a crystalline field we might anticipate that the $^3T_{2g}$ level would be of intermediate stability and, following our discussion of the splitting of D states, expect that $^3T_{1g}$ and $^3A_{2g}$ would alternate as the ground state for the d^4, d^7, and d^8 weak field cases. Detailed calculations confirm both of these predictions. It is beyond the scope of this book to give the calculations, but, given that for the ^3F term derived from the d^2 configuration the $^3T_{1g}$ state is lowest and $^3A_{2g}$ highest, we can predict the splittings of all other F terms. We shall justify both this

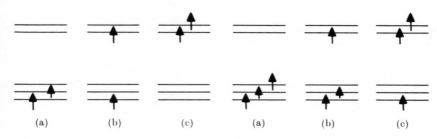

(*Left*) **Fig. 5-16**   (a) Ground and (b, c) excited states derived from the d^2 configuration. (*Right*) **Fig. 5-17**   (a) Ground and (b, c) excited states derived from the d^3 configuration.

ordering of states, and the values for the relative energies of the components, in Section 5-5.

In the ($^3T_{1g}$) ground state derived from the ^3F term of a d^2 configuration there are two electrons in the t_{2g} orbitals* (Fig. 5-16). In the ^4F (d^3) case the $^4T_{1g}$ state corresponds to the presence of two holes in the t_{2g} orbitals and so is an excited state (Fig. 5-17): the $^4A_{2g}$ state is the ground state in this case. For the ^4F state of the d^7 configuration the ground state is $^4T_{2g}$: the configuration differs from spherical symmetry by the presence of two electrons in the t_{2g} orbitals (Fig. 5-18). The ^3F state derived from the d^8 configuration gives rise to an excited $^3T_{2g}$ level (Fig. 5-19), two holes occupying the t_{2g} orbitals, and a $^3A_{2g}$ ground state.

The only other weak field case which remains to be discussed is that of the ^6S ground state of the d^5 configuration. This ground state is orbitally non-degenerate and so no crystal field splitting can occur. The behaviour of this ^6S state parallels that of the s orbital discussed earlier in this section, becoming $^6A_{1g}$ in an octahedral crystal field.

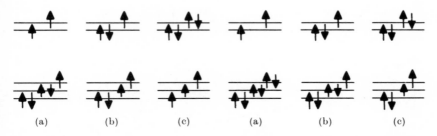

(*Left*) **Fig. 5-18**   (a) Ground and (b, c) excited states derived from the d^7 configuration. (*Right*) **Fig. 5-19**   (a) Ground and (b, c) excited states derived from the d^8 configuration.

* This statement is not quite correct, as we shall see at the end of Section 5-5. Similar errors are contained in the statements on the d^3, d^7, and d^8 configurations. These errors are made in the interests of linguistic and conceptual simplicity and in no way invalidate the general argument.

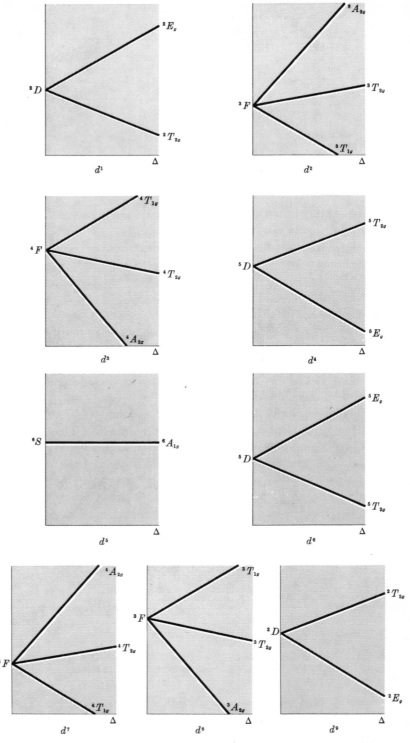

Fig. 5-20 The splittings of the weak field d^n ($n = 1 \rightarrow 9$) ground-state terms in an octahedral crystal field.

So far we have not mentioned the excited states of the d^2, d^7, and d^8 configurations which were given in Table 5-1. These excited states give rise to a T_{1g} level which is of the same spin multiplicity as the T_{1g} level derived from the free ion F ground state. These two T_{1g} levels, being of the same symmetry, may interact. In the limit of a very weak crystal field this interaction may be ignored. We draw attention to it as this point as it is referred to in Sections 5-5 and 5-6.

We summarize the arguments of this section by giving, in Fig. 5-20, the splittings, in the weak field limit, of the free ion terms listed in Table 5-1.

5-5 Strong field complexes

Strong field complexes are distinguished from weak field complexes because their crystal field splitting energy, Δ, is greater than the energies associated with electron pairing. In an actual calculation this means that instead of finding the terms arising from a d^n configuration—otherwise the first step in a calculation using the Russell–Saunders coupling scheme—one applies the crystal field perturbation. This divides the d orbitals into e_g and t_{2g} sets. A d^n configuration splits up into sets which differ in the occupancy of the t_{2g} and e_g orbitals. So, for example, the d^2 configuration splits into three sets t_{2g}^2, $t_{2g}e_g$, and e_g^2. A complete list of these sub-states is given in Table 5-2, which possesses the same sort of symmetry as Table 5-1. The number of sub-states listed for a d^n configuration is the same as that for a d^{10-n} configuration. The difference between the two sets of terms for these two configurations is only apparent. The reader should easily be able to show that, if the hole formalism is used for one of them, the difference between them disappears. For the d^8 configuration, for example, the hole formalism leads to t_{2g}^2, $t_{2g}e_g$, and e_g^2 configurations, the same as those listed for the d^2 configuration in

Table 5-2

d^n configuration	Strong-field sub-states
d^1	t_{2g}; e_g
d^2	t_{2g}^2; $t_{2g}e_g$; e_g^2
d^3	t_{2g}^3; $t_{2g}^2e_g$; $t_{2g}e_g^2$; e_g^3
d^4	t_{2g}^4; $t_{2g}^3e_g$; $t_{2g}^2e_g^2$; $t_{2g}e_g^3$; e_g^4
d^5	t_{2g}^5; $t_{2g}^4e_g$; $t_{2g}^3e_g^2$; $t_{2g}^2e_g^3$; $t_{2g}e_g^4$
d^6	t_{2g}^6; $t_{2g}^5e_g$; $t_{2g}^4e_g^2$; $t_{2g}^3e_g^3$; $t_{2g}^2e_g^4$
d^7	$t_{2g}^6e_g$; $t_{2g}^5e_g^2$; $t_{2g}^4e_g^3$; $t_{2g}^3e_g^4$
d^8	$t_{2g}^6e_g^2$; $t_{2g}^5e_g^3$; $t_{2g}^4e_g^4$
d^9	$t_{2g}^6e_g^3$; $t_{2g}^5e_g^4$

Table 5-2. The relative energies of the states given in Table 5-2 are readily evaluated and in doing this we shall see the advantage of arbitrarily placing the d orbitals of the free ions at the centre of gravity of those of the complexed ion. Adopting this convention, it is obvious (Fig. 5-10) that the t_{2g} orbitals are stabilized by $\frac{2}{5}\Delta$ and the e_g orbitals destabilized by $\frac{3}{5}\Delta$. Following the usual sign convention, the energy of the t_{2g} orbitals is $-\frac{2}{5}\Delta$ and that of the e_g orbitals $\frac{3}{5}\Delta$. That is, each electron in a t_{2g} orbital contributes $-\frac{2}{5}\Delta$, and each electron in an e_g orbital $\frac{3}{5}\Delta$, to the total d-orbital energy. Consider, for example, the t_{2g}^2, $t_{2g}e_g$, and e_g^2 states of the d^2 configuration. These have energies, respectively, of $2(-\frac{2}{5}\Delta) = -\frac{4}{5}\Delta$; $(-\frac{2}{5}\Delta + \frac{3}{5}\Delta) = \frac{1}{5}\Delta$; and $2(\frac{3}{5}\Delta) = \frac{6}{5}\Delta$.

By the end of the discussion of weak field complexes the effects of both the crystal field and electron repulsion had been included, the latter being part of the Russell–Saunders coupling scheme. To be consistent we must now consider the effects of electron repulsion in strong field complexes. Electron repulsion causes some arrangements of electrons within an unfilled shell to be more stable than others—those arrangements in which unpaired electrons are kept farthest apart and have parallel spins will be the most stable (Hund's rule). In a free atom or ion electron repulsion causes the terms arising from a configuration to have different energies. Similarly, in a crystal field, the terms arising from a configuration like t_{2g}^2 will, in general, have different energies. How does one determine the terms arising from such a configuration? What are the relative energies of these terms and how does one obtain the wavefunctions corresponding to them? Although the answers to these questions are well known, it

Table 5-3   Direct products applicable to octahedral molecules

	A_1	A_2	E	T_1	T_2
A_1	A_1	A_2	E	T_1	T_2
A_2	A_2	A_1	E	T_2	T_1
E	E	E	$A_1 + A_2 + E$	$T_1 + T_2$	$T_1 + T_2$
T_1	T_1	T_2	$T_1 + T_2$	$A_1 + E + T_1 + T_2$	$A_2 + E + T_1 + T_2$
T_2	T_2	T_1	$T_1 + T_2$	$A_2 + E + T_1 + T_2$	$A_1 + E + T_1 + T_2$

is difficult to give a complete account in an elementary text such as this, so we shall attempt only an outline of the calculations.

Table 5-3 is a table of *direct products*; its derivation is included in Appendix 1. This table is important, for it is used whenever one is simultaneously interested in two similar quantities associated with an octahedral molecule, for example, if we are interested in the symmetry properties of two electrons as a pair rather than individually. Similarly, we shall use this table to discuss spectra, for which we have to consider the ground and excited states of a molecule simultaneously. Table 5-3 does not give g and u suffixes; this could have been done, but it would have made the table four times larger with no increase in real content. We shall show shortly how these suffixes may be added.

Consider the $t_{2g}e_g$ configuration. The first electron may be fed into any one of three t_{2g} orbitals and the second into any one of two e_g. That is, there are $3 \times 2 = 6$ ways of feeding the two electrons in; there are six orbitally-different wavefunctions. Table 5-3 shows that the direct product of t_2 (extreme left-hand column) with e (top row) written $T_2 \times E$, is equal to $T_1 + T_2$ or, including suffixes in an obviously sensible way, $T_{2g} \times E_g = T_{1g} + T_{2g}$ ($T_{2g} \times E_u$ or $T_{2u} \times E_g$ would have given $T_{1u} + T_{2u}$). The other possibility, $T_{2u} \times E_u$ would have given $T_{1g} + T_{2g}$ ($g \times g = u \times u = g$; $u \times g = g \times u = u$). The sum of the degeneracies implied in T_{1g} and T_{2g} ($3 + 3 = 6$) is the same as the number of orbital wavefunctions arising from the $t_{2g}e_g$ configuration ($3 \times 2 = 6$). It will not surprise the reader to learn that these six wavefunctions divide into two sets of three each, one set of T_{1g} and one set of T_{2g} symmetry. Thus far we have not mentioned the spin of the electrons. Because the two electrons always occupy different orbitals, paired (singlet) and parallel (triplet) spin arrangements are possible. We conclude that the $t_{2g}e_g$ configuration gives rise to $^3T_{1g}$, $^3T_{2g}$, $^1T_{1g}$, and $^1T_{2g}$ states.

Now consider the $t_{2g}t_{2g}$ configuration: two electrons, each one occupying a *different* set of t_{2g} orbitals (of course, this situation does not arise in simple crystal field theory). By a discussion paralleling that above, we conclude that $^3A_{1g}$, ^3E_g, $^3T_{1g}$, $^3T_{2g}$, $^1A_{1g}$, ^1E_g, $^1T_{1g}$, and $^1T_{2g}$ states result. The t_{2g}^2 configuration is related to the $t_{2g}t_{2g}$ case, but is more restricted. First, electrons of the same spin cannot occupy the same orbital. Secondly, because the electrons are indistinguishable and occupy the same set of orbitals the number of distinct wavefunctions is halved ($A(1)B(2)$ and $B(1)A(2)$, where A and B are two of the t_{2g} orbitals and the electrons are numbered 1 and 2, do not count as distinct wavefunctions whereas $A(1)B'(2)$ and $B(1)A'(2)$, for the $t_{2g}t_{2g}$ configuration, did). We anticipate, therefore, that there are fewer states arising from the t_{2g}^2 configuration than from the $t_{2g}t_{2g}$; the number of triplet states, in particular, will be considerably reduced. The allowed states are, in fact, $^3T_{1g}$, $^1A_{1g}$, ^1E_g, and $^1T_{2g}$. The total degeneracy ($9 + 1 + 2 + 3 = 15$) is equal to the number of distinguishable and allowed ways of feeding two electrons into a set of three orbitals ($(6 \times 5)/(1 \times 2) = 15$).

These four states are all to be found amongst those arising from the $t_{2g}t_{2g}$ configuration, each symmetry species in the $T_{2g} \times T_{2g}$ direct droduct appearing once only.

The t_{2g}^3 configuration poses a problem. The most obvious way of obtaining the orbital terms arising from this configuration is to simply take each of the orbital terms arising from the t_{2g}^2 configuration and combine each with a further t_{2g} orbital function, that is, form the triple direct product $T_{2g} \times T_{2g} \times T_{2g}$ or, equivalently, consider the sum of direct products $(A_{1g} \times T_{2g}) + (E_g \times T_{2g}) + (T_{1g} \times T_{2g}) + (T_{2g} \times T_{2g})$. This would, however, be wrong. Some of the singlet wavefunctions of the t_{2g}^2 configuration represent two electrons occupying the same orbital. To form direct products blindly

Fig. 5-21 A representation of the orbital part of the $^3T_{1g}$ wavefunctions derived from the t_{2g}^2 configuration.

would, for some of the three-electron wavefunction, be to allocate all three electrons to one orbital. The simplest way to avoid this problem and obtain the correct answer is as follows. In the $^3T_{1g}$ term of the d^2 configuration we know that the electrons *must* occupy different orbitals (because of the Pauli exclusion principle). Adding a third t_{2g} electron can never give us three electrons in one orbital. Fig. 5-21 gives pictorial representations of the $^3T_{1g}$ orbital wavefunctions (we do not specify spin). The reader can easily show that all possible ways of orbitally allocating electrons in the t_{2g}^3 configuration may be obtained from those in Fig. 5-21. This suggests that the direct product $T_{1g} \times T_{2g}$ will give us the symmetries of all the sets of three-electron wavefunctions. This is so; they are A_{2g}, E_g, T_{1g}, and T_{2g}. We now have to determine the spin multiplicities of these states. It is easy to see that only one spin quartet term can exist and that this is orbitally singly degenerate—there is only one way of allocating three electrons with α spin to the three t_{2g} orbitals. The other terms must therefore be doublets; that is, we have $^4A_{2g}$, ^2E_g, $^2T_{1g}$, and $^2T_{2g}$ terms. Again, the total degeneracy $(4 + 4 + 6 + 6 = 20)$ equals the number of distinguishable and allowed ways of feeding three electrons into the t_{2g} orbitals: $(6 \times 5 \times 4)/(1 \times 2 \times 3) = 20$. Similar arguments may be applied to all the other configurations which arise, although when either or both of the t_{2g} and e_g shells are more than half full it is convenient to work in terms of holes. The results, of course, are the same as those for the similar electron configurations. Results are collected together in Table 5-4, which may appear frightening in its complexity. Fortunately Hund's rule applies to each configuration and we shall usually be interested only in the most stable states, those of highest spin multiplicity, of each configuration.

Table 5-4   Terms arising from $t_{2g}^m e_g^n$ configurations

Number of d electrons	Configuration	Terms arising
1, 9	t_{2g}; $t_{2g}^5 e_g^4$	$^2T_{2g}$
	e_g; $t_{2g}^6 e_g^3$	^2E_g
2, 8	t_{2g}^2; $t_{2g}^4 e_g^4$	$^3T_{1g}$, $^1A_{1g}$, ^1E_g, $^1T_{2g}$
	$t_{2g}e_g$; $t_{2g}^5 e_g^3$	$^3T_{1g}$, $^3T_{2g}$, $^1T_{1g}$, $^1T_{2g}$
	e_g^2; $t_{2g}^6 e_g^2$	$^3A_{2g}$, $^1A_{1g}$, ^1E_g
3, 7	t_{2g}^3; $t_{2g}^3 e_g^4$	$^4A_{2g}$, ^2E_g, $^2T_{1g}$, $^2T_{2g}$
	$t_{2g}^2 e_g$; $t_{2g}^4 e_g^3$	$^4T_{1g}$, $^4T_{2g}$, $^2A_{1g}$, $^2A_{2g}$, 2^2E_g, 2^2T_{1g}, 2^2T_{2g}
	$t_{2g}e_g^2$; $t_{2g}^5 e_g^2$	$^4T_{1g}$, 2^2T_{1g}, 2^2T_{2g}
	e_g^3; $t_{2g}^6 e_g$	^2E_g
4, 6	t_{2g}^4; $t_{2g}^2 e_g^4$	$^3T_{1g}$, $^1A_{1g}$, ^1E_g, $^1T_{2g}$
	$t_{2g}^3 e_g$; $t_{2g}^3 e_g^3$	^5E_g, $^3A_{1g}$, $^3A_{2g}$, 2^3E_g, 2^3T_{2g}, 2^3T_{1g}, $^1A_{1g}$, $^1A_{2g}$, ^1E_g, 2^1T_{1g}, 2^1T_{2g}
	$t_{2g}^2 e_g^2$; $t_{2g}^4 e_g^2$	$^5T_{2g}$, $^3A_{2g}$, ^3E_g, 3^3T_{1g}, 2^3T_{2g}, 2^1A_{1g}, $^1A_{2g}$, 3^1E_g, $^1T_{1g}$, 3^3T_{2g}
	$t_{2g}e_g^3$; $t_{2g}^5 e_g$	$^3T_{1g}$, $^3T_{2g}$, $^1T_{1g}$, $^1T_{2g}$
	e_g^4; t_{2g}^6	$^1A_{1g}$
5	t_{2g}^5; $t_{2g}e_g^4$	$^2T_{2g}$
	$t_{2g}^4 e_g$; $t_{2g}^2 e_g^3$	$^4T_{1g}$, $^4T_{2g}$, $^2A_{1g}$, $^2A_{2g}$, 2^2E_g, 2^2T_{1g}, 2^2T_{2g}
	$t_{2g}^3 e_g^2$	$^6A_{1g}$, $^4A_{1g}$, $^4A_{2g}$, 2^4E_g, $^4T_{1g}$, $^4T_{2g}$, 2^2A_{1g}, $^2A_{2g}$, 3^2E_g, 4^2T_{1g}, 4^2T_{2g}

2^2T_{1g} means that there are two different $^2T_{1g}$ terms arising within the configuration. The two sets of entries in the 'configuration' column correspond, in order, to those in the 'number of d electrons' column. Thus d^1 corresponds to t_{2g} and e_g whilst d^9 corresponds to $t_{2g}^5 e_g^4$ and $t_{2g}^6 e_g^3$.

We now have to consider the problem of the relative energies of the terms arising from a $t_{2g}^m e_g^n$ configuration. This is a precisely similar problem to calculating the relative energies of the terms arising from a d^n configuration in the Russell–Saunders coupling scheme. Indeed, identical integrals (each having the dimensions of energy) are involved. This problem was first solved by Tanabe and Sugano; the solution is not difficult but it is lengthy and so we shall make do with a qualitative answer which is given in the next section.

To conclude the present section we obtain the relative energies of the $^3T_{1g}$, $^3T_{2g}$, and $^3A_{2g}$ components of the ^3F state of the d^2 configuration, a problem postponed from the previous section. From Table 5-4 it can be seen that only one $^3T_{2g}$ and one $^3A_{2g}$ crystal field state exist for the d^2 configuration. But in the weak field limit, as we have seen (Table 5-1), both of these states are derived from the ^3F state of the free ion and, therefore, the electron repulsion contribution to the energy of each is identical. They differ only in their crystal field energies. But Table 5-4 shows that the $^3T_{2g}$ state is derived, alternatively, from the $t_{2g}e_g$ strong field configuration and therefore has an energy of $-\frac{2}{5}\Delta + \frac{3}{5}\Delta = \frac{1}{5}\Delta$. Similarly, the $^3A_{2g}$ state is derived from the e_g^2 strong field configuration and has an energy of $2 \times \frac{3}{5}\Delta = \frac{6}{5}\Delta$. Because the components of the ^3F term retain the energy of this term as their centre of gravity in the weak field case, it follows that the energy of the other component, $^3T_{1g}$, must be $-\frac{1}{3}(3 \times \frac{1}{5}\Delta + \frac{6}{5}\Delta) = -\frac{3}{5}\Delta$. This term has a different energy in the strong field limit. There, as the ground state, it is derived from the most stable configuration—t_{2g}^2—and so has an energy of $2 \times -\frac{2}{5}\Delta = -\frac{4}{5}\Delta$. Why the difference in the two cases? The explanation lies in the presence of a second $^3T_{1g}$ term, derived in the weak field limit from the ^3P term of the d^2 configuration and in the strong field limit from the $t_{2g}e_g$ configuration. In the limit of zero crystal field these two $^3T_{1g}$ states do not interact. A non-zero crystal field induces an interaction between the two states which leads to their 'repelling' each other. The $^3T_{1g}$ state derived from the ^3P term has, in the weak field limit, an energy which is independent of the magnitude of the crystal field (the ^3P term is unsplit by the field (Table 5-1); in the weak-field limit the energy of a crystal field state depends on Δ only if it is one of several states split apart by the crystal field, the magnitude of the splitting being proportional to Δ). In the strong field limit this state, usually designated $^3T_{1g}(P)$, is derived from the $t_{2g}e_g$ configuration and so has an energy of $(-\frac{2}{5}\Delta + \frac{3}{5}\Delta) = \frac{1}{5}\Delta$. In summary, the dependence on Δ of the energies of the two $^3T_{1g}$ terms in the two limits are:

	$^3T_{1g}(F)$	$^3T_{1g}(P)$
weak field limit	$-\frac{3}{5}\Delta$	0
strong field limit	$-\frac{4}{5}\Delta$	$\frac{1}{5}\Delta$
difference between the strong and the weak field limits	$-\frac{1}{5}\Delta$	$\frac{1}{5}\Delta$

The reader will notice that the effect of the interaction on the $^3T_{1g}(F)$ state is equal and opposite to that on the $^3T_{1g}(P)$ state. This is always true. The effects of a crystal field interaction are equal in magnitude but opposite in sign for the two interacting orbitals. That is, the two states repel each other equally. We may note in passing that the arguments we used to derive the energies of the $^3T_{2g}$ and $^3A_{2g}$ terms in the weak field limit depended upon the non-existence of any other terms of the same symmetry and spin multiplicity.

It is interesting to enquire into the d-orbital occupancy when a weak field d^2 ion is in its ground state (the d^7 case is similar). The energy of the $^3T_{1g}$ ground state, $-\frac{3}{5}\Delta$, must correspond to an electron distribution of $\frac{9}{5}$ electrons in the t_{2g} orbitals and $\frac{1}{5}$ in the e_g ($\frac{9}{5} \times -\frac{2}{5}\Delta$ $+ \frac{1}{5} \times \frac{3}{5}\Delta = -\frac{3}{5}\Delta$). Because electron repulsion is larger than the crystal field in weak field complexes, this repulsion forces some electron density into the e_g orbitals.

5-6 Intermediate field complexes

In the vast majority of transition-metal complexes the energies associated with electron repulsion and the crystal field are of the same order of magnitude. This means that neither the weak field limit (electron repulsion $\gg$ crystal field) nor the strong field limit (crystal field $\gg$ electron repulsion) are met with in practice. There is no separate theory for the intermediate, real life, region. One uses either the strong or the weak field approach, whichever seems the more appropriate. For d^4–d^7 complexes the choice is dictated by the distinction which we used when introducing weak and strong field complexes—by the number of unpaired electrons present on the metal ion.

The discussion of weak and strong field complexes which we have given in the previous sections was oriented towards the intermediate region. In both cases we included both crystal field and electron repulsion effects; the two cases differed only in the order in which we considered these effects. Had we in each case considered every term arising from a d^n configuration and worked out the effects of the crystal field and electron repulsion exactly* then we would have obtained the same answer no matter whether we chose the wave-functions of the strong or weak field limits as our starting point. In this way we could have included weak, intermediate and strong fields in the one discussion. Why then bother about the two different approaches? The most important reason is that a computer is usually needed to solve the complete problem so that both input and output are numerical rather than algebraic. Usually one is only interested

---

* Here, 'exactly' does not mean 'exactly in an absolute sense' but rather 'exactly within the approximations which we are making'. For example, the Russell–Saunders coupling scheme is an approximation which usually gives rather good, but not perfect, agreement with experiment.

Table 5-5 Crystal field splitting of Russell–Saunders terms arising from d^n configurations in an octahedral crystal field. The spin multiplicity, not included in this table, is the same for the crystal field terms as for the parent Russell–Saunders terms

Russell–Saunders term	Crystal field components
S	A_{1g}
P	T_{1g}
D	E_g, T_{2g}
F	A_{2g}, T_{1g}, T_{2g}
G	$A_{1g}, E_g, T_{1g}, T_{2g}$
H	$E_g, 2T_{1g}, T_{2g}$
I	$A_{1g}, A_{2g}, E_g, T_{1g}, 2T_{2g}$

in a small proportion of the total number of energy levels and it is particularly convenient to know the explicit (algebraic) dependence of these energy levels and the associated wavefunctions on the various parameters of the problem. These data have to be obtained by calculations of the sort we have described. For the interpretation of the visible and near-infrared spectra of transition metal complexes this detailed information is not needed and it is usual to compare the experimental values with the results of full calculations. That this can be done quite simply is shown in Chapter 7.

The qualitative behaviour of the energy levels in the intermediate-field region can readily be obtained from a knowledge of the energy levels in the weak and strong field limits. When discussing strong field complexes we considered every possible state arising from every possible configuration. However, for weak field complexes we discussed only the states arising from the lowest free ion Russell–Saunders term. First, then, we must extend the weak field treatment to include the states arising from all of the other Russell–Saunders terms. This information is given in Table 5-5, which also includes the splittings of those Russell–Saunders terms which we have already considered in detail. The Russell–Saunders terms arising from d^n configurations are listed in Table 5-6. The relative energies of the components of these terms in a crystal field may be obtained

Table 5-6 Terms arising from d^n configurations

Configuration	Terms
d^1, d^9	^2D
d^2, d^8	$^3F, {}^3P, {}^1G, {}^1D, {}^1S$
d^3, d^7	$^4F, {}^4P, {}^2H, {}^2G, {}^2F, 2{}^2D, {}^2P$
d^4, d^6	$^5D, {}^3H, {}^3G, 2{}^3F, {}^3D, 2{}^3P, {}^1I, 2{}^1G, {}^1F, 2{}^1D, 2{}^1S$
d^5	$^6S, {}^4G, {}^4F, {}^4D, {}^4P, {}^2I, {}^2H, 2{}^2G, 2{}^2F, 3{}^2D, {}^2P, {}^2S$

$2{}^2D$ means that there are two distinct ^2D terms.

by the methods which we have already described or by others which are related to them. Two problems arise. First, as we have already noted, for a given d^n configuration there is usually more than one state of a given spin multiplicity and symmetry. These interact, the cross-terms between them being important unless the field is very weak. Second, if we wish to show the transition from weak to strong fields diagrammatically, the diagrams will be rather complicated. For the d^4 and d^6 configurations there are 43 energy levels the behaviour of which would have to be shown (see Table 5-6).

As we wish to use diagrammatic representations of the behaviour of these energy levels we shall make simplifications. We know which are the more stable states in the weak and strong field limits and we will show only these. If we do not wish to solve the problem of the interactions between terms exactly, the non-crossing rule (the energy levels of states of the same symmetry and spin degeneracy do not cross) gives a qualitative idea of what happens. It is convenient first to consider the behaviour of the ground and low-lying states of the weak-field limit as the crystal field increases.

The behaviour of the T_{2g} and E_g states derived from the D term of highest spin multiplicity for the d^1, d^4, d^6, and d^9 configurations is given in Fig. 5-22, which summarizes the relevant discussion of the

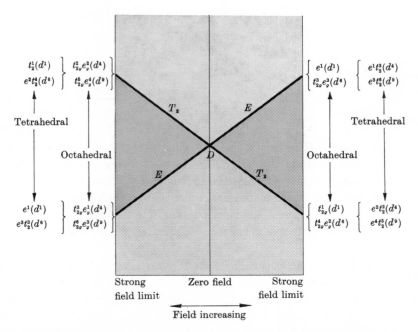

Fig. 5-22 A modified Orgel diagram for weak field complexes with free ion D ground states.

two previous sections and, in particular, Fig. 5-20. Fig. 5-22 is a modified form of a type of diagram first introduced by Orgel and usually called 'Orgel diagrams'. It will be noted that we have dropped some of the g suffixes in Fig. 5-22. The reason for this will appear in the next section.

The ground and low-lying weak field states of the d^2, d^3, d^7, and d^8 configurations are given in Fig. 5-23. Again, this figure summarizes

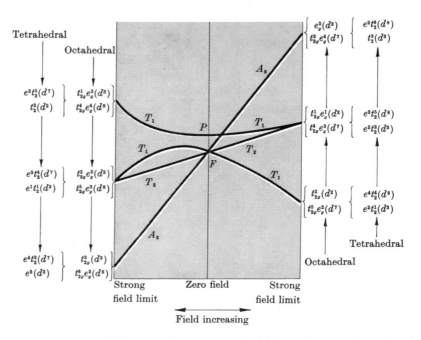

Fig. 5-23 A modified Orgel diagram for weak field complexes with free ion F ground states.

the relevant discussion in the previous sections. In particular, the interaction between the $T_{1g}(P)$ and $T_{1g}(F)$ terms has been included and is responsible for the appearance of curved lines in the figure.

The d^5 case is trivial and we do not give a diagram for it. The latter would consist of a single straight line joining the ^6S free ion term to the $t_2^3e^2$ strong field configuration (again we omit the g suffixes).

The next step is to include in these diagrams additional terms appropriate to strong field complexes for those cases where these have different ground-state spin multiplicities from the corresponding weak field complexes. Fig. 5-24, 5-25, and 5-26 include the additions, the last named showing the d^5 case. The reader will notice that the suffixes have been reinstated in these figures.

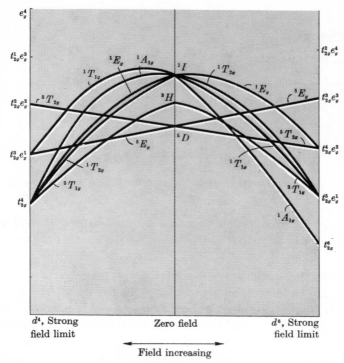

Fig. 5-24   A modified Tanabe–Sugano diagram for d^4 and d^6 octahedral complexes.

Figs. 5-21–5-26 show in a qualitative fashion the crystal field energy levels for the intermediate region and for weak and strong field limits. Additionally, the close relationship between the d^n and d^{10-n} configurations is brought out. Unfortunately, these diagrams have a serious limitation. The scale along the horizontal axis cannot be defined. To interpret spectra, in particular, it is convenient to have

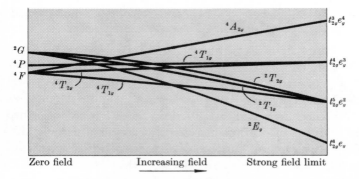

Fig. 5-25   A modified Tanabe–Sugano diagram for d^7 octahedral complexes.

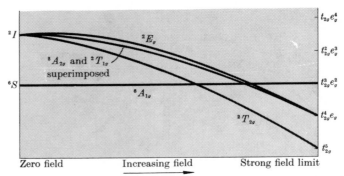

Fig. 5-26 A modified Tanabe–Sugano diagram for d^5 octahedral complexes.

the scale along this axis proportional to Δ. In Chapter 7 we shall introduce diagrams similar to those above but with a scale linear in Δ.

5-7 Non-octahedral complexes

So far this chapter has been concerned entirely with octahedral complexes. Whilst the majority of complexes are octahedral, almost all of them display some slight deviation from the ideal geometry. Other complexes have quite different geometries, as we saw in Chapter 2. For the moment we discuss only tetrahedral and square planar complexes.

5-7-1 Tetrahedral complexes

In tetrahedral complexes the five d orbitals of a transition metal ion are again split into a set of three (d_{xy}, d_{yz}, and d_{zx}), denoted t_2, and a set of two ($d_{x^2-y^2}$ and d_{z^2}), denoted e. These labels are those obtained by dropping the g suffix from the labels given to these orbitals in the octahedral group, but the reader must be wary for this is not always the case. In the next chapter we shall use the label t_{1u} when discussing octahedral complexes. This becomes t_2, not t_1, when carried over to tetrahedral complexes.

That the d orbital split into t_2 and e sets in tetrahedral complexes may be seen from Fig. 5-27. The key is to recognize that a tetrahedron is closely related to a cube. If the Cartesian axes are drawn as in Fig. 5-27, then $x \equiv y \equiv z$ so that d_{xy}, d_{yz}, and d_{zx} must be degenerate. The degeneracy of $d_{x^2-y^2}$ and d_{z^2} follows from the same argument used for octahedral complexes (Section 5-3 and Appendix 2). The relative ordering of these two sets energetically may also be seen from Fig. 5-27. One may say, loosely, that each lobe of a t_2 orbital is half a cube edge away from each ligand (regarded as a

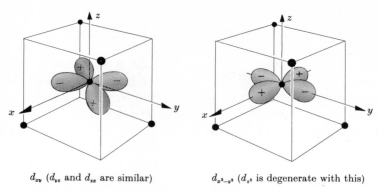

d_{xy} (d_{yz} and d_{zx} are similar) $d_{x^2-y^2}$ (d_{z^2} is degenerate with this)

Fig. 5-27 d orbitals in a tetrahedral ligand field.

point) but each lobe of the $d_{x^2-y^2}$ orbital is half a cube diagonal away. As for the octahedral case, this argument must be regarded as indicative only. The conclusion that the e set is less destabilized by the ligand field than the t_2 set (Fig. 5-28) is confirmed by experiment and by detailed calculations. These calculations also show that, for a given metal and ligand and constant metal–ligand distance, the magnitude of the splitting in a tetrahedral complex is $\frac{4}{9}$ of that in an octahedral. That is, $\Delta_{\text{tet.}} = -\frac{4}{9}\Delta_{\text{oct.}}$. Experimentally, this relationship has been found to hold remarkably well.

The next step is to obtain crystal field splitting diagrams of the type that we gave in the last section. We already have some of these: when discussing, for example, the d^8 weak field case we obtained the energy levels from those of the d^2 case by noting that we could talk of 'holes' rather than electrons. For these holes the crystal field splitting of the d orbitals is, effectively,* $-\Delta$ (energetically, the holes are more stable in e_g than t_{2g} orbitals). That is, the

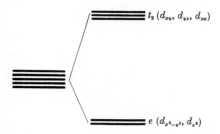

t_2 (d_{xy}, d_{yz}, d_{zx})

e ($d_{x^2-y^2}$, d_{z^2})

Fig. 5-28 d orbital splitting in a tetrahedral ligand field.

* As in previous sections we shall use Δ without any suffix to denote the octahedral case. Other cases (and the octahedral also, when in the interest of clarity) carry suffixes.

d^8 case is obtained from the d^2 by replacing Δ by $-\Delta$. Now, the crystal field splitting (for electrons) in tetrahedral complexes is $-\frac{4}{9}\Delta_{oct.}$. That is, the splitting diagram for a d^2 ion in a tetrahedral crystal field is the same as that for a d^8 ion in an octahedral field provided we include a scale factor of $\frac{4}{9}$. It was for this reason that we dropped some of the g suffixes in Figs. 5-22 and 5-23. Fig. 5-22 shows the energy levels of d^1, d^4, d^6, and d^9 weak field complexes in both octahedral and tetrahedral ligand fields. Similarly, Fig. 5-23 shows the energy levels of d^2, d^3, d^7, and d^8 weak field complexes in both of these fields. The reader should be able to show easily that $d^3 \rightarrow d^6$ ions would be expected to form both weak and strong field tetrahedral complexes, differing in the spin multiplicity of their ground states. No case of a strong field tetrahedral complex has yet been recognized so we shall not discuss them further. In particular, no attempt is made to include tetrahedral complexes in Figs. 5-24–5-26.

5-7-2   Square planar complexes

There are two conceptually different approaches to square planar complexes. One may regard the d-orbital splitting as being that obtained when two *trans* ligands are simultaneously removed from an octahedral complex. Alternatively, one may use the same approach as that used for octahedral and tetrahedral complexes and consider the splitting of the free ion d orbitals by a square planar ligand field. Since, in a square planar complex, $x \equiv y\,(\neq z)$ (Fig. 5-29), d_{zx} and d_{yz} are degenerate. This is the only symmetry-enforced degeneracy amongst the d orbitals. Adopting the first of the two approaches mentioned above, the d_{z^2} orbital of an octahedral complex is found to be relatively more stable in a square planar environment. Similarly, d_{zx} and d_{yz} will be more stable than d_{xy}, leading to the qualitative d-orbital splitting pattern shown in Fig. 5-30. The symmetry labels used for square planar complexes are different from those used for octahedral complexes. The correlation between

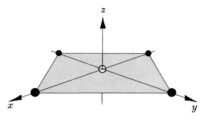

Fig. 5-29

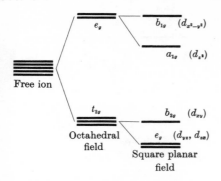

Fig. 5-30 Correlation of the d-orbital splitting in a square planar ligand field with those in an octahedral ligand-field.

the two sets is shown in Table 5-7. We include some symmetry labels which we have not yet used, anticipating a need for them in later chapters. The g and u suffixes have been omitted in both geometries in order to keep Table 5-7 compact. (The rule, of course, is $g \rightarrow g$ and $u \rightarrow u$.) There is some freedom about the choice of the B_1 and B_2 labels in square planar complexes in that they may be interchanged. What one author calls B_1, another may call B_2. In this book we consistently use the choice shown in Table 5-7.

Table 5-7 may be used for either orbitals or states. For example, the $^2T_{2g}$ state of a d^1 configuration in an octahedral ligand field splits into two, $^2A_{1g}$ and ^2E_g, if the ligand field is reduced to square planar (Fig. 5-30). Of these the ^2E_g is the more stable because it corresponds to the single d electron occupying the d_{zx} and d_{yx} orbitals (which are more stable than d_{xy}, cf. Fig. 5-30).

The relative energies of the components of other octahedral crystal field terms can be discussed in the same way, but we will

Table 5-7

Octahedral	Square planar
A_1	A_1
A_2	B_1
E	$A_1(z^2) + B_1(x^2 - y^2)$
T_1	$A_2 + E$
T_2	$B_2(xy) + E(zx, yz)$

Although g and u suffixes are not given, the brackets indicate how the various d orbitals transform. Thus d_{z^2} has A_{1g} symmetry in a square planar complex.

Table 5-8

Octahedral	*Trigonally distorted octahedral field*	*Digonally distorted octahedral field*
A_1	A_1	A
A_2	A_2	A
E	E	$A(z^2) + A(x^2 - y^2)$
T_1	$A_2 + E$	$B_1 + B_2 + B_3$
T_2	$A_1(xy) + E(zx, yz)$	$B_1(xy) + B_2(yz) + B_3(zx)$

As for Table 5-7, g and u suffixes are omitted. $A_1(xy)$ and $A(z^2)$ mean, respectively, that d_{xy} transforms as A_{1g} (trigonally distorted octahedron) and d_{z^2} transforms as A_g (digonal distortion). For digonally distorted complexes the labels B_1, B_2, and B_3 (with g or u suffixes) may be used differently by different workers, although those with g suffixes are never interchanged with those with u suffixes.

content ourselves with noting that the final energies depend on the magnitude of a) the splitting between the d_{z^2} and $d_{x^2-y^2}$ orbitals and b) the splitting between d_{xy} and d_{xz}, d_{yz} as well as Δ.

5-7-3 Other stereochemistries

The d-orbital splitting patterns in low-symmetry geometries other than those which we have discussed are most readily obtained in the way outlined for square planar complexes. The results for two important geometries are given in Table 5-8. However, care must be exercised in using this table. First, as for square planar complexes, some choice exists in the allocation of symmetry labels for digonally distorted octahedral complexes (Fig. 5-31). Secondly, the choice of z axis for an octahedral complex is not consistent with the usual

Fig. 5-31 A digonally distorted octahedral complex. The form of the distortion is shown by arrows.

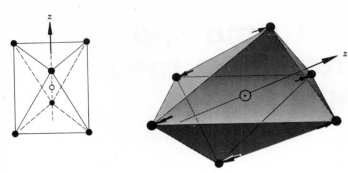

Fig. 5-32 A trigonally distorted octahedral complex. The form of the distortion is shown by arrows. A different view of the distorted structure is shown in the smaller diagram.

choice for trigonally distorted octahedral complexes, for which the threefold axis is chosen as z axis (Fig. 5-32). This means that, for example, the d_{z^2} orbital in the latter geometry is not the same d_{z^2} as that in the corresponding octahedral complex, but is a mixture of the octahedral d_{xy}, d_{yz}, and d_{zx} orbitals.

Problems

5-1 The ion $[\text{PaF}_8]^{3-}$ has a cubic arrangement of ligands around the Pa atom. What is the d-orbital splitting pattern in this ion? Assuming that it is possible to prepare a series of such molecules with different d^n configurations, for which would you expect a sharp distinction between weak and strong field complexes?

5-2 Consider the hypothetical series discussed in question 5-1 and investigate how their energy level patterns could be included in Figs. 5-22 to 5-26.

5-3 Explain in detail why the $^3T_{1g}(F)$ state arising from the d^2 configuration has energies of $-\tfrac{3}{5}\Delta$ and $-\tfrac{4}{5}\Delta$ in the weak and strong field limits, respectively.

5-4 Show, using Table 5-3, that the terms arising from the e_g^2 configuration are either $^3A_{2g}$, $^1A_{1g}$, and ^1E_g or $^1A_{2g}$, $^3A_{1g}$, and ^1E_g. Determine which of these is correct, using Tables 5-5 and 5-6. The answer is given in Table 5-4.

5-5 The splitting of an incompletely filled f shell of electrons by a crystal field is usually very small. Assuming, however, that it is large, construct a diagram analagous to Fig. 5-11.

6 Ligand field theory of transition metal complexes

6-1 Introduction

In the previous chapter we discussed the electronic structure of transition metal complexes assuming that the ligands' only effect is to produce an electrostatic field which relieves the degeneracy of the d orbitals of the central metal ion. The most serious defect of this model is that it does not recognize the existence of overlap and, hence, the existence of specific bonding interactions between the ligand and metal orbitals. Yet calculations which assume reasonable sizes for the orbitals (together with a considerable body of physical evidence which will be reviewed in Chapter 9) point to the existence of overlap. How should we take account of it?

In a non-linear polyatomic system one cannot strictly talk of σ, π, δ, etc. interactions. (Draw a σ bond between two atoms and then allow a third, non-collinear, atom to participate. The interactions between the orbital of this third atom with those forming the σ bond will not be purely σ unless all three are s orbitals.) For simplicity, we shall neglect ligand–ligand overlap (although some workers hold that this is of importance) and consider only ligand–metal interactions. From the point of view of the *metal* each such diatomic interaction may be classified as either σ or π. First, we consider the case of octahedral complexes.

6-2 Octahedral complexes

6-2-1 Metal–ligand σ interactions

We have to consider here the interactions between the six ligand σ orbitals, one on each ligand, and the valence shell orbitals of the metal atom, and shall discuss the case of a complex formed by a metal ion of the first transition series so that the valence shell orbitals are $3d$, $4s$, and $4p$. The ligand σ orbitals are all formally occupied by two electrons, which, in a very simple picture, one might regard as being 'donated' to the transition metal ion.

A considerable simplification results if we exploit the fact that only orbitals of the same symmetry type have non-zero overlap integrals. That is, if we have two sets of orbitals of e_g symmetry, (one on the ligands, the other on the metal), they will in general be non-orthogonal (i.e. have a non-zero overlap integral) and therefore interact. On the other hand both will have zero overlap with all orbitals of a_{1g}, t_{1u}, t_{2g}, etc. symmetry and will not interact with them.

The valence shell atomic orbitals of the central metal atom were classified according to their symmetry in the previous chapter. The $4s$ orbital has a_{1g} symmetry, the $4p$ orbitals have t_{1u}, and the d orbitals split into two sets, one with t_{2g}, the other with e_g symmetry. Evidently, the next step is to classify the ligand orbitals according to their symmetry types. Two problems arise. First, for a regular octahedral complex, all six ligand orbitals 'look alike'—How then can they be classified differently? Secondly, we have seen that a characteristic of a symmetry-classified set is that all of those symmetry operations which send an octahedron into itself send one member of the set into either itself or another member or a mixture of members (this was used to demonstrate the degeneracy of $d_{x^2-y^2}$ and d_{z^2}). As these symmetry operations send one ligand σ orbital into another, why do they not at once constitute a complete set? The answer is, they do. However, this set can be broken down into smaller sets and it is to these latter that we attach symmetry labels.* In these sets the individuality of the ligand σ orbitals is lost. We talk of the wavefunctions of various groups of ligand orbitals rather than of the wavefunctions corresponding to individual ligand orbitals. The members of the symmetry-classifiable sets are linear combinations of the ligand σ orbitals and are sometimes referred to as 'ligand group orbitals' or 'symmetry-adapted wavefunctions'). The explicit form of these ligand group orbitals is given in Table 6-1. The individual σ orbitals are identified by the labels $\sigma_1 \rightarrow \sigma_6$, as shown in Fig. 6-1. As mentioned earlier, we have assumed that the ligand σ orbitals do not overlap each other, although non-zero ligand–ligand overlap integrals would only affect the normalization factors given in the table, not the general form of the wavefunctions.

The ligand group orbitals listed in Table 6-1 will overlap with metal orbitals of the same symmetry, so that the $4s(a_{1g})$, $4p(t_{1u})$, and $3d(e_g)$ orbitals of the metal will be involved in bonding. Of the basis set on the metal atom only the $3d(t_{2g})$ orbitals are not involved in σ bonding. Fig. 6-2 shows schematically the sort of energy level pattern obtained as a result of these σ interactions. The a_{1g}, t_{1u}, and e_g interactions are shown pictorially in Figs. 6-3, 6-4, and 6-5, where

---

* Appendix 4 shows how these sub-sets may be obtained.

Table 6-I   Ligand group orbitals of six octahedrally-oriented ligands

Symmetry	Ligand group orbital
a_{1g}	$\frac{1}{\sqrt{6}}(\sigma_1 + \sigma_2 + \sigma_3 + \sigma_4 + \sigma_5 + \sigma_6)$
t_{1u}	$\frac{1}{\sqrt{2}}(\sigma_1 - \sigma_4)$ $\frac{1}{\sqrt{2}}(\sigma_2 - \sigma_5)$ $\frac{1}{\sqrt{2}}(\sigma_3 - \sigma_6)$
e_g	$\frac{1}{2}(\sigma_2 - \sigma_3 + \sigma_5 - \sigma_6)$ $\frac{1}{\sqrt{12}}(2\sigma_1 + 2\sigma_4 - \sigma_2 - \sigma_3 - \sigma_5 - \sigma_6)$

it can be seen that there is a close matching between ligand group orbitals and the corresponding metal orbitals. At the present time many research groups are trying to carry out reasonably accurate calculations aimed, in part, at obtaining molecular orbital energy level schemes (such as that in Fig. 6-2) accurately. Fig. 6-2 indicates that the idea that the ligands function as electron donors is correct. Electrons which, before the interaction was 'switched on', were in pure ligand orbitals are really in delocalized molecular orbitals. The consequences of this for the concept of formal valence states will be discussed later. The most important feature of Fig. 6-2 is the fact that the two lowest 'unoccupied' orbital sets are, in order, t_{2g} and $e_g(2)$ (which is weakly antibonding). Further, the number of electrons occupying these orbitals is the same as the number present

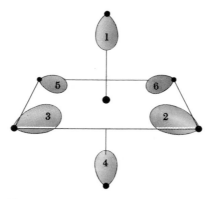

Fig. 6-1

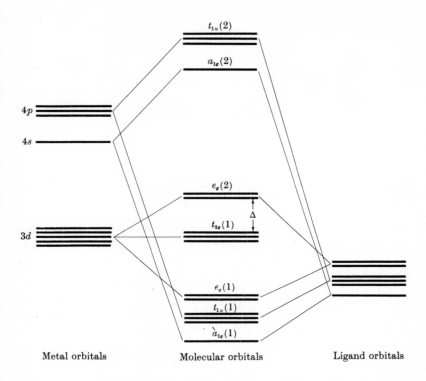

Fig. 6-2 A schematic molecular orbital energy level scheme for octahedral complexes (only σ interactions are included).

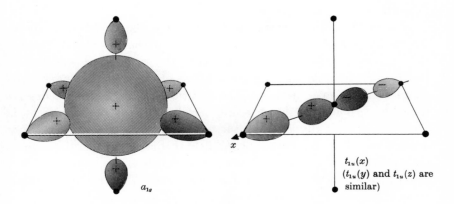

(*Left*) **Fig. 6-3** The interaction between the metal s orbital and the a_{1g} ligand group orbital. (*Right*) **Fig. 6-4** The interaction between the metal p_x orbital and the corresponding t_{1u} ligand group orbital.

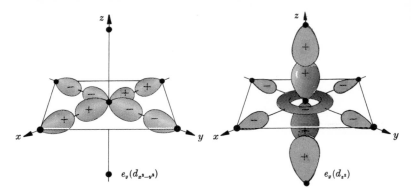

Fig. 6-5 The interaction between the metal $d_{x^2-y^2}$ and d_{z^2} orbitals and the corresponding ligand group orbitals.

in the valence shell orbitals of the metal before the interaction was 'switched on'. In practice, this means the number originally present in the metal d orbitals. That is, the d electrons of the uncomplexed metal ion may be regarded as being distributed between the t_{2g} and e_g molecular orbitals. This is precisely the situation discussed in the previous chapter where, it will be recalled, we were careful to state that Δ, the separation of the t_{2g} and e_g sets, was an experimental quantity. Evidently, Δ is determined partially by crystal field and partially by molecular orbital effects. Provided that we replace e_g, wherever it appears in Chapter 5, by e_g (antibonding) then all the discussion in that chapter remains valid. It should be noted that the 'metal' electrons in the e_g (antibonding) orbitals are to some extent delocalized over the ligands.

We conclude that crystal field theory may be modified to allow for the effects of covalency. This modified theory, called 'ligand field theory', differs from crystal field theory in that additional parameters are introduced; we shall meet them in the next two chapters. The magnitudes of the additional parameters are determined experimentally, but the number of independent experimental observables is usually less than the total number of parameters. One cannot, therefore, assert that ligand field theory, is in general, proven. One may say only that it provides a consistent explanation for experimental data using parameters which, almost invariably, have physically reasonable values.

6-2-2   Metal–ligand π interactions

So far we have only considered σ bonding in an octahedral complex. What of π bonding? It appears usually to be true that π bonding is rather weaker than σ bonding. Thus, there is no compound known in which it has been established that, in the ground state, there is a π bond but no σ bond. On the other hand, the vast majority of molecules have at least one σ bond with, apparently, no associated π bond. Consequently we can assume that the effects of π bonding will be to modify, but probably not drastically alter, Fig. 6-2.

The treatment of π bonding is similar to that of σ bonding. We suppose that there are two orbitals available for π bonding on each ligand (Fig. 6-6), a total of 12 in all. The symmetry-adapted combinations of these consist of four sets with three ligand group orbitals in each set. The sets have t_{1g}, t_{1u}, t_{2g}, and t_{2u} symmetries. There are

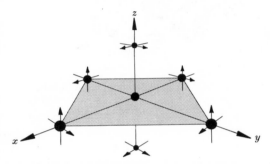

Fig. 6-6   Ligand π orbitals in an octahedral complex. The arrow heads represent the lobe of each orbital with positive phase.

no metal orbitals of the t_{1g} and t_{2u} symmetries within our chosen valence set (one set of f orbitals transforms as t_{2u} and one set of g orbitals as t_{1g}). These π ligand group orbitals are therefore carried over, unmodified, into the full molecular orbital description. The t_{1u} set will interact with the metal p orbitals (also of t_{1u} symmetry), but it is simpler to think of their effect on the occupied t_{1u} molecular orbitals in Fig. 6-2 and to consider three cases.

Case 1: The ligand π orbitals are occupied. In this case the t_{1u} combination of the molecular orbitals is also occupied. Interaction with the $t_{1u}(1)$ molecular orbitals of Fig. 6-2 will raise or lower this latter set depending on whether its energy is higher or lower than that of the ligand $\pi(t_{1u})$ set. As long as we retain two occupied t_{1u} sets the orbital occupancy is unaffected by this interaction and, because the t_{2g}–$e_g(2)$ separation is our concern, we may neglect it.

Case 2: The ligand t_{1u} set is unoccupied. In this case interaction between the ligand and $t_{1u}(1)$ sets will result in a 'repulsion' between the two energy levels and the orbital occupancy will remain unchanged.

Case 3: *Interactions involving the* $t_{1u}(2)$ *set in Fig.* 6-2.   We need only consider the interaction between the $t_{1u}(2)$ molecular orbital set and the ligand $\pi(t_{1u})$ set if it leads to one of them becoming occupied. In fact, there is no recognized case in which the ligand $\pi(t_{1u})$ set, whether occupied or not, needs to be considered.

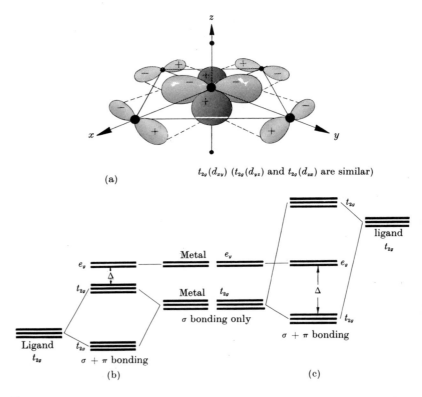

$t_{2g}(d_{xy})$ $(t_{2g}(d_{yz})$ and $t_{2g}(d_{zx})$ are similar)

(a)

(b)   (c)

Fig. 6-7   (a) The interaction between the metal d_{xy} orbital and the corresponding t_{2g} ligand π-group orbital; (b), (c) alternative consequences of this interaction.

We are left with the ligand $\pi(t_{2g})$ set. This, of course, may interact with the metal t_{2g} set (d_{xy}, d_{yz}, d_{zx}) which, in the absence of this π bonding, is non-bonding. The consequences of this interaction, shown in Fig. 6-7a, depend upon which of the two t_{2g} sets is higher in energy. The alternative situations are shown in Figs. 6-7b and c. If the ligand $\pi(t_{2g})$ set is the higher in energy then the metal t_{2g} set is pushed down; if the ligand set is the lower, the metal set is raised in energy. That is, the magnitude of Δ depends, in part, on π bonding. The halide anions provide an example of the situation shown in Fig. 6-7b. For these ligands, two of the filled p orbitals in their valence shell will be the orbitals involved in π bonding. This explains partially at least why the halide anions exert relatively weak crystal fields (see the spectrochemical series given in Section 5-3). The cyanide anion possesses two sets of π orbitals both of which will interact with the metal orbitals. The effect of the occupied C≡N π-bonding orbitals will be similar to that of the occupied p orbitals of the halides. However, these π orbitals have energies well removed from those of the metal d orbitals and so their effect is small. Much more important are the empty C≡N π-antibonding orbitals, which behave as shown in Fig. 6-7c. Again, this behaviour is consistent with the position of the cyanide anion in the spectrochemical series—it exerts a very large crystal field.

At this point it is worthwhile to reconsider the crystal field splitting parameter Δ, since it is evidently more complicated than we at first supposed. We have encountered three factors which influence the magnitude of Δ.

First, it depends on the electrostatic field generated by the ligands—the crystal field.

Second, it depends on ligand–metal σ bonding because the energy of the 'metal' e_g orbitals depends on this.

Third, it depends on the ligand–metal π bonding, since this affects the energy of the 'metal' t_{2g} set. This does not exhaust the list of factors influencing the magnitude of Δ, but there are at present believed to be no others of comparable importance. For a constant metal charge and metal–ligand distance, the metal will only influence Δ through the second and third factors.

6-3   Tetrahedral complexes

In this and the next section we consider the bonding in complexes with other-than-octahedral stereochemistries. For tetrahedral complexes we shall use the nomenclature discussed in Section 5-7-1 and remind the reader that crystal field theory predicts that the d_{xy}, d_{yz}, and d_{zx} orbitals, of t_2 symmetry, are less stable than d_{z^2} and $d_{x^2-y^2}$ (e symmetry). The other metal orbitals in the valence set are $4s(a_1)$ and $4p_x$, $4p_y$, and $4p_z(t_2)$, again considering a first-row transition element. The four ligand σ orbitals give a_1 and t_2 symmetry-adapted combinations, so that the σ-bonding-only molecular orbital diagram is as given schematically in Fig. 6-8. As in octahedral complexes, the more stable d-orbital set according to crystal-field theory, that of e symmetry, is not involved in σ bonding. Many tetrahedral complexes involve the oxide anion as a ligand (e.g. the permanganate, chromate, and ferrate anions) and contain a metal atom in a high formal valence state. Since oxygen is usually regarded as forming two covalent bonds and because a

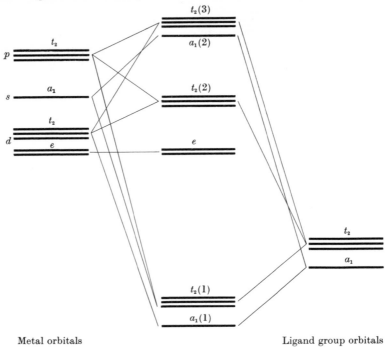

Fig. 6-8 A schematic molecular orbital energy level diagram for tetrahedral complexes (only σ interactions are considered).

high metal charge will favour ligand $\rightarrow$ metal charge migration, we anticipate that π bonding is of potential importance for tetrahedral complexes. Unfortunately, the consequences of π bonding are not as clear-cut as for octahedral complexes. The ligand π-orbital symmetry-adapted combinations are of t_1, t_2, and e symmetry. That is, π bonding involves *all* of the metal d orbitals, not just one set (as in the octahedral case), and it is impossible to give a simple diagram analogous to Fig. 6-7. Both the $t_2(2)$ and e levels of Fig. 6-8, which crystal field theory regarded as pure d orbitals, will change with varying π bonding and it is not possible to discuss the behaviour of their separation, $\Delta_{\text{tet.}}$, in general terms. A schematic molecular orbital pattern for a tetrahedral complex with a significant π-bonding contribution is shown in Fig. 6-9. It is emphasized that the relative energies shown for the molecular orbitals in Fig. 6-9 are to be regarded as flexible.

6-4 Complexes of other geometries
Other geometries will not be discussed in detail as there are none for which we could arrive at firm general conclusions. Instead, we

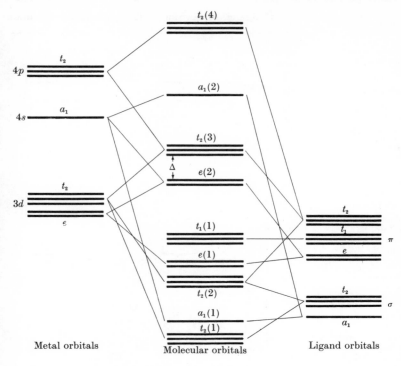

$t_2(4)$

$4p$ t_2

$a_1(2)$

$4s$ a_1

$t_2(3)$

Δ $e(2)$

$3d$ t_2

e

$t_1(1)$

t_2

t_1

π

$e(1)$

e

$t_2(2)$

t_2

$a_1(1)$

σ

$t_2(1)$

a_1

Metal orbitals   Molecular orbitals   Ligand orbitals

Fig. 6-9 A schematic molecular orbital energy level diagram for tetrahedral complexes including π bonding.

list in Table 6-2 the symmetries of the σ and π ligand group orbitals for common geometries and compare these with the symmetry of the orbitals comprising the valence set of the transition metal ion. In the table we introduce a convenient and widely used shorthand description for each symmetry type. The label consists of an uppercase symbol, often in **bold** type, with one or two subscripts of the sort already encountered. Almost any textbook on spectroscopy or on group theory explains how these symbols are arrived at. Note that the shorthand does not always distinguish between apparently quite different geometries. For completeness octahedral and tetrahedral complexes are also listed in Table 6-2.

6-5 Formal oxidation states

In crystal field theory a complex ion is assumed to be composed of a cation, M^{n+}, surrounded by, but not overlapping with, a number of ligands. What is the effect of covalency on the electronic nature of the cation? Let us consider two complex ions, one of $Fe^{3+}(d^5)$, the other of $Fe^{2+}(d^6)$, both assumed to be high spin, with identical

Table 6-2 The symmetries of ligand σ, π, and metal orbitals for common

Molecular geometry	Shorthand symmetry symbol	s	p_z	p_x	p_y	d_{z^2}	$d_{x^2-y^2}$	d_{xy}	d_{yz}	d_{zx}
Octahedral, ML_6	$\mathbf{O_h}$	a_{1g}	t_{1u}			e_g		t_{2g}		
Tetrahedral, ML_4	$\mathbf{T_d}$	a_1	t_2			e		t_2		
$trans$-Octahedral, ML_4L_2'	$\mathbf{D_{4h}}$	a_{1g}	a_{2u}	e_u		a_{1g}	b_{1g}	b_{2g}	e_g	
Square planar, ML_4	$\mathbf{D_{4h}}$									
Octahedral with a bidentate chelating ligand, $M(L_2)_3$	$\mathbf{D_3}$	a_1	a_2	e		a_1	e		e	
Trigonal bipyramid, ML_5	$\mathbf{D_{3h}}$	a_1'	a_2''	e'		a_1'	e'		e''	
All cis-octahedral, ML_3L'	$\mathbf{C_{3v}}$									
Tetrahedral, ML_3L'	$\mathbf{C_{3v}}$	a_1	a_1	e		a_1	a_1	a_2	e	
Face-centred octahedron, ML_7	$\mathbf{C_{3v}}$									
Square based pyramid, ML_4L'	$\mathbf{C_{4v}}$									
Octahedral, ML_5L', or $trans$ $ML_4L'L''$	$\mathbf{C_{4v}}$	a_1	a_1	e		a_1	b_1	b_2	e	
cis-Octahedral, ML_4L_2'	$\mathbf{C_{2v}}$									
Tetrahedral, ML_2L_2'	$\mathbf{C_{2v}}$	a_1	a_1	b_1	b_2	a_1	a_1	a_2	b_2	b_1
Square face-centred trigonal prism, ML_7	$\mathbf{C_{2v}}$									
Dodecahedral, ML_8	$\mathbf{D_{2d}}$	a_1	b_2	e_1		a_1	b_1	b_2	e	
Square antiprism, ML_8	$\mathbf{D_{4d}}$	a_1	b_2	e_1		a_1	e_2		e_3	

ligands. Fig. 6-10 gives schematic molecular orbital energy level diagrams for the two complexes. The electrons in the $a_{1g}(1)$, $t_{1u}(1)$, and lower $e_g(1)$ orbitals 'originated' on the ligands but in the complex ions occupy molecular orbitals and are therefore delocalized onto the cations to some extent.

Because of its higher charge and smaller size the polarizing power of the Fe^{3+} cation would be expected to be greater than that of Fe^{2+} so that the transfer of electron density from the ligands to the cation will be greater for Fe^{3+} than for Fe^{2+}. Let us suppose that an effective transfer of two electrons occurs for the former and one for the latter (we choose integers for simplicity and ignore the rather difficult problem of how to calculate the number of electrons transferred). The resultant charges on the two cations are therefore *both* $+1$ $[(+3 - 2)$ and $(+2 - 1)]$. The charges we assumed, $3+$ and $2+$, are *formal* charges. The absolute magnitude of an actual charge is always less than the absolute magnitude of a formal charge, for both ligands and cation. This, of course, is a restatement of Pauling's

Symmetry of the ligand orbitals		Comments
σ	π	
$a_{1g} + e_g + t_{1u}$	$t_{1g} + t_{1u} + t_{2g} + t_{2u}$	
$a_1 + t_2$	$e + t_1 + t_2$	
$2a_{1g} + a_{2u} + b_{1g} + e_u$	$a_{2u} + b_{1u} + 2e_g + e_u$	$\left.\begin{array}{l} b_{1g} \\ b_{1u} \end{array}\right\}$ may be encountered $\left(\begin{array}{l} b_{2g} \\ b_{2u} \end{array}\right.$ exchanged with
$a_1 + a_2 + 2e$	$2a_1 + 2a_2 + 4e$	
$2a_1' + e'$	$a_2' + a_2'' + 2e' + 2e''$	
$2a_1 + 2e$	$2a_1 + 2a_2 + 4e$	the three-fold axis is the z-axis
$2a_1 + e$	$a_1 + a_2 + 3e$	
$3a_1 + 2e$	$2a_1 + 2a_2 + 5e$	
$2a_1 + b_1 + e$	$a_1 + a_2 + b_1 + b_2 + 3e$	
$3a_1 + b_1 + e$	$a_1 + a_2 + b_1 + b_2 + 4e$	
$3a_1 + a_2 + b_1 + b_2$	$2a_1 + 2a_2 + 4b_1 + 4b_2$	$\left.\begin{array}{l} b_1 \\ b_2 \end{array}\right\}$ may be encountered $\left(\begin{array}{l} b_2 \\ b_1 \end{array}\right.$ exchanged with
$2a_1 + b_1 + b_2$	$2a_1 + 2a_2 + 2b_1 + 2b_2$	
$3a_1 + a_2 + 2b_1 + b_2$	$3a_1 + 3a_2 + 4b_1 + 4b_2$	
$2a_1 + 2b_2 + 2e$	$2a_1 + 2a_2 + 2b_1 + 2b_2 + 4e$	
$a_1 + b_2 + e_1 + e_2 + e_3$	$a_1 + a_2 + b_1 + b_2 + 2e_1 + 2e_2 + 2e_3$	

Electroneutrality Principle. Contemporary calculations indicate that whilst the actual charge on a Fe^{3+} ion is likely to be rather greater than that on a Fe^{2+} ion, if the ligands are identical, the difference between them is only of the order of one-third of an electron. The actual charges themselves would be of the order of unity (positive).

Although the charges indicated by the symbols Fe^{3+} and Fe^{2+} are misleading this representation is not valueless. In particular these formal charges lead to the correct number of electrons being placed in the t_{2g} and upper e_g orbitals (Fig. 6-10). It is therefore usual to refer to Fe(III) and Fe(II), as we have done throughout this book rather than Fe^{3+} and Fe^{2+}, thereby avoiding the difficult problem of the actual charge distribution within the molecule. At one or two points in the text we have, usually for emphasis, reverted to the Fe^{3+}, Fe^{2+} convention.

It is common practice to assign a formal charge to species such as $[Fe(H_2O)_6]^{2+}$. This assumes that there is no covalent interaction between the complex ion and surrounding molecules. For example,

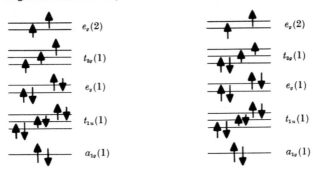

Fe^{3+} complex (high spin)   Fe^{2+} complex (high spin)

Fig. 6-10

we assume that in aqueous solution $[Fe(H_2O)_6]^{2+}$ either does not hydrogen bond with the solvent or that any hydrogen bonding does not affect the electron distribution within the complex ion. When attention is focussed on the metal ion in these species, this approximation introduces no difficulties. For quantitative work on the interaction of a complex ion with its environment it may in the future become necessary to further modify the nomenclature and to call this species $[Fe(H_2O)_6]^{II}$ or something similar.

Problems

6-1 Use Table 6-2 to construct schematic σ-only molecular orbital energy level diagrams for (a) a tetragonally distorted octahedral complex, (b) a square planar complex.

6-2 If you had a probe which would measure the total electron density at any point in a molecule what differences would you expect it to show for the complex ions $[Co(NH_3)_6]^{3+}$ and $[Co(NH_3)_6]^{2+}$?

6-3 Use Table 6-2 to construct a table which shows how symmetry labels change going from one symmetry to another (related) one. Such a table is called a correlation table.

6-4 Modify the discussion of this chapter to obtain schematic molecular energy level diagrams for the (octahedral) $[SiF_6]^{2-}$ and (tetrahedral) $[BF_4]^-$ anions.

6-5 Give a molecular orbital interpretation of the 'rule of average environment' (see section 7-9).

6-6 Compare the factors affecting the splitting of the d orbitals of octahedral and tetrahedral complexes.

Electronic spectra of transition metal complexes

7-1 Introduction

In this chapter we shall be concerned with the electronic spectra of transition metal complexes. The energy required for the promotion of an electron from one orbital to another or, more precisely, the excitation of a molecule from its electronic ground state to an electronic excited state, corresponds to absorption of light in the near-infrared, visible or ultraviolet regions of the spectrum. For transition metal complexes the absorption bands in the first two of these regions are relatively weak and are associated with transitions largely localized on the metal atom.

The ultraviolet bands are intense. They are associated with the transfer of an electron from one atom to another and so are called charge-transfer bands. These bands are usually responsible for the absorption of indicators involving inorganic species, such as the thiocyanate test for Fe^{3+} or the indicators used in EDTA (compleximetric) titrations.

We shall discuss the intense bands later in this chapter and for the moment concern ourselves with the weaker bands. While these are most simply explained by crystal field theory, a more detailed comparison of the data with the theoretical predictions will show that ligand field theory provides a more appropriate explanation.

The explanation provided by crystal field theory for the weak transitions is presented in diagrams such as Fig. 7-1, which shows the effect of an octahedral crystal field on the energy levels of a d^2 ion such as vanadium(III). The ground state is $^3T_{1g}$ and spin-allowed transitions (those in which the spin state is the same in both ground and excited states) may occur to the $^3T_{2g}$, $^3T_{1g}$, and $^3A_{2g}$ excited states, this being the usual order of increasing energy. Experimentally, two transitions are observed. Calculations (*vide infra*) indicate that the third, high energy, band is obscured by an intense charge-transfer transition. We shall also see that this third band should, in any case, be particularly weak. It thus appears that we can account, qualitatively, for the spectrum. Whether we can also do so quantitatively is discussed in the next section.

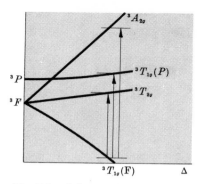

Fig. 7-1 d–d transitions in an octahedral d^2 complex.

7-2   The electronic spectrum of vanadium(III) complexes

We need explicit expressions for the energies of the excited states of the vanadium(III) ion relative to that of the ground state. These energies depend on three quantities, the crystal field splitting parameter Δ, the magnitude of the ^3F–^3P separation in the free ion, and the magnitude of the interaction between the two $^3T_{1g}$ states. The second of these quantities is usually denoted $15B$, where B is a sum of electron repulsion integrals which it is convenient not to evaluate explicitly and which is referred to as a 'Racah parameter'. Other Racah parameters, also composed of electron repulsion integrals, which the reader may encounter elsewhere, are denoted A and C. The third of the quantities mentioned above, the energy of interaction of the two $^3T_{1g}$ states, is, fortunately, a function of Δ and B only, so that these two quantities are all that is needed to interpret the spectrum of octahedral vanadium(III) complexes. $15B$ is the separation of the ^3F and ^3P free ion terms, so it should be possible to obtain the value of B from atomic spectral data. This corresponds to the pure crystal field approach, but agreement between experiment and theory is only obtained if B is treated as a parameter, the value of which may be varied. B has to be given a value rather smaller than that obtained from the free ion data. This parameterization of B is part of the ligand field method and is consistent with one's ideas of the consequences of covalency. Covalency implies a) that the 'metal' electrons will be partially delocalized onto the ligands, and b) the effective positive charge on the transition metal will be smaller than in the free ion. Both these effects mean that the 'metal' electron clouds will be more diffuse in the complex than in the free ion and electron repulsion therefore reduced. This conclusion is confirmed by a more detailed analysis.

     The energies of the crystal field spin triplet terms of the d^2

configuration, relative to the ^3F free ion term as zero, are given explicitly below. We give these expressions without proof, but the reader may readily check that they reduce to those given near the end of Section 5-5 for both the weak field limit* $\Delta \to 0$ (expand the square root using the binomial theorem in the form $(y^2 + xy)^{1/2} \simeq y + x/2$; note that the $15B$ term was not included in the energies given in Section 5-5) and that in the strong field limit $B = 0$. The square root terms are those which allow for the mixing of the $^3T_{1g}(F)$ and $^3T_{1g}(P)$ levels by the crystal field. Indeed, it should be evident from the form of these two energy level expressions that they are obtained as the roots of a quadratic equation:

Term	Energy
$^3T_{1g}(F)$	$\frac{1}{2}[15B - \frac{3}{5}\Delta - (225B^2 + 18B\Delta + \Delta^2)^{1/2}]$
$^3T_{2g}$	$\frac{1}{5}\Delta$
$^3T_{1g}(P)$	$\frac{1}{2}[15B - \frac{3}{5}\Delta + (225B^2 + 18B\Delta + \Delta^2)^{1/2}]$
$^3A_{2g}$	$\frac{6}{5}\Delta$

It follows that the two observed bands, assigned to the $^3T_{2g} \leftarrow T_{1g}(F)$ and $^3T_{1g}(P) \leftarrow {}^3T_{1g}(F)$ transitions, have energies:

Transition	Energy
$^3T_{2g} \leftarrow {}^3T_{1g}(F)$	$\frac{1}{2}[\Delta - 15B + (225B^2 + 18B\Delta + \Delta^2)^{1/2}]$
$^3T_{1g}(P) \leftarrow {}^3T_{1g}(F)$	$(225B^2 + 18B\Delta + \Delta^2)^{1/2}$

We have experimental transition energies to fit to these expressions, so we can now obtain values for Δ and B. This task is not as difficult as it seems. Let us divide the two expressions above by B. We then have:

$$\frac{E(^3T_{2g} \leftarrow {}^3T_{1g}(F))}{B} = \frac{1}{2}\left[\frac{\Delta}{B} - 15 + \left(225 + 18\frac{\Delta}{B} + \frac{\Delta^2}{B^2}\right)^{1/2}\right] \qquad 7\text{--}1$$

$$\frac{E(^3T_{1g}(P) \leftarrow {}^3T_{1g}(F))}{B} = \left(225 + 18\frac{\Delta}{B} + \frac{\Delta^2}{B^2}\right)^{1/2} \qquad 7\text{--}2$$

The right-hand-side expressions are functions of Δ/B. Similarly, the energies of the terms themselves, divided by B, may be expressed as functions of Δ/B. Tanabe and Sugano have published diagrams which show these relationships; they take as their energy zero the energy of the ground state, so that they effectively plot the functions:

$$\frac{E(^3T_{2g} \leftarrow {}^3T_{1g}(F))}{B} \qquad \text{and} \qquad \frac{E(^3T_{1g}(P) \leftarrow {}^3T_{1g}(F))}{B}$$

---

* Strictly, of course, the weak field limit is $\Delta = 0$. However, substituting this value simply gives the ^3F–^3P separation in the free ion, $15B$.

against Δ/B for the d^2 case. It should be noted that, because of this, the ground state is coincident with the abscissa in these diagrams. If a change in ground state occurs there is a discontinuity in the diagram. Fig. 7-2 is a Tanabe and Sugano diagram for the octahedral d^2 case.

Let us now consider as a specific example the $[V(H_2O)_6]^{3+}$ ion, which has the spectrum shown in Fig. 7-3 with weak peaks at *ca*

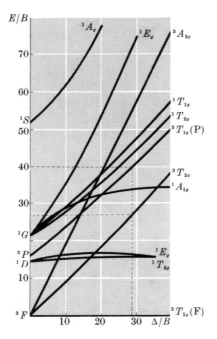

Fig. 7-2 A Tanabe–Sugano diagram for octahedral d^2 complexes.

$17,200\ \text{cm}^{-1}$ and $25,600\ \text{cm}^{-1}$. We conclude that $E(^3T_{2g} \leftarrow {}^3T_{1g}(F)) = 17,200\ \text{cm}^{-1}$ and $E(^3T_{1g}(P) \leftarrow {}^3T_{1g}(F)) = 25,600\ \text{cm}^{-1}$. We can use Eqns. 7-1 and 7-2 and therefore Fig. 7-2 provided that we can eliminate the Bs appearing on the left-hand side of each equation. This can be done if Eqn. 7-1 is divided by Eqn. 7-2, to give:

$$\frac{E(^3T_{2g} \leftarrow {}^3T_{1g}(F))}{E(^3T_{1g}(P) \leftarrow {}^3T_{1g}(F))} = \frac{\dfrac{\Delta}{B} - 15 + \left(225 + 18\dfrac{\Delta}{B} + \dfrac{\Delta^2}{B^2}\right)^{1/2}}{2\left(225 + 18\dfrac{\Delta}{B} + \dfrac{\Delta^2}{B^2}\right)^{1/2}} \qquad 7\text{-}3$$

In the case of $[V(H_2O)_6]^{3+}$ the value of this quotient is $17,200/25,600 = 0\cdot672$.

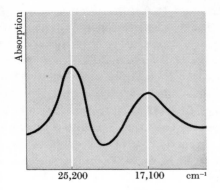

Fig. 7-3   The d–d spectrum of the $[V(H_2O)_6]^{3+}$ cation.

We can now proceed in one of two ways. We may apply a trial and error process to Fig. 7-2, until we find the correct value of Δ/B (in our case $\Delta/B = 28$, shown dotted in Fig. 7-2). Alternatively we may plot the right-hand side of Eqn. 7-3 against Δ/B. Such plots are useful when a large number of data have to be analysed. The one appropriate to the d^2 configuration is shown in Fig. 7-4, where again the $[V(H_2O)_6]^{3+}$ case is indicated by dotted lines. Having determined Δ/B from Fig. 7-4, we return to Fig. 7-2 and use this ratio to obtain $E(^3T_{2g} \leftarrow {}^3T_{1g}(F))/B$ and $E(^3T_{1g}(P) \leftarrow {}^3T_{1g}(F))/B$ (alternatively, and more accurately, we could substitute for Δ/B in Eqns. 7-1 and 7-2). These have values of 25·9 and 38·6 respectively so, using the experimental transition energies, both give $B = 665$ cm^{-1}. Since $\Delta/B = 28$, it follows that $\Delta = 18,600$ cm^{-1}. This analysis follows the ligand field approach, with B regarded as a parameter.

In the crystal field approach we use the free ion value of B, 860 cm^{-1}. It follows that $E(^3T_{2g} \leftarrow {}^3T_{1g}(F))/B = 17,200/860 = 20$ and $E(^3T_{1g}(P) \leftarrow {}^3T_{1g}(F))/B = 25,600/860 = 29\cdot8$. Using Fig. 7-2

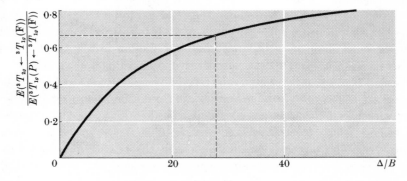

Fig. 7-4

these lead to values of Δ/B of 22·5 and 18·0 respectively; that is, Δ values of 19,400 and 15,500 cm^{-1}. This internal inconsistency does not occur in ligand field theory. However, it is only removed by introducing an additional parameter and, consequently, there are no additional data with which to test the theory, for we have used two experimental quantities (transition energies) to define the two parameters Δ and B. Only if the $^3A_{2g} \leftarrow ^3T_{1g}(F)$ transition could be observed could we test the theory. Using the Δ and B values obtained above, together with the expression for orbital energies given earlier, we predict this transition to lie at ca 36,000 cm^{-1}, where it is obscured by charge-transfer bands. However, a weak band has been

Table 7-1   Free ion values of the electron repulsion parameter B for first-row transition elements with d^n configurations

Charge on the metal atom				*Metal atom*				
	Ti	V	Cr	Mn	Fe	Co	Ni	Cu
0	560	579	790	720	805	789	1,025	—
+1	681	660	710	872	870	879	1,038	1,218
+2	719	765	830	960	1,059	1,117	1,082	1,239
+3	—	860	1,030	1,140				
+4	—	—	1,040		1,144			

A blank indicates that the value is not known; a dash indicates that the configuration has either one or no electrons outside a closed shell, so that electron repulsion does not occur within the valence shell. The data given are an average of literature values.

observed in this region in closely related complexes. Those cases in which there are sufficient data to provide a test of ligand field theory show that it leads to good agreement between observed and calculated band positions. It will be noted that we have confined our discussion to spin-allowed bands (both ground and excited states were spin triplets). Other, extremely weak, bands also occur and are assigned to spin-forbidden transitions (for example $^1T_{2g} \leftarrow ^3T_{1g}(F)$).

The spin-allowed spectral bands of all other cases, weak field and strong field alike, may be analysed in a similar way to that given above. Tanabe and Sugano have given diagrams for all other d^n cases (except d^1 and d^9 which are trivial having only one excited state at an energy Δ above the ground state) and a complete set is given in Appendix 5. As we have demonstrated, both Δ and B may be obtained from these diagrams with sufficient accuracy for most purposes. The physical reasonableness of the results obtained may be assessed by reference to the spectrochemical series (for Δ) and the free ion value of B. The latter are given in Table 7-1 for ions of the first-row transition elements. It is assumed that an incorrect assignment of the spectral bands will lead either to an incompatibility with the Tanabe–Sugano diagram or to physically unreasonable values of Δ and B. As an example of this, the reader should attempt to work out Δ and B for $[V(H_2O)_6]^{3+}$ if the two observed bands are assigned to the $^3A_{2g} \leftarrow {}^3T_{1g}(F)$ (25,600 cm^{-1}) and $^3T_{2g} \leftarrow {}^3T_{1g}(F)$ (17,200 cm^{-1}) transitions.

7-3 Spin-forbidden transitions

As mentioned above, extremely weak bands, assigned to spin-forbidden transitions, may sometimes be observed in the spectra of transition metal ions. Indeed, for the d^5 weak field case, the ground state is the only sextet spin state ($^6A_{1g}$) and so all the observed transitions are spin-forbidden. Evidently, the spin selection rules are not absolute; similarly, most of this chapter is concerned with transitions which, in large measure, are $d \leftarrow d$ transitions and therefore forbidden. Later we shall return to the problem of why these forbidden transitions occur.

   The problem of accounting quantitatively for the spin-forbidden bands is rather more difficult than that for their spin-allowed counterparts. Not surprisingly, a new parameter has to be introduced. This is the Racah parameter C, which, like B, is numerically smaller than the free ion value. If we follow the treatment given above for the d^2 case, C appears in the final expressions for (Transition energy)$/B$ as the quotient C/B. Before a Tanabe–Sugano diagram which includes state of all multiplicities can be constructed it is necessary to give a numerical value to C/B (or, as it is sometimes called, γ). For different values of C/B the Tanabe–Sugano diagram will be different. However, this parameter only affects the inter-scaling between states of different multiplicities, so that, for example, the relative energies of the $^3A_{2g}$, $^3T_{1g}(P)$, $^3T_{2g}$, and $^3T_{1g}(F)$ states of the d^2 configuration are independent of C/B. The Tanabe–Sugano diagrams which are commonly encountered are plotted for $C/B \simeq$ 4·5. This value is rather larger than the free ion ratio which, for the first-row transition elements, has an average value of ca 4·0 (but which varies from 3·2 to 4·8). It is common practice to assign spin-forbidden bands in a spectrum using whatever Tanabe–Sugano diagram is to hand. This procedure should be used with caution, since the C/B ratio is not then used as a parameter and it is most unlikely that the best fit between experiment and theory will be obtained. Those cases for which the job has been done properly have shown that it is possible to obtain an excellent agreement between theory and experiment, comparable with that found between the predictions of the Russell–Saunders coupling scheme and measurements on atomic spectra.

It is convenient at this point to complete our discussion of the reduction in the free ion value of the Racah parameter B which occurs on complex formation. This, it will be recalled, appears to be a consequence of the 'metal' electrons being delocalized over a larger volume of space in the complex than in the free ion. It has proved possible to arrange ligands in a series such that, for a given metal ion, the B value required to fit the spectrum of the $[ML_6]^{n+}$ ions decreases down the series:

$$F^- > H_2O > NH_3 > en > Cl^- > CN^- > Br^- > I^-$$

This series has been called the 'nephelauxetic series' (nephelauxetic = 'cloud expanding'). It should be noted that what are probably the most polarizable ligands give the lowest B values and *vice versa*.

7-4 The effect of spin–orbit coupling

The spin-allowed d–d bands which dominate the visible spectrum of complexes of many transition metal ions are rather broad, with half-widths of *ca* $3,000$ cm^{-1}. This means that if there is some inter-action within the complex which we have overlooked, its presence will not be apparent from the electronic spectrum unless it causes splittings in the energy levels of *ca* $1,000$ cm^{-1}. In fact we have over-looked two such effects—spin–orbit coupling and the Jahn–Teller effect (see Section 7-5).

In the Russell–Saunders coupling scheme (Appendix 3) it is assumed as a first approximation that we can talk of the orbital properties of the electrons of a given configuration as something quite separate from their spin. This separation is reflected in the symbolism of the theory: in the symbol ^3F, for example, the 3 refers to the spin multiplicity and the F to the orbital multiplicity. Now, as is well known, the electron has an intrinsic magnetic moment. Similarly, there is an orbital-derived magnetic moment for all but S states which may be likened to the magnetic moment of a solenoid, the circulation of the electron around the nucleus being akin to the circulation of a current through the turns of a solenoid. We see that the separation of orbital and spin properties of the electrons, which is the basis of the simple Russell–Saunders coupling scheme, is equivalent to assuming that two magnets, spin- and orbital-derived, will not interact. Of course, they couple together to some extent, and this is reflected in the phenomenon of spin–orbit coupling. It should be pointed out, however, that a more formal theory of spin–orbit coupling treats the phenomenon as one of the coupling of two angular momenta rather than bar magnets. The consequences of spin–orbit coupling are discussed in more detail in the next chapter. At this point it is sufficient to state simply that spin–orbit coupling causes splitting of the degeneracies implicit in the orbital energy level diagrams encountered so far. For example, a $^4T_{1g}$ state is 12-fold degenerate (4×3). This splits into three sub-levels as a consequence of spin–orbit coupling because, loosely, some arrangements of spin and orbital magnets are energetically more stable than others. The number of spin–orbit components of crystal field terms depends only on their spin and orbital multiplicities and these are shown in Table 7-2. The magnitude of the actual splitting caused

Table 7-2   Spin–orbit components of crystal-field terms

Crystal field state	$^1A_{1g}$	$^6A_{1g}$	$^2A_{2g}$	$^3A_{2g}$	$^4A_{2g}$	^2E_g	^5E_g
Spin–orbit components	1	1	1	1	1	1	1
Crystal field state	$^3T_{1g}$	$^4T_{1g}$	$^5T_{1g}$	$^2T_{2g}$	$^3T_{2g}$	$^4T_{2g}$	$^5T_{2g}$
Spin–orbit components	3	3	3	2	3	3	3

by spin–orbit coupling depends on the metal (for identically charged ions along any one transition series it varies roughly as Z^8, where Z is the atomic number; for identically charged ions with the same d^n configuration in different transition series it is roughly proportional to Z) and on the charge on the atom (for each unit increase in positive charge it increases, very roughly, by 25% of the neutral atom value).

For Ti^{3+} the free ion value of the spin–orbit coupling constant, denoted by ζ, is 155 cm^{-1}, so fine structure caused by spin–orbit coupling is most unlikely to be seen in the spectrum. For Ni^{2+} the value is 630 cm^{-1}, which means that small splittings might be caused by this effect. Spin–orbit coupling is more likely to be of importance in the assignment of the weak spin-forbidden transitions. As we shall see, these are frequently much narrower than spin-allowed transitions and, consequently, smaller splittings will be visible. For Rh^{3+} and Ir^{3+}, both of which form stable complexes, ζ has values of *ca* 1,600 and 4,000 cm^{-1} respectively so, for these complexes, spin–orbit splitting of d–d bands is to be expected. Indeed, spin–orbit coupling is of potential importance for all ions of the second and third transition series (this is why our discussion of the crystal and ligand field theories has been exemplified by complexes formed by elements of the first transition series).

7-5   The Jahn–Teller effect

The second effect which we have neglected is that due to low-symmetry crystal fields. As we have confined our discussion to octahedral ML_6 complexes one might assume that low-symmetry fields could be ignored, but this is not so. A theorem due to Jahn and Teller states that any non-linear ion or molecule which is in an orbitally degenerate state will distort to relieve this degeneracy. This means that all E_g, T_{1g}, and T_{2g} states of d^n configurations are unstable with respect to some distortion, which reduces the symmetry. Of course, as we have discussed above, some of the orbital degeneracy may be lost because of spin–orbit coupling. If this mechanism were to totally relieve the orbital degeneracy then there would be no need to consider the Jahn–Teller theorem.

The Jahn–Teller theorem tells us that a regular octahedral complex will often be unstable with respect to a distortion, but it says nothing at all about the magnitude of the distortion. An exceedingly small distortion, small enough to escape detection, would satisfy the Jahn–Teller requirement. Indeed, it is difficult to find unambiguous crystallographic evidence of the phenomenon. The most convincing evidence for the operation of the Jahn–Teller effect is found in studies on copper(II) complexes in the ground state (*vide infra*).

Physically, the Jahn–Teller effect may be regarded as operating as follows. Suppose that an octahedral complex is momentarily distorted as a result of a molecular vibration and has the shape shown in Fig. 7-5. This vibration will cause d_{z^2} and $d_{x^2-y^2}$ to lose their degeneracy (Table 6-2, the *trans*-octahedral case).

Suppose, too, that in the undistorted complex the e_g orbitals were occupied by a single electron and that in the distorted complex it occupies the $d_{x^2-y^2}$ orbital. The whole basis of crystal field theory is that this electron will be repelled by the ligand electrons and the metal–ligand bonding in the xy-plane thereby weakened. Because there is no corresponding reduction in the metal–ligand bonding along the z-axis we would expect the complex to be stable in the distorted shape shown in Fig. 7-5. Alternatively, if the odd electron occupies the d_{z^2} orbital, the opposite distortion (Fig. 7-6) is expected to be stable. The reader should readily be able to convince himself that similar possibilities for distortion exist when the parent e_g

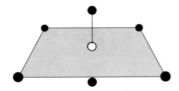

Fig. 7-5

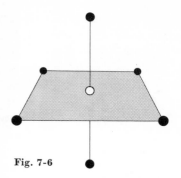

Fig. 7-6

orbitals are occupied by three electrons. These conclusions are equally valid in the ligand field approach, for this recognizes that the 'd_{z^2}' and '$d_{x^2-y^2}$' orbitals are weakly antibonding.

There remains a problem inseparable from the Jahn–Teller theorem. We predict that the octahedron will distort, but can neither choose between the alternative forms for this distortion nor say how large the distortion will be. There have been attempts to remove these uncertainties, but an account of this work is beyond the scope of the present text. There is one result of the general theory which should be mentioned, however. It can be shown that in a regular octahedron the Jahn–Teller effect only operates via vibrations of E_g symmetry* for electronic states of ^nE_g symmetry (the spin multiplicity is irrelevant) and vibrations of either E_g or T_{2g} symmetry for $^nT_{1g}$ and $^nT_{2g}$ states. The form of the two E_g metal–ligand vibrational modes is shown in Fig. 7-7 together with a representative mode of T_{2g} symmetry. It should be evident that in our discussion of the Jahn–Teller effect the two distorted structures considered were distorted by the first of the E_g vibrations shown in Fig. 7-7. Note that orbital degeneracy in an octahedral complex may be relieved by distortions other than those shown in Fig. 7-7. However, in such cases we may conclude that whatever is responsible for the distortion it is not the Jahn–Teller effect.

The account which we have given of the Jahn–Teller effect indicates why it is of little importance when the t_{2g} orbitals are unequally occupied. Occupation of these orbitals involves less electron repulsion destabilization than does occupation of the e_g orbitals and they are, to a first approximation, non-bonding. The 'octahedral' complexes of copper(II) are almost invariably distorted, commonly in the manner shown in Fig. 7-6. This behaviour is

* Vibrations may be classified by symmetry labels. As will be evident from figures such as Fig. 7-7 and Fig. 7-10 there is a similarity between the form of a vibration and the nodal properties of an orbital of the same symmetry.

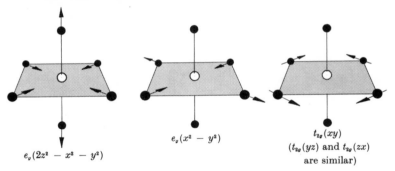

$e_g(2z^2 - x^2 - y^2)$

$e_g(x^2 - y^2)$

$t_{2g}(xy)$
($t_{2g}(yz)$ and $t_{2g}(zx)$
are similar)

Fig. 7-7   Jahn–Teller active vibrations.

entirely consistent with the operation of the Jahn–Teller effect because the ground-state configuration of a copper(II) ion in an octahedral field is $t_{2g}^6 e_g^3 ({}^2E_g)$.

The Jahn–Teller effect is of importance in the spectra of octahedral metal complexes because the transitions observed usually involve the excitation of an electron from a t_{2g} to an e_g orbital. (The exceptions are some spin-forbidden bands and those bands associated with two-electron jumps, both of which are discussed later.) It follows, therefore, that there must be an odd number of electrons in the e_g orbitals either before or after the transition. That is, if the ground state is not subject to a Jahn–Teller distortion, the excited state is, and *vice versa*. To discover the effect of a Jahn–Teller distortion on the electronic spectrum of a complex we shall consider a simplified model.

Suppose that the Jahn–Teller effect is operative in the excited state and that molecular vibrations have momentarily distorted the molecule in its electronic ground state so that it has the shape shown in Fig. 7-6. Suppose, too, that the stable molecular geometry in the electronic excited state is also that shown in Fig. 7-6 (i.e. that momentarily assumed by the ground state). Then there also exists a less stable excited state for which the molecular geometry is as shown in Fig. 7-5 (i.e. the two excited states have the odd 'e_g' electron

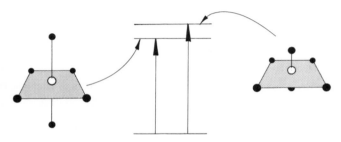

Fig. 7-8

in d_{z^2} and $d_{x^2-y^2}$, respectively). If, whilst the ground state has the molecular geometry of Fig. 7-6, it absorbs light and assumes an electronically excited state, then we have to consider two possibilities (Fig. 7-8). First, the excited state could be the more stable one, so that the excited molecule finds itself in its vibrational ground state (we assume that the nuclei do not move during the excitation—the Franck–Condon principle). Second, the molecule could assume the less stable excited state but would then find itself well away from its equilibrium molecular geometry—it is vibrationally excited, possibly by several quanta. As these quanta may each have an energy of *ca*

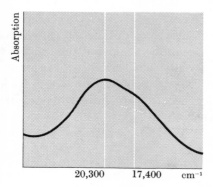

Fig. 7-9   The visible spectrum of the $[\text{Ti}(\text{H}_2\text{O})_6]^{3+}$ cation.

200 cm^{-1} and as one has to remember the intrinsic difference in energy between the two excited levels (in their vibrational ground states), one concludes that Jahn–Teller distortions may well be spectrally apparent. For example, this is believed to be the explanation of the asymmetry in the $^2E_g \leftarrow {}^2T_{2g}$ transition of the $[\text{Ti}(\text{H}_2\text{O})_6]^{3+}$ ion (Fig. 7-9).

If the Jahn–Teller effect operates on the electronic ground state of a complex it is unlikely to be apparent in the visible and near-infrared spectrum. If the two 'ground' states are split sufficiently far apart for transitions to the excited state to be resolvable, the upper of the two 'ground' states will not be sufficiently thermally populated for transitions from it to be seen. On the other hand, in this situation there will be additional transition in the infrared region of the spectrum. This will correspond to a simultaneous electronic and vibrational excitation from the lower of the 'ground' states to the upper.

A Jahn–Teller distortion may be either static or dynamic and so far we have considered only the former. The latter occurs when the potential barrier separating, for example, the three equivalent distortions of the type shown in Fig. 7-6 (elongation along the x-, y- or

z-axes), is of the order of kT. The distortion then rapidly alternates between the possibilities. In this way a small Jahn–Teller effect may be unobserved; the time average is a regular structure (however, as we shall see in Chapter 8, small distortions may be detected by magnetic measurements). Because the time taken to jump from one configuration to another is of the same order as the time taken for a simple vibration, a measurement taking much longer than this to perform will give only an average. A measurement of 10^{-10} s duration takes too long! The dynamic Jahn–Teller effect does not affect the appearance of the visible spectrum of transition metal complexes, but this is because of the energetics of the effect, not because of the time scale.

The reader may inquire whether there exists a theorem analogous to the Jahn–Teller theorem which requires that spin degeneracies should be relieved. The answer is yes. The author knows of no simple explanation of the effect, so we content ourselves with remarking that an orbitally non-degenerate state with either a four- or six-fold spin degeneracy is expected to split. This means, for example, that the $^4A_{2g}(d^3$ and $d^7)$ and $^6A_{1g}(d^5)$ states must, in principle, be split.

7-6   Band contours

The d–d bands of transition metal complexes are weak, sometimes very weak. Some of the bands are sharp, some broad and some so broad that it is difficult to be certain that they exist. In the next section we shall discuss the problem of intensities; in this section, the problem of band shapes. The two are related. The very weak peaks are usually sharp. If they were not, they would escape detection and no doubt many broad, very weak, peaks do pass undetected.

When discussing the Jahn–Teller effect we introduced a refinement into our model of a transition metal complex: we allowed it to vibrate. This is an important refinement for it enables us to understand both band intensities and shapes.

Let us consider an octahedral complex in which the totally symmetrical metal–ligand stretching mode (the breathing mode) is excited. That is, the complex retains its octahedral geometry because all the M—L bonds are contracting and elongating in phase. The essential point is that the repulsion between the ligands and metal d electrons, and, therefore, the crystal field splitting parameter, Δ, will vary with the metal–ligand distance. Alternatively, if the reader prefers the molecular orbital model, the overlap between the metal and ligand orbitals will vary with the M—L distance. We conclude that Δ is, in practice, not a fixed quantity but rather a quantity which is modulated by the vibrations of the molecule, and so at any instant differs from one molecule to another. A convenient way of thinking of this is to regard a collection of the molecules as being represented, not by a line in a Tanabe–Sugano diagram (as in Fig. 7-2), but by a band, covering a range of values of Δ/B. The absorption peak will then consist not of a narrow line but usually a broad one (a superposition of a multitude of sharp lines). The relative breadths of the spectral lines will be determined by the relative slopes of the lines which, in a Tanabe–Sugano diagram, represent the excited states. For example, we anticipate that transitions to the $^3T_{1g}(P)$ and $^3T_{2g}$ levels of the d^2 configuration will give bands of similar widths (Fig. 7-2). As Fig. 7-3 shows, this prediction is roughly confirmed by experiment. We further predict that the transition to the $^3A_{2g}$ excited state will give a band which is about twice as broad as the other two. This, together with its inherent low intensity (*vide infra*), is no doubt why it is so difficult to observe.

On the other hand, some of the lines in a Tanabe–Sugano diagram are almost parallel to that representing the ground state. These lines are invariably amongst those derived from the same strong field configuration as the ground state. For example, in the d^2 configuration the Δ dependence of the $^1A_{1g}$, ^1E_g, and $^1T_{2g}$ states is roughly parallel to that of the $^3T_{1g}(F)$ ground state. These four states are those which arise from the t_{2g}^2 strong field configuration. That is, a transition from the ground to another of these states corresponds to a rearrangement of electrons within the t_{2g} orbitals and so does not depend on the t_{2g}–e_g separation, Δ. This statement is rigorously true in the strong field limit but is only approximately so in weak fields, for in the latter case mixing of the $^1A_{1g}$, ^1E_g, and $^1T_{2g}$ states derived from the $t_{2g}e_g$ and e_g^2 configurations into the lowest $^1A_{2g}$, ^1E_g, and $^1T_{2g}$ states makes the members of this set each have a different dependence on Δ. However, in intermediate and strong ligand fields it is true that the energies of transitions to these states are scarcely modulated by the Δ variations caused by ligand vibrations. It follows that transitions to these excited states will appear as sharp lines in the spectrum. They are, however, very weak and for this reason are not easy to detect.

The existence of these transitions is exploited in the ruby laser. Ruby is an Al_2O_3 lattice containing a small amount of chromium(III) (d^3) ions as impurity, the chromium ions being approximately octahedrally surrounded by oxygen atoms. The energies of the transitions from the ground state ($^4A_{2g}$) to the lowest ^2E_g, $^2T_{1g}$, and $^2T_{2g}$ levels are essentially independent of Δ and so the bands are sharp. Emission of light from chromium(III) ions in the ^2E_g excited state gives rise to the essentially monochromatic laser beam.

In this section we have considered only the effect of the totally symmetric breathing vibration on the value of Δ. Similar conclusions follow if vibrations of other symmetries are considered in detail. Indeed, as we shall see in the next section, some of these other vibrations are responsible for the appreciable intensity in formally forbidden $d \to d$ transitions.

7-7 Band intensities

The fact that very weak $d \to d$ transitions may be observed in atomic spectroscopy indicates the approximate nature of the rule that only

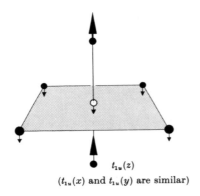

$t_{1u}(z)$

$(t_{1u}(x)$ and $t_{1u}(y)$ are similar)

Fig. 7-10   A t_{1u} vibration of an octahedral complex.

$s \to p$, $p \to d$, $d \to f$, etc. orbital transitions are allowed. The spin-allowed $d \to d$ transitions in an octahedral metal complex are of much higher intensity than their atomic counterparts so that some new intensity-generating mechanism exists in the complex which is not present in a free ion. It should not surprise the reader to learn that one such mechanism involves the metal–ligand vibrations. Consider, for example, an octahedral complex which has momentarily been distorted by the vibration of T_{1u} symmetry, shown in Fig. 7-10. This vibration destroys the centre of symmetry of the molecule together with all of the three-fold and all but one four-fold axis (that along which the vibration takes place). The molecular symmetry is, in fact, the same as that of a *trans*-$ML_4L'L''$ complex, C_{4v}. As Table 6-2 shows, in this symmetry p_z, s, and d_{z^2} carry the same symmetry labels (a_1) and so may mix. Similarly, p_x and p_y together have the same symmetry as d_{xz} and d_{yz} (e) and so these orbitals may also mix. In the distorted environment of Fig. 7-10 what we have called 'd_{z^2}' becomes a mixture of d_{z^2} with a little bit of p_z (and s). The 'contamination' by these other orbitals disappears when the molecule becomes accurately octahedral again. Similarly, what we have called 'd_{xz}' is contaminated by p_x and 'd_{yz}' by p_y. This means that, if an electronic excitation occurs whilst the molecule is distorted, a transition in which an electron jumps formally from $d_{xz} \to d_{z^2}$ also contains components in which the electron jumps from $d_{xz} \to p_z$ and $p_x \to d_{z^2}$, both of which are allowed by the selection rules. The '$d \to d$' transition, therefore, gains intensity because it is not entirely $d \to d$. The intensity depends on the extent of d–p mixing and, in turn, this depends on the nature of the distortion at the moment of excitation. Any distortion which fails to remove the centre of symmetry of the molecule will not introduce any intensity, for the essential requirement is that the vibration mixes atomic orbitals of g and u types (d and p orbitals, respectively).

The most general selection rule for electric-dipole transitions (which is the type that we are considering) is the following:

An electronic transition is electric-dipole allowed if the direct product of the symmetries of the ground and excited electronic states of a molecule contains the symmetry species of one or more coordinate axes, both ground and excited states having the same spin multiplicity.

Consider the $^3T_{2g} \leftarrow {}^3T_{1g}(F)$ transition in the d^2 case. Here the ground-state orbital symmetry is T_{1g} and the excited state T_{2g}. The direct product $T_{1g} \times T_{2g}$ is $A_{2g} + E_g + T_{1g} + T_{2g}$ (Table 5-3). Now, the Cartesian coordinate axes, x, y, and z have the same symmetry properties as the corresponding p orbitals which in our case is T_{1u}. As T_{1u} is not contained in the $T_{1g} \times T_{2g}$ direct product $(A_{2g} + E_g + T_{1g} + T_{2g})$ the $^3T_{2g} \leftarrow {}^3T_{1g}(F)$ transition is orbitally forbidden. As we have just seen, a vibration of T_{1u} symmetry can remove this forbiddenness. This is seen by taking a triple direct product:

$$T_{1g} \times T_{2g} \times T_{1u} = (A_{2g} + E_g + T_{1g} + T_{2g}) \times T_{1u}$$
$$= A_{2g} \times T_{1u} + E_g \times T_{1u} + T_{1g} \times T_{1u} + T_{2g} \times T_{1u}$$
$$= A_{1u} + A_{2u} + 2E_u + 3T_{1u} + 4T_{2u}$$

This final direct product contains T_{1u} three times so, as T_{1u} is the symmetry species of the coordinate axes, the intervention of the T_{1u} vibration not only makes the $^3T_{2g} \leftarrow {}^3T_{1g}(F)$ transition allowed but also splits it into three separate transitions. These will differ slightly in energy and so contribute to the breadth of the observed peaks.

The picture is further complicated when it is recognized that there are two distinct sets of T_{1u} metal–ligand vibrations in an octahedral complex and, further, there is a set of T_{2u} vibrations which may also give intensity to the d–d transitions via four sub-peaks. We therefore conclude that the $^3T_{2g} \leftarrow {}^3T_{1g}(F)$ transition observed is composed of no less than ten $(3 + 3 + 4)$ sub-peaks, which may be separated by energies of the order of magnitude of the energy of metal–ligand vibrations (ca $200\ \text{cm}^{-1}$). Each of these peaks is broadened by the vibrational modulation of Δ discussed in the previous section, so the peak half-widths observed are understandable.

The discussion which we have just given is associated with a breakdown in the Born–Oppenheimer approximation. This states that electronic, vibrational and rotational energy levels may be treated separately so that an electronic transition is something quite separate from a vibrational transition. However, in the case we have discussed we had to consider the coupling between vibrational and electronic states. This is called *vibronic* coupling.

The intensity introduced by vibronic coupling into a $d \rightarrow d$ transition cannot appear from nowhere. It is, in fact, 'stolen' from what in a regular octahedron is an allowed transition—for example, the equivalent in the complex to the free ion $d \rightarrow p$ transition (which will lie in the ultraviolet region). A more detailed analysis shows that the magnitude of the 'stolen' intensity is an inverse function of the energy separation between the $d \rightarrow d$ and the allowed bands. This means that the highest-energy d–d bands, with the smallest separation from the allowed bands, will generally be the most intense; see, for example, Fig. 7-3.

We now consider the intensity of the spin-forbidden $d \rightarrow d$ transitions. In electron spin and nuclear magnetic resonance (e.s.r. and n.m.r.) measurements electromagnetic radiation is used to 'turn over' the spin of either an electron or nucleus (this simple view of the process is adequate for our present purpose). The electromagnetic radiation does this by virtue of its associated magnetic vector and we talk of the process as one which is magnetic-dipole allowed. Although a similar process undoubtedly contributes to the intensity of the spin-forbidden $d \rightarrow d$ bands, detailed calculations indicate that its contribution is small. Much more important is spin–orbit coupling. The reader will recall that spin–orbit coupling allows for the fact that the spin and orbital properties of an electron are not completely independent of each other. We have just discussed a mechanism whereby an orbital transition becomes weakly allowed, so spin–orbit coupling may in turn transfer some of this allowedness into what is, formally, a spin-forbidden transition. Let us consider a specific case.

The ground state of an octahedral d^8 complex is $^3A_{2g}$. A low-lying spin-forbidden transition is to a ^1E_g level and a spin-allowed transition is to the $^3T_{2g}$ level (Fig. 7-11). Now spin–orbit coupling has the effect of contaminating two of the nine wavefunctions of the $^3T_{2g}$ state with those of the ^1E_g state (which are also two in number) and *vice versa*.

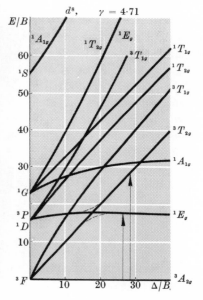

Fig. 7-11 A Tanabe–Sugano diagram for the d^8 configuration, modified to include the effect of spin–orbit coupling on the $^3T_{2g}$ and ^1E_g states.

When the energy separation between these two states is small $\Delta/B \simeq 18$) the contamination becomes gross pollution! The result is that for these four coupled wavefunctions the two lines on a Tanabe–Sugano diagram should not cross, but 'repel' each other and behave as shown by the dotted lines in Fig. 7-11, so that those two wavefunctions which in a weak field belonged to $^3T_{2g}$ become ^1E_g in a strong field and *vice versa*. This means that some of the intensity of what was the $^3T_{2g} \leftarrow {}^3A_{2g}$ transition (before we included spin–orbit coupling) is transferred to the $^1E_g \leftarrow {}^3A_{2g}$ transition once spin–orbit coupling is included. All other spin-forbidden transitions are believed to gain intensity by analogous mechanisms. Two points should be mentioned. First, although the $^1E_g \leftarrow {}^3A_{2g}$ transition of the above example would, by the arguments of the previous section, be expected to be sharp, mixing with the $^3T_{2g} \leftarrow {}^3A_{2g}$ transition will broaden it. The lower the intensity of a spin-forbidden band the narrower it is likely to be. Secondly, the greater the spin–orbit coupling, the more important the spin-forbidden transitions. The relative magnitudes of spin–orbit coupling constants has been discussed earlier (Section 7-4).

We conclude this section by considering transitions such as $^3A_{2g} \leftarrow {}^3T_{1g}(F)$ of the d^2 case. In the strong field limit this corresponds to a transition from the t_{2g}^2 to the e_g configuration. Now the effect of electromagnetic radiation is to excite one electron at a time, not two. In the strong field limit the above transition is therefore forbidden (rigorously, within the general approximation scheme that we are using). In the intermediate and weak field regions the $^3T_{1g}(F)$ level is a mixture of the t_{2g}^2 and $t_{2g}e_g$ configurations (we first met this in Section 5-5) and so the $^3A_{2g} \leftarrow {}^3T_{1g}(F)$ transition has a $t_{2g}e_g \rightarrow e_g^2$ component which, of course, corresponds to a one-electron jump. This component can acquire intensity by a vibronic mechanism. It follows that the most favourable situation for observing the $^3A_{2g} \leftarrow {}^3T_{1g}(F)$ transition of the d^2 configuration will be with very weak field complexes. In this case it will lie at a relatively long wavelength and, hopefully, will not be obscured by charge-transfer bands.

7-8   Tetrahedral complexes

So far in this chapter we have considered only octahedral transition metal complexes. However, all of what we have said may at once be carried over to the tetrahedral case, provided that we remember that $\Delta_{\text{tet.}}$ is of opposite sign to $\Delta_{\text{oct.}}$. This means, for example, that the spectrum of a tetrahedral d^2 complex can be interpreted using a Tanabe–Sugano diagram for the octahedral d^8 case (dropping g suffixes, of course). There is only one point of difference which should be discussed, and this concerns the intensities of the $d \rightarrow d$ bands of tetrahedral complexes. These are at least an order of magnitude greater than those of their octahedral counterparts. Evidently, some new intensity-generating mechanism is available in tetrahedral complexes.

One important aspect of the electronic structure of tetrahedral complex ions which we did not discuss in Chapter 6, although it is contained in Table 6-2, is that, unlike the octahedral case, the metal p orbitals have the same symmetry (t_2) as do the metal d_{xy}, d_{yz}, and d_{zx} orbitals. It will be recalled that in a tetrahedral crystal field the metal d orbitals split into two sets, of e and t_2 symmetries. Because they are of the same symmetry, the t_2 set of d orbitals will be mixed by the crystal field with the metal p orbitals. This in turn means that an $e \rightarrow t_2$ transition contains some $d \rightarrow p$ character and so is allowed.

Evidently, the intensity of the transition is related to the extent of d–p mixing so that this may be assessed, at least qualitatively. Notice both the similarity and difference between these intensity-generating mechanisms for $d \rightarrow d$ transitions in octahedral and tetrahedral complexes. Both depend on d–p mixing but only for the tetrahedral case does this occur for the non-distorted molecule.

7-9 Complexes of other geometries

The $d \rightarrow d$ transitions of complexes of other geometries can only be discussed by introducing further parameters which take account of the loss of degeneracy, and consequent increase in number of spectral bands, passing from a cubic geometry (tetrahedral, octahedral, etc.) to one of lower symmetry. For square planar complexes, for example, two additional parameters must be introduced.

The number of observed spectral bands is seldom sufficient to allow all the parameters to be simultaneously determined. Commonly, therefore, one has to be content either with tentative band assignments or with parameters obtained from an oversimplified model. A useful first approximation to the assignment of the spectra of coordination compounds in which the symmetry is low by virtue of the coordination of several different ligands is provided by the *rule of average environment*. This states, for example, that Δ for the octahedral complex $[ML_3L'_3]$ will be approximately the mean of Δ for $[ML_6]$ and $[ML'_6]$; for $[ML_4L'_2]$, Δ will be about $\frac{1}{3}[2\Delta([ML_6]) + \Delta([ML'_6])]$. However, the ligand non-equivalence may manifest itself by a slight splitting of the bands expected for an octahedral complex with this value of Δ.

7-10 Charge-transfer spectra

If the absorption of light is to cause an electronic transition within an atom or molecule, it is essential that the absorption results in a charge density displacement. This displacement may be localized on one atom (as it is, to a first approximation, in the $d \rightarrow d$ spectra which we have been discussing) or it may be the displacement of charge from one atom to another. Electronic transitions which can be ascribed to the latter process are termed charge-transfer transitions. At least three categories of charge-transfer processes may be distinguished in coordination compounds:

1. *Intra-ligand transitions.* A ligand such as SCN^- has internal charge-transfer transitions, usually located in the ultraviolet region of the spectrum. Corresponding transitions occur in the coordinated ligand but can usually be identified by comparison with the spectrum of the free ligand. We shall not discuss this class further.

2. *Ligand → metal (reduction) transitions.* These are a common type
of transition, in which a 'ligand' electron is transferred to a metal
orbital and the charge separation within the complex thereby
reduced. One problem associated with this class is the lack of certainty about which orbital the electron comes from. Thus, one is
tempted to discuss a transition of this type in terms of molecular
orbital energy level diagrams such as those of Figs. 6-2 or 6-9.
Fig. 6-9 is more complete than Fig. 6-2 because the former
includes both ligand σ and π electrons, a total of six on each ligand.
Yet a monatomic ligand such as F^- or O^{2-} has eight valence electrons.
The two which have not been included are in a σ orbital which points
away from the metal atom. These σ orbitals give rise to ligand
group orbitals which are probably higher in energy than most of the
occupied 'ligand' orbitals of Figs. 6-9 and 6-2 because they are not
stabilized by interaction with the metal orbitals and might be
expected to give the lower-energy charge-transfer bands. This is
probably the case but, as the intensity of charge-transfer bands is a
function of the overlap of the orbitals between which the transfer
occurs, the corresponding intensities are small. These bands may,
however, be confused with d–d transitions. This is in contrast with
most charge-transfer bands, which are very intense.

3. *Metal → ligand (oxidation) transitions.* An example of this type
of transition probably occurs in the aquo ions of divalent ions of the
first transition series, for which Dainton has shown that the energy
of the first charge-transfer band is linearly related to the redox
potential of the system:

$$M^{2+}(aq.) \rightarrow M^{3+}(aq.) + e^-$$

It is not always easy to decide whether category 2 or 3 is
involved in a particular transition. If it is 2, then, for an allowed
transition in an octahedral complex, the excitation must be from
a ground-state orbital of u symmetry (and therefore either t_{1u} or
t_{2u} as there are no other occupied u orbitals) and the electron must
be excited into either a t_{2g} or e_g orbital. If both t_{2g} and e_g sets are
incompletely filled then both processes may occur, and two bands
are to be expected. If the t_{2g} set is full, only excitation to the e_g set
will occur. This is probably the explanation of a long-wavelength
charge-transfer band in $[Fe(CN)_6]^{3-}(d^5)$ which is absent from
$[Fe(CN)_6]^{4-}(d^6)$. A similar phenomenon is observed in $[IrBr_6]^{2-}(d^5)$
and $[IrBr_6]^{3-}(d^6)$. In both cases the band in the d^5 complex which
'disappears' is about Δ away from that which 'remains', as the
above explanation would lead us to expect.

Because the charge-transfer process involves electron transfer the spectra are sometimes called 'redox spectra' and, certainly, their position correlates with the relative ease of oxidation or reduction of the metal ion and ligand. Fig. 7-12 shows the charge-transfer spectra of $[Co(NH_3)_5X]^{2+}$, X = Cl^-, Br^-, and I^-. As one would expect, the transition energies decrease in the order $Cl^- >$ $Br^- > I^-$.

Usually, the charge-transfer process does not lead to permanent oxidation or reduction. However, in the series $[CuCl_4]^{2-}$, $[CuBr_4]^{2-}$, and $[CuI_4]^{2-}$ charge-transfer absorption occurs at longer and longer wavelength until, for the latter, the process becomes irreversible.

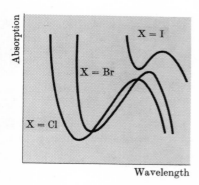

Fig. 7-12 The lowest-energy charge-transfer band of $[Co(NH_3)_5X]^{2+}$ complexes (X = Cl, Br, and I).

Similarly, $[FeF_6]^{3-}$ is virtually colourless, but replacement of the fluoride ion with the heavier halogens leads first to yellow solutions (Cl^-) then brown (Br^-) and finally to spontaneous reduction of Fe(III) by I^-.

It has been found possible to calculate the position of charge-transfer bands by assuming that they depend on an electronegativity difference between the ligand and metal ion. The values of these optical electronegativities indicate, as observed, that the first charge-transfer band in the spectrum moves to lower energies in the order

Pt(IV) > Rh(III) > Cu(II) > Co(III) > Ir(III) > Ni(II)

> Co(II) > Cr(III) > Mn(II)

although there is at present no evident explanation for this order.

7-11 Conclusions

The reader must not be misled by this chapter into believing that the interpretation of the spectrum of a transition metal coordination compound is always straightforward. This is usually the case for complexes of the first-row transition series, but for the others the larger values of Δ mean that there is more overlapping of $d \to d$ and charge-transfer bands. Further, the larger values of spin–orbit coupling constants make intensity criteria for distinguishing between spin-allowed and spin-forbidden transitions less reliable.

Even more problematical is the case of complexes of less-than-octahedral symmetry. It is probably true that the spectrum of no transition metal complex species has been studied in the same detail as has that of the square planar $[PtCl_4]^{2-}$ ion. Despite this work, however, there is not universal agreement on the assignment of the spectrum and few would regard as completely improbable a revision of the current interpretation.

Problems

7-1   An octahedral vanadium(III) complex has d–d bands at 20,000 and 30,000 cm^{-1}. Interpret these data in terms of (a) the crystal field, (b) the ligand field approach.

7-2   Modify the discussion of Section 7-2 to make it applicable to octahedral nickel(II) complexes (d^8). (This is a fairly difficult problem and so the answer to it is given after the problems at the end of Chapter 8.)

7-3   The $^1T_{1g}$ state of the d^2 configuration has an energy of $12B + 2C$ (it is independent of Δ). Extend the discussion of Section 7-2 to include this state.

7-4   A mechanism by which a 'd–d' transition may acquire intensity, but which has not been discussed in detail in the text, is that intensity may be stolen from a ligand–ligand transition. How might you, experimentally, attempt to assess the importance of this mechanism?

7-5   Discuss the spectral consequences of (a) the Jahn–Teller effect, (b) spin–orbit coupling.

7-6   Use the Tanabe–Sugano diagrams given in Appendix 5 to suggest transitions which might provide monochromatic (laser) light.

Magnetic properties of transition metal complexes

8-1   Introduction

When an atom or molecule is placed in a magnetic field any spin degeneracy may be removed. So, a level which is orbitally non-degenerate but which is a spin doublet may be split. If there is orbital degeneracy this too may be removed by the magnetic field. The splittings produced are very small, ca 1 cm^{-1} for a field of 5,000 gauss, and are, for the vast majority of cases, proportional to the magnetic field. Because the splittings are so small, any particular atom or molecule may be in any one of several closely spaced states. For a macroscopic sample, however, there will be a Boltzmann distribution between the levels. We can now recognize the essential features of a discussion of the effect of a magnetic field on a complex ion. Because the effect of the magnetic field is small we must consider interactions much smaller than that caused by the crystal field if they involve energies corresponding to more than about 1 cm^{-1}. This is because such interactions will play a part in determining the ground state of the complex in the absence of a magnetic field. Two of these interactions—spin–orbit coupling and the presence of low-symmetry components in what is otherwise an octahedral crystal field—have already been discussed in outline. The latter effect can seldom be neglected. One might think, for example, that an isolated $[Co(NH_3)_6]^{3+}$ ion would be accurately octahedral. This is not so, for there is an incompatibility between the three-fold axis of each NH_3 molecule and the coincident four-fold axis of the CoN_6 octahedron. Add to this the effects of the environment (i.e. do not consider an isolated molecule) and recall the Jahn–Teller effect, and it becomes evident that a regular octahedral environment is, from the point of view of magnetism, a rare species. An octahedral model is, however, a very good first approximation and may be refined to take account of the above effects.

At this point we must introduce some of the vocabulary of magnetism. Closed shells of electrons have neither spin nor orbital degeneracy and are represented by a single wavefunction. A magnetic field, therefore, produces no splitting. It does, however, distort the electron clouds slightly in a manner akin to that predicted by Lenz's law in classical electrodynamics. That is, effectively, a small current is produced, the magnetic effect of which opposes the applied magnetic field. Because there is no resistive damping, the 'current' remains until the magnetic field is removed. Molecules with closed shells are therefore repelled by a magnetic field and are said to exhibit *diamagnetism* or to be *diamagnetic*.

Suitably oriented magnets are attracted into the magnetic field of a stronger magnet and the same is true for any orbital magnet and the intrinsic (spin) magnet associated with an unpaired electron (we first met these magnets when discussing spin–orbit coupling in Section 7-4). Molecules with unpaired electrons are therefore attracted into a magnetic field* and are said to exhibit *paramagnetism* or to be *paramagnetic*. For any transition metal ion which has both closed shells and unpaired electrons the two effects are opposed. All that can be measured is their resultant. Fortunately, the effect of paramagnetism is about 100 times as great as that of diamagnetism so it takes a great deal of the latter to swamp the former. Fortunately, too, it is found that the effects of diamagnetism are approximately additive—each atom makes a known, and approximately constant, contribution to the diamagnetism of any molecule in which it is present and so diamagnetism may be fairly accurately allowed for once the empirical formula of a complex ion is known. This means that it is possible to deduce the intrinsic paramagnetism of a complex ion and to compare it with the theoretical predictions. Finally, a discussion in terms of an isolated molecule requires that the (para)magnetic units do not interact; in other words, these units must be well separated spatially. That is, the sample must be *magnetically dilute*. The detailed theory of non-magnetically dilute substances is beyond the scope of this book.

8-2 Classical magnetism

A theory of magnetism was well developed long before the advent of quantum mechanics. In the present section we give an outline of this theory and define some of the experimental quantities which may be encountered.

When a substance is placed within a magnetic field H, the field within the substance, B, usually differs from H. One writes:

$$B = H + 4\pi I$$

where $4\pi I$ is the field induced within the sample. The factor 4π appears because of the definition of a unit pole (at a distance of 1 cm

---

* Exceptions to this rule occur at very low temperatures.

from a unit pole there is a field of 1 oersted over the surface of a sphere of area 4π cm²; hence 4π lines of force leave a unit north-seeking pole). I is the intensity of magnetization and is equal to the induced magnetic moment per unit volume. This equation may be written

$$\frac{B}{H} = 1 + 4\pi\,\frac{I}{H}$$

$$= 1 + 4\pi\kappa$$

where κ is the volume susceptibility (the ratio of the induced magnetic moment per unit volume to the applied field). A more useful quantity is the susceptibility per gramme, χ, called the specific susceptibility, which is given by:

$$\chi = \frac{\kappa}{\rho}$$

where ρ is the density of the substance. Alternative forms of χ which are encountered are χ_A and χ_M, the atomic and molecular susceptibilities. These are obtained by multiplying χ by the atomic and molecular weights, respectively, of the magnetically active atom or molecule. They are the susceptibilities per gramme-atom and gramme-mole, respectively. Because one is frequently interested in the paramagnetism of a species, some correction has to be made for the underlying diamagnetism (see Appendix 6). If such a correction has been made it is indicated by a prime, thus:

$$\chi'_A, \qquad \chi'_M$$

Now:

$$\chi_M = \frac{\kappa}{\rho}\,.\,M = \frac{I}{H}\,.\,V$$

where M is the molecular weight and V the molar volume. So:

$$\chi_M = \frac{\text{total magnetic moment per mole}}{H}$$

$$= \frac{\text{average magnetic moment per molecule}\,.\,N}{H}$$

or

$$\chi_M = \frac{\bar{m}N}{H}$$

where $\bar{m}$ is the average moment per molecule and N is Avogadro's number.

If we have a collection of identical molecules, each of magnetic moment μ and each free to orient itself in a magnetic field, then in such a field there will be some alignment, but this will be opposed by the thermal motion of the molecules. That is, the measured moment will decrease with increasing temperature although μ itself is a constant.

Langevin showed that in this situation the average (measured) magnetic moment, $\bar{m}$, and the actual moment, μ, per molecule are related by:

$$\bar{m} = \frac{\mu^2}{3kT} \cdot H$$

(the derivation of this relationship will be found in any university text on magnetism). His derivation contains the assumption that $B = H$, so the theory can only be expected to hold for gaseous molecules. Combining the two last equations, we have:

$$\chi_M = \frac{N\mu^2}{3kT} = \frac{N^2\mu^2}{3RT} = \frac{C}{T}$$

where C, the Curie constant, equals $N^2\mu^2/3\mathbf{R}$. The equation $\chi_M = C/T$ is known as the *Curie Law*—susceptibility is inversely proportional to the absolute temperature. Surprisingly, this law is obeyed by many liquids and solids, in particular, by complexes of the first-row transition elements. Rearranging the above equation we find:

$$\mu = \frac{(3RT\chi_M)^{1/2}}{N}$$

It is convenient to express μ in units of Bohr magnetons,* β, and so we write:

$$\mu = \mu_{\text{eff.}}\beta$$

* The Bohr magneton is a fundamental quantity in the quantum theory of magnetism. Bohr's explanation of atomic structure and spectra was based on the assumption that the angular momentum of an electron circulating about the nucleus of an atom was quantized and equal to $nh/2\pi$, where n is an integer and h Planck's constant. That is, $nh/2\pi = ma^2\omega$, where m is the mass of the electron, a the radius of its orbit and ω its angular velocity. The area of the orbit is πa^2 and the current to which the electron circulation is equivalent is e . $(\omega/2\pi)$ (ω is measured in terms of radians). From the theory of a current flowing through a circular loop of wire, the magnetic moment associated with the circulating electron is equal to the product:

$$\text{(current} \times \text{area)} = \frac{e\omega}{2\pi} \times \pi a^2 = \frac{ea^2\omega}{2}$$

From Bohr's postulate, this equals:

$$\frac{ea^2}{2} \times \frac{nh}{2\pi ma^2} = n\left(\frac{he}{4\pi m}\right) = n\beta, \qquad \text{where} \qquad \beta = \frac{he}{4\pi m}$$

That is, the magnetic moment is an integer times β, where β is the Bohr magneton. Its value is 0.927×10^{-20} erg gauss^{-1}. It turns out that β is also the fundamental unit in the more modern quantum theory.

Combining the last two equations we find:

$$\mu_{\text{eff.}} = \frac{(3RT\chi_M)^{1/2}}{N\beta}$$

Notice that, defined in this way, $\mu_{\text{eff.}}$ is a number, the Bohr magneton number, which refers to a single molecule. It is otherwise dimensionless. It is therefore not strictly correct to call it 'the effective magnetic moment', and it is certainly incorrect to express it in units of Bohr magnetons, although this is sometimes done.

8-3   The orbital contribution to a magnetic moment

We turn now to the quantum-mechanical approach to the phenomenon of paramagnetism and discuss first the orbital contribution to a magnetic moment. It is convenient at this point to make a few general statements which will be explained by the subsequent discussion.

We used the phrase 'any orbital moment' in Section 8-1, thereby implying that one may or may not exist. If in a free ion (in the absence of a magnetic field) there is orbital degeneracy (that is, if we have anything but an S-state ion) the free ion would have an orbital 'magnet'. If the orbital degeneracy is lost in a real environment the orbital contribution to the total magnetic moment is zero— the orbital contribution is *quenched*. If the orbital contribution is merely reduced, the orbital contribution is partially or incompletely quenched. Orbital degeneracy, however, although a necessary condition for an orbital moment, is not a sufficient condition.

The reader will recall that in Section 7-4 we likened the orbital moment to that produced by a current in a solenoid; an even better analogy would be with the magnetic moment associated with a current flowing around a circular ring of superconducting material. If the superconducting ring is rotated by 90° (or any other angle) about its unique axis one is left with a physically identical situation (for a solenoid the ends of the wire would be in a different position after the rotation). The requirement for a non-zero orbitally-derived moment is similar. We need orbital degeneracy (which only occurs when orbitals are unequally occupied), but this orbital degeneracy must be such that there exist two or more degenerate orbitals which can be interconverted by rotation about a suitable axis or axes. Consider the d_{xz} and d_{yz} orbitals in an octahedral complex (Fig. 8-1). Rotation by 90° about the z-axis interconverts them, so that if an electron were initially in the d_{xz} orbital it could circulate about the z-axis by jumping into the d_{yz} orbital. This circulation is equivalent to a current flowing and so it produces a magnetic effect. The circulation may take place in either direction (clockwise or anticlockwise) and, in the absence of a magnetic field, the two possibilities are degenerate (this is implicit in the orbital degeneracy). On application of a magnetic field the two possibilities have different energies, and this is associated with the loss of orbital degeneracy which may occur in a magnetic field. Similarly, the d_{xy} and d_{xz} orbitals are interconverted by a rotation about the x-axis and the d_{xy} and d_{yz} by a rotation about the y-axis.

Three comments are relevant at this point. First, the d_{xy} and $d_{x^2-y^2}$ orbitals are interconverted by a rotation of 45° about the

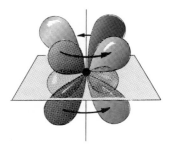

Fig. 8-1 The circulation of electron density around a coordinate axis in an incompletely filled t_{2g} shell of an octahedrally coordinated transition metal atom.

z-axis. However, they are not degenerate and so give rise to no magnetic effect. In a free atom, on the other hand, they are degenerate and so contribute to an orbital magnetic moment. Second, a more detailed analysis shows that an electron in the d_{xz} orbital does not have to 'jump' 90° to 'get into' the d_{yz} orbital because these orbitals overlap each other (note that this statement is not inconsistent with the fact that these two orbitals have a zero overlap *integral*). A continuous range of rotations is allowed, so that the electron cloud experiences no barrier to free rotation about the z-axis. Third, the Jahn–Teller theorem (Section 7-5) requires that the orbital degeneracy which we have just invoked never exists! However, any Jahn–Teller splitting of the d_{xy}, d_{yz}, and d_{zx} orbitals is small and the orbital contribution to the moment is only slightly quenched. Physically, this means that an electron circulating about the z-axis in the d_{xz} and d_{yz} orbitals *does* experience a barrier to free rotation, but this barrier is usually small compared with thermal energies.

We have seen that the stabilization produced by the application of a magnetic field to a paramagnetic complex ion may be composed of an orbital-derived part and, certainly, a spin-derived part. In order to discuss this in more detail the simple picture of an octahedral complex ion must now be modified to allow for spin–orbit coupling and low-symmetry fields. For any particular case we then arrive at a family of energy levels any member of which may be thermally populated. Since this thermal population varies with temperature, a study of the temperature dependence of the magnetic behaviour of a complex ion provides useful additional data on the relative splittings of the energy levels.

Because this book is essentially non-mathematical we shall not explain in detail how the various energy levels arise, although their derivation will not be found difficult by the student with a good background in quantum mechanics.*

8-4   Spin–orbit coupling

Spin–orbit coupling has to be included in a discussion of the magnetic properties of transition metal complexes whenever a spin-derived magnetic moment and an orbitally derived magnetic moment coexist. It turns out that, for octahedral transition metal ions, only ground states of T_{1g} and T_{2g} orbital symmetries give rise to orbital-derived magnetic moments. E_g ground states have no such moment.†️ Spin–orbit coupling splits states with both spin and orbital degeneracy into a number of sub-states. We have already encountered this and listed in Table 7-2 the number of components obtained.

When discussing spectra we recognized that two states could be coupled together by spin–orbit coupling (Section 7-4). It often happens that a ground state, although it is not split by spin–orbit coupling, is coupled to an excited state by it. Because magnetic moments are very sensitive to such couplings it is necessary to include them in the discussion. When the excited state is well removed from the ground state the coupling gives rise to the phenomenon of temperature-independent paramagentism (T.I.P. for short). Thus, the permanganate anion, although in a spin and orbitally non-degenerate ground state, is weakly paramagnetic because of T.I.P. Physically, because of spin–orbit coupling, the magnetic field pushes some electron density into an excited state

---

* See FIGGIS, B. N., *Introduction to Ligand Fields*. Interscience, New York, 1966, p. 248 *et seq.*
† Because we are here discussing states rather than orbitals, there is no simple proof of this assertion as it stands. There exists, however, a close relationship between t_{2g} orbitals and T_{2g} states, e_g orbitals and E_g states, t_{1g} orbitals and T_{1g} states—we exploited this in Section 5-3 *et seq.* Because of this isomorphism and the fact that one member of a t_{2g} set may be rotated into another (members of t_{1g} sets are similarly interconverted) but the members of an e_g set cannot, the assertion follows.

which has both orbital and spin degeneracy. The effect is temperature-independent because the thermal population of the excited state, being essentially zero, does not change appreciably with temperature. When the state which is mixed with the ground state by spin–orbit coupling is not well removed from the ground state, the effects of the mixing become more pronounced and more complicated, although in the limit when the energy difference between ground and 'excited' states is zero the problem simplifies to that of the splitting of T_{1g} and T_{2g} states discussed earlier.

There is a simple method by which one may discover whether spin–orbit coupling mixes two orbitals of the same type. If two orbitals differ by either one or zero in the number of their nodal planes which also contain the z-axis, then the two orbitals may be mixed by spin–orbit coupling. Using this rule it can readily be seen that spin–orbit coupling mixes the d orbitals as indicated below. Numbers in brackets indicate the number of nodal planes which, in a particular orbital, contain the z-axis.

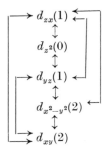

The magnitude of the spin–orbit coupling for a particular ion is usually given in terms of one of two so-called spin–orbit coupling constants, ζ (zeta) and λ. The former is the one-electron spin orbit coupling constant and is useful when comparing the relative magnitudes of the coupling between spin and orbital for different ions (as we did in Section 7-4). In practice, for many-electron ions, one measures the coupling between a resultant spin magnetic moment and a resultant orbital magnetic moment, and this many-electron spin–orbit coupling constant is given the symbol λ. The two constants are related: $\lambda = \zeta/2S$ where S is the spin multiplicity of the ion. Values for λ (and ζ) are obtained for free ions from atomic spectral data and for complex ions from magnetic measurements of the type discussed in this chapter.

The literature and text-books on the subject occasionally contain errors about the various spin–orbit coupling constants which may be defined. The following paragraph is included to help those who wish to study magnetism in more detail and may be omitted by other readers.

There exist *two* one-electron spin–orbit coupling parameters. ξ (xi), which is a function of r, the electron–nucleus separation, and ζ. The former occurs in the definition of the perturbation Hamiltonian $\mathscr{H}'_{\text{s.o}} = \sum_i \xi_i(r) \mathbf{l}_i \cdot \mathbf{s}_i$ where the summation is over the i electrons outside a closed shell. One usually assumes that $\xi_i(r)$ is a constant for, say, all $3d$ electrons (the is) and replaces it by $\xi(r)$. Matrix elements of the type $\langle \psi_1 | \xi(r) \mathbf{l} \cdot \mathbf{s} | \psi_2 \rangle$ will involve an integration over radial functions $\int R^2_{\text{nl}} \xi(r) \cdot r^2 \, dr$ and so it is simpler to define $\zeta_{\text{nl}} = \hbar^2 \int R^2_{\text{nl}} \xi(r) r^2 \, dr$. $\hbar = h/2\pi$ is included in the definition to simplify the description of the effect of the $\mathbf{l} \cdot \mathbf{s}$ operator. That is, ζ_{nl}, unlike $\xi(r)$, involves an implicit integration over the radial coordinate. In the text we have used ζ to stand for any of ζ_{3d}, ζ_{4d} and ζ_{5d}.

8-5 Low-symmetry crystal fields

We saw in Chapter 5 how the degeneracies of members of the octahedral t_{2g} and e_g orbital sets may be relieved by a low-symmetry crystal field. Similarly, we saw how the corresponding energy levels split. Unfortunately, estimating the relative magnitudes of the splittings is rather difficult, even within a point-charge model. It is usually strictly necessary to work with at least two splitting parameters although, commonly, only one is employed; as we shall see, so many parameters are introduced into the theory of magnetism that economy is practised wherever possible!

A point which must be emphasized is that although small asymmetries may usually be neglected (when discussing electronic spectra, for example) they are magnetically of great importance. However, because of their small size it may not be possible to detect the distortion by the usual methods of structure determination. In this case the additional splitting becomes something of a 'fudge factor'—it is given the value which produces the best agreement between experiment and theory.

There is an important theorem due to Kramer, which states that when the ground-state configuration has an odd number of unpaired electrons there exists a degeneracy which a low-symmetry crystal field cannot remove. This degeneracy, usually known as Kramer's degeneracy, arises from the fact that an orbital may be occupied by one electron in two ways—the spin may be 'up' or 'down'. In the absence of a magnetic field these two arrangements have the same energy. The application of a magnetic field may cause the two arrangements to differ in energy (by *ca* 1 cm^{-1}) and it is the greater occupation of the more stable situation in a macroscopic sample which causes the sample to be attracted into the magnetic field. When there is an even number of unpaired electrons a low-symmetry ligand field can relieve degeneracies, but then the application of a magnetic field causes the lowest state to become even more stable.

8-6 Experimental results

If there were no orbital contribution to the magnetic moment of a complex ion, then one would have to worry a great deal less about the effects of spin–orbit coupling and low-symmetry fields. Table 8-1 lists the moments that would be expected for ions of the first transition series if there were no orbital contribution (spin-only moments) and compares these with experimental data. It is also indicated whether an orbital contribution is to be expected (i.e. whether there is a ground-state T_{1g} or T_{2g} term). In Section 8-9 we shall derive the 'spin-only' equation used to predict moments in Table 8-1. On the whole, the agreement in this table is not bad and if all one is interested in is whether a complex is high or low spin then, if the valence state is known, a magnetic susceptibility measurement on a tetrahedral or octahedral complex of a first-row transition element may readily be interpreted using Table 8-1. In Appendix 6 we describe how these measurements are made. The reasonable agreement between spin-only and experimental moments shown in Table 8-1 is somewhat fortuitous. For d^1–d^4 ions spin–orbit coupling has the effect of reducing the observed moment and, roughly, cancels any orbital contribution. For d^6–d^9 ions spin–orbit coupling increases the observed moment and adds to the orbital contribution. This, together with the increased magnitude of the spin–orbit coupling constant for these ions, explains the few gross disagreements between spin-only and experimental values. Because of the very large spin–orbit coupling constants of elements of the second and third transition series, their complexes usually have moments much smaller than the spin-only values. We shall see why this is so in Section 8-8.

8-7 The orbital contribution reduction factor, k

So far in this chapter we have adopted a crystal field approach. How has it to be modified to take account of covalency? One way is to let the spin–orbit coupling constant λ become a parameter, rather than giving it its free ion value. Because a molecular orbital differs from an atomic orbital, we would expect them to be associated with different magnetic moments. Following the reasoning of Section 7-4 we would expect different λs. A second way is to recognize that

Table 8-1　Comparison of calculated spin-only moments and experimental data for magnetic moments of ions of the first transition series

Ion	Configuration	Orbital contribution expected?	Theoretical spin-only value	Experimental value
Octahedral complexes				
Ti^{3+}	d^1	Yes	1·73	1·6–1·7
V^{4+}	d^1	Yes	1·73	1·7–1·8
V^{3+}	d^2	Yes	2·83	2·7–2·9
Cr^{4+}	d^2	Yes	2·83	ca 2·8
V^{2+}	d^3	No	3·88	3·8–3·9
Cr^{3+}	d^3	No	3·88	3·7–3·9
Mn^{4+}	d^3	No	3·88	3·8–4·0
Cr^{2+}	d^4 h.s.	No	4·90	4·7–4·9
Cr^{2+}	d^4 l.s.	Yes	2·83	3·2–3·3
Mn^{3+}	d^4 h.s.	No	4·90	4·9–5·0
Mn^{3+}	d^4 l.s.	Yes	2·83	ca 3·2
Mn^{2+}	d^5 h.s.	No	5·92	5·6–6·1
Mn^{2+}	d^5 l.s.	Yes	1·73	1·8–2·1
Fe^{3+}	d^5 h.s.	No	5·92	5·7–6·0
Fe^{3+}	d^5 l.s.	Yes	1·73	2·0–2·5
Fe^{2+}	d^6 h.s.	No	4·90	5·1–5·7
Co^{2+}	d^7 h.s.	Yes	3·88	4·3–5·2
Co^{2+}	d^7 l.s.	No	1·73	1·8
Ni^{3+}	d^7 l.s.	No	1·73	1·8–2·0
Ni^{2+}	d^8	No	2·83	2·9–3·3
Cu^{2+}	d^9	No	1·73	1·7–2·2
Tetrahedral complexes (note that low-spin tetrahedral complexes are very rare—if any exist at all—and are not included in this table)				
Cr^{5+}	d^1	No	1·73	1·7–1·8
Mn^{6+}	d^1	No	1·73	1·7–1·8
Cr^{4+}	d^2	No	2·83	2·8
Mn^{5+}	d^2	No	2·83	2·6–2·8
Fe^{5+}	d^3 h.s.	Yes	3·88	3·6–3·7
—	d^4 h.s.	Yes	4·90	—
Mn^{2+}	d^5 h.s.	No	5·92	5·9–6·2
Fe^{2+}	d^6 h.s.	No	4·90	5·3–5·5
Co^{2+}	d^7	No	3·88	4·2–4·8
Ni^{2+}	d^8	Yes	2·83	3·7–4·0

h.s. = high spin (weak field); l.s. = low spin (strong field)

what we have assumed to be orbitals of the metal ion are, in fact, mixtures of metal and ligand orbitals. In particular, the t_{2g} orbitals are mixtures of metal and ligand π orbitals. Now, we have associated with the t_{2g} set the possibility of an orbital contribution to the magnetic moment. What happens when the t_{2g} set contains a ligand component? Evidently, the arguments used to justify an orbital contribution from the metal orbitals apply equally well to the ligand π orbitals (the appropriate ligand combinations can be interchanged by suitable rotations). The real question, therefore, is whether there is any reason to expect the ligand contribution to the moment to be equivalent to that part of the metal contribution which it has replaced (in the pure metal orbital t_{2g} set). There is no such reason and so the ligand and crystal field models predict different orbital contributions. If we are going to use a crystal field model for our calculations we must allow for this difference. This is most simply done by multiplying the orbital contribution calculated by crystal field theory by a parameter, usually denoted k, which is generally less than unity and is frequently about $0 \cdot 7$; k is obtained by choosing that value which gives the best agreement with experiment. This procedure is open to objections—in particular, that too many parameters are being obtained from one set of experimental data. Although other methods, theoretical and quasi-experimental, are available for the determination of k, none can be said, at the moment, to represent an improvement on the best-fit procedure generally adopted.

8-8   An example

In order to illustrate the preceding points we shall consider a specific case in some detail. The reader should recognize that we are not giving a detailed mathematical treatment but only sketching an outline of one in an attempt to remove some of the mystique which surrounds these calculations. As far as possible we shall justify the individual steps in the calculation.

The example chosen is fairly simple—a single d electron confined to the 't_{2g}' set of orbitals in a tetragonally distorted octahedral complex. The effect of the (pure) octahedral crystal field is to give us three degenerate orbitals each of which may be occupied by an electron with spin 'up' or 'down'. That is, we have six degenerate wave functions. We now apply a tetragonal distortion (a trigonal distortion would be mathematically similar). As Table 6-2 indicates, this separates the orbitals into two sets, d_{zx} and d_{yz} (which are degenerate), and d_{xy}. We take the distortion as occurring along the z-axis. If the total tetragonal splitting is t, then we have two orbital wavefunctions (d_{zx} and d_{yz}) of energy $-t/3$ and one (d_{xy}) at $2t/3$. We have here assumed that the distortion is such that d_{xy} is destabilized relative to d_{xz} and d_{yz} and, for simplicity, have neglected the crystal field stabilization term $\frac{2}{5}\Delta$—it is the same for all three orbitals. Including spin, we have four wavefunctions of energy $-t/3$ and two of energy $2t/3$. The next step is to allow for spin–orbit coupling. This is more difficult but we may anticipate the form of the result by recalling the rule given in Section 8-4. This indicates that spin–orbit coupling causes the degenerate orbitals, d_{zx} and d_{yz}, to interact (and thus lose their degeneracy). Further, spin–orbit coupling causes each of these orbitals to interact with d_{xy}. Detailed calculations show that the resultant energies are as given below (check that when $\zeta = 0$ they give the energy levels detailed above). Note that, once spin–orbit coupling energies have been included, it is no longer possible to refer to the resultant orbitals by labels such as d_{xz}.

$$E_3 = \tfrac{1}{2}(\tfrac{1}{2}\zeta + \tfrac{1}{3}t + (t^2 - t\zeta + \tfrac{9}{4}\zeta^2)^{1/2}) \quad \text{(doubly degenerate)}$$

$$E_2 = -\tfrac{1}{3}t - \tfrac{1}{2}\zeta \quad \text{(doubly degenerate)}$$

$$E_1 = \tfrac{1}{2}(\tfrac{1}{2}\zeta + \tfrac{1}{3}t - (t^2 - t\zeta + \tfrac{9}{4}\zeta^2)^{1/2}) \quad \text{(doubly degenerate)}$$

The spin orbit coupling parameter* for the d^1 case is equal to λ. Had we worked with the full d-orbital set, instead of the t_{2g} set above, these expressions would have been slightly modified because of spin–orbit coupling between the t_{2g} and e_g sets. The final result would have been qualitatively the same—the six 't_{2g}' spin functions would have split into three pairs. Each pair is a Kramer's doublet, the degeneracy within which may be removed by a magnetic field.

The effect of the application of a magnetic field to this set of energy levels is, from the point of view of a calculation, conveniently divided into two parts. The first part consists of the effect of the magnetic field on the three individual Kramer's doublets and the second consists of the mixing of these doublets together (it is at this point that T.I.P. is covered by the calculation). The two effects are known, respectively, as the first- and second-order Zeeman effects. The first-order effect in our problem leads to the following energy levels (listed in order of increasing stability). Because $z \neq x \equiv y$, we assume that the magnetic field is applied along the z-axis; k is the orbital reduction factor.

$$E_3(b) = \tfrac{1}{2}(\tfrac{1}{2}\zeta + \tfrac{1}{3}t + (t^2 - t\zeta + \tfrac{9}{4}\zeta^2)^{1/2}) + \frac{1 - w^2(1 + k)}{1 + w^2} \cdot \beta H$$

$$E_3(a) = \tfrac{1}{2}(\tfrac{1}{2}\zeta + \tfrac{1}{3}t + (t^2 - t\zeta + \tfrac{9}{4}\zeta^2)^{1/2}) - \frac{1 - w^2(1 + k)}{1 + w^2} \cdot \beta H$$

$$E_2(b) = -\tfrac{1}{3}t - \tfrac{1}{2}\zeta + (1 - k)\beta \cdot H$$

$$E_2(a) = -\tfrac{1}{3}t - \tfrac{1}{2}\zeta - (1 - k)\beta \cdot H$$

$$E_1(b) = \tfrac{1}{2}(\tfrac{1}{2}\zeta + \tfrac{1}{3}t - (t^2 - t\zeta + \tfrac{9}{4}\zeta^2)^{1/2}) + \frac{w^2 - (k + 1)}{1 + w^2} \cdot \beta H$$

$$E_1(a) = \tfrac{1}{2}(\tfrac{1}{2}\zeta + \tfrac{1}{3}t - (t^2 - t\zeta + \tfrac{9}{4}\zeta^2)^{1/2}) - \frac{w^2 - (k + 1)}{1 + w^2} \cdot \beta H$$

---

* It is not necessary to decide at this point whether ζ has the free ion value or whether it is being used as a parameter.

In these expressions, w is a numerical coefficient which is a complicated function of both ζ and t. H is the field strength—that is, the first-order Zeeman splitting is proportional to the field strength—and β is the Bohr magneton. The first-order Zeeman effect has removed all degeneracies.

Inclusion of the second-order Zeeman effect gives:

$$E_3(b) = \tfrac{1}{2}(\tfrac{1}{2}\zeta + \tfrac{1}{3}t + (t^2 - t\zeta + \tfrac{9}{4}\zeta^2)^{1/2}) + \frac{1 - w^2(1 + k)}{1 + w^2} \cdot \beta H$$

$$+ \frac{1}{(t^2 - t\zeta + \tfrac{9}{4}\zeta^2)^{1/2}} \cdot \left(\frac{w(k + 2)}{1 + w^2}\right)^2 \cdot \beta^2 H^2$$

$$E_3(a) = \tfrac{1}{2}(\tfrac{1}{2}\zeta + \tfrac{1}{3}t + (t^2 - t\zeta + \tfrac{9}{4}\zeta^2)^{1/2}) - \frac{1 - w^2(1 + k)}{1 + w^2} \cdot \beta H$$

$$+ \frac{1}{(t^2 - t\zeta + \tfrac{9}{4}\zeta^2)^{1/2}} \cdot \left(\frac{w(k + 2)}{1 + w^2}\right)^2 \cdot \beta^2 H^2$$

$$E_2(b) = -\tfrac{1}{3}t - \tfrac{1}{2}\zeta + (1 - k)\beta H$$

$$E_2(a) = -\tfrac{1}{3}t - \tfrac{1}{2}\zeta - (1 - k)\beta H$$

$$E_1(b) = \tfrac{1}{2}(\tfrac{1}{2}\zeta + \tfrac{1}{3}t - (t^2 - t\zeta + \tfrac{9}{4}\zeta^2)^{1/2}) + \frac{w^2 - (k + 1)}{1 + w^2} \cdot \beta H$$

$$- \frac{1}{(t^2 - t\zeta + \tfrac{9}{4}\zeta^2)^{1/2}} \cdot \left(\frac{w(k + 2)}{1 + w^2}\right)^2 \cdot \beta^2 H^2$$

$$E_1(a) = \tfrac{1}{2}(\tfrac{1}{2}\zeta + \tfrac{1}{3}t - (t^2 - t\zeta + \tfrac{9}{4}\zeta^2)^{1/2}) - \frac{w^2 - (k + 1)}{1 + w^2} \cdot \beta H$$

$$- \frac{1}{(t^2 - t\zeta + \tfrac{9}{4}\zeta^2)^{1/2}} \cdot \left(\frac{w(k + 2)}{1 + w^2}\right)^2 \cdot \beta^2 H^2$$

The second-order Zeeman effect is characterized by terms which depend on the square of the magnetic field strength. These final expressions for the energy levels are rather complicated, and we have considered a particularly simple case. The splittings of the six 't_{2g}' functions we have just discussed are shown schematically in Fig. 8-2.

The final step is to consider the thermal population of these energy levels. At this stage we shall simplify the problem, first by neglecting the deviation of the crystal field from pure octahedral. We do this by setting $t = 0$ in the energy level expressions. This simplification also has the effect that w becomes equal to $\sqrt{2}$. Secondly, we shall drop the orbital reduction factor k, setting it equal

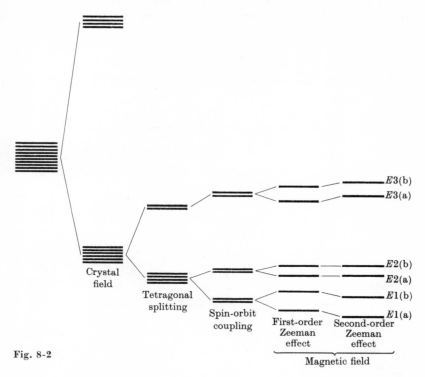

Fig. 8-2

to unity. With these simplifications, the energy levels become:

$$E_3(\text{b}) = \zeta + \beta H + \frac{4}{3}\frac{\beta^2 H^2}{\zeta}$$

$$E_3(\text{a}) = \zeta - \beta H + \frac{4}{3}\frac{\beta^2 H^2}{\zeta}$$

$$E_2(\text{b}) = -\tfrac{1}{2}\zeta$$

$$E_2(\text{a}) = -\tfrac{1}{2}\zeta$$

$$E_1(\text{b}) = -\tfrac{1}{2}\zeta - \frac{4}{3}\frac{\beta^2 H^2}{\zeta}$$

$$E_1(\text{a}) = -\tfrac{1}{2}\zeta - \frac{4}{3}\frac{\beta^2 H^2}{\zeta}$$

These expressions were first derived by Kotani (by a less circuitous route!), and the simple theory which neglects distortion and orbital reduction factors is called Kotani theory. Note that levels which are split apart in the more detailed theory are degenerate in the Kotani treatment.

We have now to derive an equation for the susceptibility in terms of the thermal population of these levels. To do this we first write the energy levels in the general form:

$$E_n = E_n(0) + E_n(1)H + E_n(2)H^2$$

Table 8-2 gives the above set of energy levels written in this form.

Table 8-2

E_n	$E_n(0)$	$E_n(1)$	$E_n(2)$
$E_3(b)$	ζ	β	$\dfrac{4\beta^2}{3\zeta}$
$E_3(a)$	ζ	$-\beta$	$\dfrac{4\beta^2}{3\zeta}$
$E_2(b)$	$-\frac{1}{2}\zeta$	0	0
$E_2(a)$	$-\frac{1}{2}\zeta$	0	0
$E_1(b)$	$-\frac{1}{2}\zeta$	0	$-\dfrac{4\beta^2}{3\zeta}$
$E_1(a)$	$-\frac{1}{2}\zeta$	0	$-\dfrac{4\beta^2}{3\zeta}$

An important property of the magnetic moment of a molecule is that it is proportional to the decrease in energy of the molecule with increase in the applied magnetic field. Provided that we use the correct units we can write:

$$\mu_n = -\frac{dE_n}{dH}$$

The correct units are atomic units, in which the energy is written in terms of β. Combining the last two mathematical expressions gives:

$$\mu_n = -E_n(1) - 2HE_n(2) - \ldots$$

an expression that we shall use shortly.

We have seen (Section 8-2) that χ_M is given by:

$$\chi_M = \frac{N}{H} \cdot (\text{average magnetic moment per molecule})$$

The average magnetic moment per molecule will be given by an expression of the form:

$$\frac{\displaystyle\sum_{\text{all molecules}} (\text{magnetic moment of an ion}) \cdot (\text{number with this moment})}{(\text{total number of molecules})}$$

Remembering that the population of a set of energy levels will be governed by a Boltzmann distribution law, it follows that

$$\chi_M = \frac{N \sum_n \mu_n \exp\left(-E_n/kT\right)}{H \sum_n \exp\left(-E_n/kT\right)}$$

We now expand the exponentials:

$$\exp\left(-E_n/kT\right) = \exp\left(-\frac{1}{kT}[E_n(0) + E_n(1)H + \dots]\right)$$

$$= \exp\left(-E_n(0)/kT\right).\exp\left(-E_n(1)H/kT\right)\dots$$

where further terms, omitted in the last expression, will (except at very low temperatures or high fields) be approximately $\exp\left(-0/kT\right) = \exp\left(0\right) = 1$, and so may be neglected. Using the expansion:

$$\exp\left(x\right) = 1 + x + \frac{x^2}{2!} + \frac{x^3}{3!} + \dots$$

for the second exponential above, we have, approximately:

$$\exp\left(-E_n/kT\right) \simeq \exp\left(-E_n(0)/kT\right).\left(1 - \frac{E_n(1)H}{kT}\right)$$

Putting this, together with the expression for μ_n given earlier, into the equation for χ_M gives, approximately:

$$\chi_M = \frac{N.\sum_n \left(-E_n(1) - 2HE_n(2)\right)\left(1 - \frac{E_n(1)H}{kT}\right).\exp\left(-E_n(0)/kT\right)}{H.\sum_n \exp\left(-E_n(0)/kT\right)}$$

We now expand the numerator but first note that when the magnetic field is zero the average magnetic moment per molecule must be zero and so the numerator must be zero also. It follows that the term:

$$\sum_n -E_n(1).\exp\left(-E_n(0)/kT\right) = 0$$

We have, then:

$$\chi_M = \frac{N\sum_n \left[\frac{(E_n(1))^2H}{kT} - 2HE_n(2) + \frac{2H^2E_n(1)}{kT}\right].\exp\left(-E_n(0)/kT\right)}{H.\sum_n \exp\left(-E_n(0)/kT\right)}$$

Cancelling the Hs and neglecting the term $2HE_n(1)/kT$ (which will be very small except at low temperatures or high fields) we have, finally:

$$\chi_M = \frac{N\sum_n \left[\frac{(E_n(1))^2}{kT} - 2E_n(2)\right].\exp\left(-E_n(0)/kT\right)}{\sum_n \exp\left(-E_n(0)/kT\right)}$$

Or, using the relationship derived in Section 8-2:

$$\mu_{\text{eff.}}^2 = \frac{3RT\chi_M}{N^2\beta^2} = \frac{3kT\chi_M}{N\beta^2}$$

we have, for $\mu_{\text{eff.}}^2$:

$$\mu_{\text{eff.}}^2 = \frac{3kT \sum_n \left[\dfrac{(E_n(1))^2}{kT} - 2E_n(2) \right] . \exp\left(-E_n(0)/kT\right)}{\beta^2 \sum_n \exp\left(-E_n(0)/kT\right)}$$

These expressions for χ_M and $\mu_{\text{eff.}}^2$ are known as the van Vleck relationships.

It is a simple matter to apply these formulae to our case;* we have only to sum over the six different E_ns using the values for $E_n(0)$, $E_n(1)$, and $E_n(2)$ given in Table 8-2. This gives:

$$\mu_{\text{eff.}}^2 = \frac{3kT}{\beta^2} \times$$

$$\frac{2\left(-\dfrac{\beta^2}{kT} - \dfrac{8\beta^2}{3\zeta}\right)\exp\left(-\zeta/kT\right) + 2\left(0-0\right)\exp\left(\zeta/2kT\right) + 2\left(0 + \dfrac{8\beta^2}{3\zeta}\right)\exp\left(\zeta/2kT\right)}{2\exp\left(-\zeta/kT\right) + 2\exp\left(\zeta/2kT\right) + 2\exp\left(\zeta/2kT\right)}$$

where the factors of two arise because $E_1(a)$ and $E_1(b)$, for example, make the same contribution to the summation. This expression simplifies to:

$$\mu_{\text{eff.}}^2 = \frac{\left(3\dfrac{\zeta}{kT} - 8\right)\exp\left(-3\zeta/2kT\right) + 8}{\dfrac{\zeta}{kT}\left(\exp\left(-3\zeta/2kT\right) + 2\right)}$$

or, by putting $\zeta/kT = x$:

$$\mu_{\text{eff.}}^2 = \frac{(3x - 8)\exp\left(-3x/2\right) + 8}{x(\exp\left(-3x/2\right) + 2)}$$

another expression first derived by Kotani.

We can now plot the value of $\mu_{\text{eff.}}$ (given by the positive square root of the above expression) against x, or, more conveniently, $1/x$ (a so-called 'Kotani plot'). This has been done in Fig. 8-3. We have also indicated on this figure the values of ζ/kT for some d^1 ions at 300°K, ζ being given the free ion value.

---

* Their application to the energy level set which includes k and t is similar but more complicated.

It is seen that $\mu_{\text{eff.}}$ is almost independent of temperature at high enough temperatures (the larger ζ, the higher the temperature); room temperature measurements on first row transition metal ions give, essentially, their 'plateau' values. It is under these limiting conditions that simple formulae like

$$\mu_{\text{eff.}} = \sqrt{(n(n+2))}$$

the spin-only formula (which we shall derive in the next section), in which n is the number of unpaired electrons, become applicable. For complexes of elements of the second and third transition series

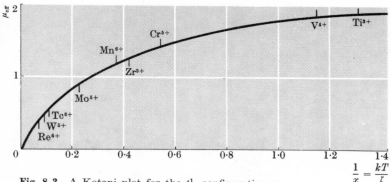

Fig. 8-3 A Kotani plot for the t_{2g}^1 configuration.

magnetic measurements over a temperature range are absolutely essential, even if it is only the number of unpaired electrons which is to be determined.

For electronic configurations other than the one we have discussed, analogous calculations lead to relationships which are roughly similar to that shown in Fig. 8-3: $\mu_{\text{eff.}}$ does not generally drop to zero at $0°K$, and, down to $\lambda/kT \simeq 1\cdot5$, $\mu_{\text{eff.}}$ may increase slightly with decreasing temperature, decreasing as the temperature is lowered further. When k and t (or related functions) are included in the final energy-level expressions, the temperature dependence of $\mu_{\text{eff.}}$ is less than in the corresponding case where they are omitted.

As an illustration of the use of this approach we show in Fig. 8-4 a comparison between the predicted and experimental results for $[VCl_6]^{2-}$, the cation being the pyridinium ion, pyH⁺. Simple Kotani theory is roughly followed if the spin–orbit coupling constant is reduced to 190 cm^{-1} from the free ion value of 250 cm^{-1} (Fig. 8-4a), but excellent agreement is obtained if distortion and covalency are allowed for (Fig. 8-4b). The theoretical curve is that calculated for $k = 0.75$, $\zeta = 150$ cm^{-1}, and $t = -150$ cm^{-1}. The negative sign on t implies that the orbital singlet lies lowest (not the orbital doublet; the distortion of the octahedron is the opposite to that which we assumed). The job of fitting a theoretical curve to the experimental results is best done by a computer; the need for high experimental accuracy is evident.

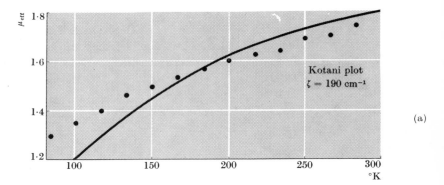

(a)

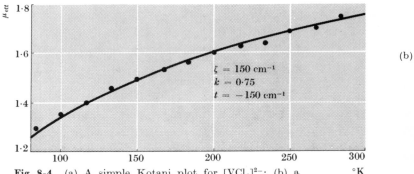

(b)

Fig. 8-4   (a) A simple Kotani plot for $[VCl_6]^{2-}$; (b) a Kotani plot modified to include tetragonal distortion and orbital reduction factors.

8-9   The spin-only formula

We have seen in the preceding section that even if there is an orbital contribution to the magnetic moment it may be reduced by covalency and by distortions. What if we assume that there is no orbital contribution at all—that it is completely quenched? In this section we consider this problem, which will lead us to the 'spin-only' formula mentioned earlier.

The unpaired electrons within an isolated ion couple to give a resultant S ($= n/2$, where n is the number of unpaired electrons). The allowed components of S along the direction of the magnetic field are $S_z = S, S - 1, S - 2, \ldots -S + 1, -S$.

These will have energies $-2S\beta H$, $-2(S-1)\beta H$, $-2(S-2)\beta H$, ... in a magnetic field (the factor two is the Landé g factor for the electron—the splittings in a magnetic field are twice as great as one would expect from the magnitude of the spin angular momentum). Assuming a Boltzmann distribution of ions over the various S_z values in a macroscopic sample, we have, by arguments analogous to those used in the derivation of the van Vleck relationships:

$$\mu_{\text{eff.}}^2 = \frac{3kT}{H\beta^2} \cdot \frac{\sum\limits_{S_z=S}^{-S} 2S_z \cdot \beta \cdot \exp(2S_z\beta H/kT)}{\sum\limits_{S_z=S}^{-S} \exp(2S_z\beta H/kT)}$$

Expanding the exponentials:

$$\mu_{\text{eff.}}^2 = \frac{6kT}{H\beta} \cdot \frac{\sum\limits_{S_z=S}^{-S} S_z\left(1 + \frac{2S_z\beta H}{kT}\right)}{\sum\limits_{S_z=S}^{-S}\left(1 + \frac{2S_z\beta H}{kT}\right)}$$

Now:

$$\sum\limits_{x=a}^{-a} x = 0, \qquad \text{and} \qquad \sum\limits_{x=a}^{-a} x^2 = \frac{a}{3}(a+1)(2a+1)$$

so:

$$\mu_{\text{eff.}}^2 = \frac{6kT}{H\beta} \cdot \frac{2\beta H}{kT} \cdot \frac{S}{3} \cdot (S+1) = 4S(S+1)$$

That is:

$$\mu_{\text{eff.}} = 2\sqrt{(S(S+1))} = \sqrt{(n(n+2))}$$

As we have seen, this relationship holds quite well for the first transition series. For the second- and third-row elements, it gives totally misleading results, because the spin–orbit coupling energy of these ions is much greater than kT—the 'plateau' of the Kotani plot has not been reached (with the exception of d^3 systems).

8-10 Magnetically non-dilute compounds

When a simple Curie law plot χ_M against T^{-1} (Section 8-2) does not give a straight line it is often found that a modified form, the *Curie–Weiss* law, does:

$$\chi_M = \frac{C}{T+\theta}$$

Here θ is a constant, the Weiss constant, which has the dimensions of temperature and is measured in degrees. Despite its widespread applicability it is difficult to give a quantum-mechanical interpretation of this relationship. In the limiting cases where this is possible, θ is associated with the breakdown of the Langevin assumption $B = H$, and values of $\theta \neq 0$ are generally regarded as indicative of magnetic interaction between discrete molecules in condensed phases.

This brings us back to an assumption made at the beginning of this chapter: that we could restrict our discussion to magnetically dilute materials. Magnetically non-dilute materials fall into one of three classes. Of these ferromagnetic behaviour is well known. As with the other two classes, the individual magnetic centres must be considered together, not separately, the correct 'building block' being the lattice unit cell. In ferromagnetic materials, such as metallic iron, the electron spins on each of the atoms couple together to form a resultant unit cell magnetic moment.

Iron has a cubic unit cell so let us suppose that the unit cell moment is perpendicular to one of the faces of the unit cell. There are six such faces and in a 'perfect' crystal of non-magnetized iron there are domains within each of which there is magnetic alignment between unit cells, but in the whole crystal there is a random distribution over all of the six orientations. The process of magnetization brings these moments into alignment. These features make ferromagnetic materials quite different from most of those which concern a chemist, and we shall not consider them further here. The second class consists of ferrimagnetic materials. While ferromagnetic materials are usually metals or alloys, ferrimagnetic substances are compounds, the best-known example being Fe_3O_4 'magnetic oxide of iron'. In this and other ferrimagnetic materials there is a coupling, and parallel alignment between the spins of the metal ions on similar sites in the lattice. In ferrimagnetics there are two sets of sites occupied by the metal ions. These have opposed spin arrangements but as they do not cancel each other out there is a resultant permanent moment. Fe_3O_4 ($\equiv 2Fe^{3+} + Fe^{2+} + 4O^{2-}$) is more complicated than this because one site contains (formally) Fe^{2+} and Fe^{3+} in equal amounts, whilst the other site contains only Fe^{3+}.

The third and most important case for the chemist is that of antiferromagnetism. In antiferromagnetic materials transition metal ions are usually separated by small ligands so that many transition metal oxides and halides are antiferromagnetic. In such compounds adjacent metal ions couple with their spins parallel or antiparallel; there are always equal numbers with the two arrangements so, unlike antiferrimagnetic materials, there is no resultant magnetization.

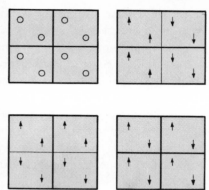

Fig. 8-5   Crystallographic and magnetic unit cells.

As an example of one complicating feature of antiferromagnetism consider the sets of four crystallographic unit cells shown in Fig. 8-5, the magnetic centres being represented by circles in the first diagram and arrows. representing spin orientations, in the others. In this figure we give three possible arrangements of spin orientations within this block of four cells. It can be seen that these are all different; two of the arrangements only contain two *magnetic unit cells*. Compared with the 32 point groups and 230 space groups of classical crystallography there are 90 magnetic point groups and 1,651 magnetic space groups. Neutron diffraction data are capable of allocating an antiferromagnetic material to its correct magnetic space group. If this is not known, it is not possible to give a

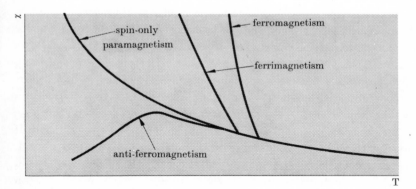

Fig. 8-6   Idealized temperature–susceptibility plots for the various types of magnetic behaviour. Very low temperatures are not included in this diagram. The applied magnetic field is, in all cases, assumed to be moderate (saturation phenomena may exist at high magnetic fields).

complete theoretical discussion of the magnetic properties of an antiferromagnetic material. In this respect, those examples of antiferromagnetism in which there is coupling between two atoms adjacent to each other (cupric acetate falls into this class*) are much simpler than those for which the interactions are more delocalized. In either case there is a maximum in a plot of χ_M vs T (at the so-called Néel point—see Fig. 8-6), that for intra-molecular antiferromagnetism being more rounded than that for the intermolecular case. Below the Néel point the susceptibility is to some extent field-dependent. These properties provide an

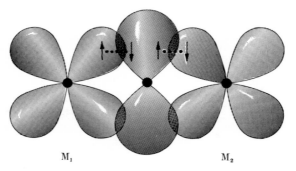

Fig. 8-7 The superexchange mechanism of antiferro-magnetic coupling.

indication of the existence, or absence, of antiferromagnetism. Other tests include a comparison of the results of solution and solid-state measurements and the technique of dilution by substitution in the lattice of an isomorphous non-magnetic material. At temperatures sufficiently above the Néel point, antiferromagnetic materials follow a Curie–Weiss law. Even if the Néel point is at too low a temperature to be conveniently measured, the observation that a material follows the Curie–Weiss law may imply a residual antiferromagnetic coupling.

The coupling between adjacent magnetic centres, which char-acterizes antiferromagnetic materials, is believed to occur by a so-called 'superexchange' mechanism. Consider Fig. 8-7. Suppose that an electron on metal ion M_1 has its spin 'up' as shown, then, if overlap with the central ligand orbital shown were to lead to a bond, of the two electrons in the ligand orbital that with spin 'down' would have to be selected to pair with that on M_1. This would leave an

---

* It has been shown that the antiferromagnetism of cupric acetate is the result of a *ferromagnetic* coupling (a parallel arrangement of spins is preferred) between electrons in molecular orbitals based on the two copper atoms in the (dimeric) molecule. That is, antiferromagnetic behaviour does not necessarily imply anti-ferromagnetic coupling!

electron with spin 'up' to pair with the electron on the metal ion M_2, which would therefore have to have its spin 'down', that is in the opposite direction to that on M_1. Even if the overlap between the metal ions and the central ligand is relatively small, as long as it exists at all, the relative spins of M_1 and M_2 will remain opposed, and the essentials of the above argument remain true.

Problems

8-1   Draw a diagram to show which d orbitals are *not* coupled together by spin–orbit coupling.

8-2   How would you expect to be able to distinguish magnetically between octahedral, tetrahedral and square planar complexes of nickel(II)?

8-3   Explain what is meant by the following:
(a) Temperature-independent paramagnetism;
(b) 'The orbital contribution to the susceptibility is partially quenched';
(c) Antiferromagnetism

8-4   What can be deduced from the following magnetic moments (all measurements at room temperature)?

Complex of	$\mu(B.M.)$
cobalt(II)	4·9
nickel(II)	diamagnetic
nickel(II)	3·9
copper(II)	1·41
iron(III)	2·2
osmium(IV)	1·3

8-5   Outline the magnetic consequences of (a) spin–orbit coupling, (b) the Jahn–Teller effect, and (c) covalency.

Answer to Problem 7-2

Because of the electron–hole parallel, wherever Δ appears in Section 7-2 it must be replaced by $-\Delta$. Comparison with the appropriate energy level diagram (such as that in Fig. 5-23) leads to the following energy levels

$^3A_{2g}$ $\qquad -\frac{6}{5}\Delta$

$^3T_{2g}$ $\qquad -\frac{1}{5}\Delta$

$^3T_{1g}(F)$ $\qquad \frac{1}{2}[15B + \frac{3}{5}\Delta - (225B^2 - 18B\Delta + \Delta^2)^{1/2}]$

$^3T_{1g}(P)$ $\qquad \frac{1}{2}[15B + \frac{3}{5}\Delta + (225B^2 - 18B\Delta + \Delta^2)^{1/2}]$

Taking differences and dividing through by B we find

$$\frac{E(^3T_{2g} \leftarrow {}^3A_{2g})}{E(^3T_{1g}(F) \leftarrow {}^3A_{2g})} = \frac{2\dfrac{\Delta}{B}}{15 + 3\dfrac{\Delta}{B} - \left(225 - 18\dfrac{\Delta}{B} + \dfrac{\Delta^2}{B^2}\right)^{1/2}}$$

9 Other methods of studying coordination compounds

9-1 Introduction

In preceding chapters we have discussed some of the methods which have been used to characterize and identify coordination compounds. This chapter outlines further methods which are similarly used.

If one only wishes to determine whether a complex is formed in a particular system, relatively crude methods often suffice. The evolution of heat, the crystallization of a product or other changes in solubility, a change in colour or chemical properties (failure to undergo a characteristic reaction, for example) are all simple but useful indications. When these indications are undetectable more sensitive methods must be used, which usually involve the study of some physical property of the system as a function of its composition. Examples of methods used for non-transition metal complexes are the measurement of colligative properties such as vapour pressure (or boiling point) and freezing point. Less commonly, measurements of quantities such as viscosity and electrical conductivity have been employed (by a suitable choice of temperature it is always possible to study the system in the liquid phase). For example, a sharp maximum in plot of viscosity against composition is a good indication of the formation of a complex, although ill-defined maxima are not. Measurements of electrical conductivity, based on the assumption that the conductivity of a complex differs from that of its components, similarly show maxima or minima. However, these may be caused either directly (by a change in concentration of some conducting species) or indirectly (by the viscosity changes, which alter ionic mobilities).

Besides conductivity measurements (to which we shall return), another electrical measurement which has been used is pH change. Most ligands may be protonated at their coordination site so that, for example, corresponding to the NH_3 ligand there is the protonated species NH_4^+. This means that, if in the same solution there is free ligand L, the acceptor species A, and acidic protons (which we shall, for simplicity, write as H^+), there will be two important equilibria:

$$H^+ + L \rightleftharpoons HL^+$$
$$A + L \rightleftharpoons [AL].$$

If the second equilibrium exists (that is, if a complex is formed), addition of more A will cause the first equilibrium to be displaced to the left so that the pH of the solution will decrease. Measurement of pH not only allows the formation of complexes to be detected but may also be used to determine the stability constants of the species formed (Chapter 4). In a similar way, half-cell potential and polarographic measurements may be used both to detect complex formation and to determine stability constants.

We shall now consider in detail six techniques which not only indicate the formation of coordination compounds but also provide insights into their structure.

9-2   Infrared spectroscopy

The excitation of molecular vibrations and rotations gives rise to absorption bands in the infrared regions of the spectrum. The spectra themselves are determined by the arrangement of atoms in space— their masses, bond lengths and angles—and by the forces between the atoms. When a ligand is coordinated, at least one additional atom—the atom to which the ligand coordinates—is introduced into the ligand's vibrating system and bond lengths and angles, and interatomic forces within the ligand would be expected to alter slightly. This means that the infrared spectrum of a coordinated ligand will differ from that of the free ligand, and it should be possible to correlate the changes in spectra with the changes in geometry. In this way information about the structure of the complex may be obtained. Similarly, there will be changes in the vibrations of the system to which the ligand becomes attached, but a study of these is usually less rewarding than a study of those associated with the ligand.

The differences between the spectra of free ligand and complex fall into three categories:

1. Band positions may change.

2. Relative band intensities may change. The most noticeable feature here is the appearance of new, often weak, bands.

3. Single peaks in the free ligand may split into several, closely-spaced, bands in the complex.

However, it is seldom possible to place a unique interpretation on the changes observed, because even with simple ligands it is not always possible to uniquely associate spectral bands with the vibrational modes of the molecule. In practice, therefore, we usually compare a spectrum with that of a compound in which the ligand is coordinated in a known way. The results obtained may conveniently be exemplified and discussed under the three headings listed above.

9-2-1   Changes in band position

Vibrational bands associated with the stretching of bonds involving the coordinated atom(s) usually move to longer wavelength (lower energy) on coordination. Thus, the carbonate ion may function either as a unidentate or bidentate (chelating) ligand. A vibration of the free CO_3^{2-} anion which absorbs at *ca* 890 cm^{-1} appears at *ca* 850 cm^{-1} and *ca* 830 cm^{-1} when CO_3^{2-} functions as a unidentate and bidentate ligand, respectively, and is indicative of the mode of coordination. An example of a ligand frequency which moves to higher energy on coordination is provided by the cyanide anion. In KCN this shows absorption at 2,080 cm^{-1}, but on coordination it appears anywhere from 2,040 cm^{-1} to 2,170 cm^{-1}, although usually above 2,100 cm^{-1}.

When linkage isomerism (Section 2-4-7) occurs, infrared spectroscopy may provide a simple method of determining the coordination. Thus, when the thiocyanate anion is S-bonded the C—S stretching vibration commonly occurs at *ca* 700 cm^{-1}, but for N-bonding it appears at *ca* 820 cm^{-1}. Similarly, a N—O stretching mode of the NO_2^- anion occurs at *ca* 1,300 cm^{-1} when N-bonded, but at *ca* 1,050 cm^{-1} when O-bonded. However, the more complicated the ligand the less likely it is that infrared spectroscopy will unambiguously indicate its mode of coordination.

9-2-2   Altered relative band intensities

Although band intensities have been used to predict the molecular geometries of metal carbonyls this technique has been applied only rarely to other systems. This stems, in part, from the difficulties of assignment referred to above. One feature which has been recognized is that, if hydrogen bonding is more important within a complex than in the free ligand, bands involving the hydrogen atoms show considerable intensification.

Of more general interest has been the appearance of new bands in the spectrum. These may originate in several ways. Most important are new chemical bonds formed as a result of coordination, from which corresponding vibrations are to be expected. Unfortunately, some of these 'metal–ligand' modes produce relatively weak bands and may be difficult to distinguish from intra-ligand absorptions. In favourable cases, where assignment has been possible—for example, in the case of metal–halogen stretching frequencies—the number and wavelength of the bands have been shown to reflect both the coordination symmetry and the bond strength changes. These bands occur in the 600–100 cm^{-1} region, which, at the long-wavelength end, presents some instrumental difficulties.

Coordination usually reduces the effective symmetry of the

ligand and so alters the vibrational selection rules. As a consequence vibrations which were infrared inactive in the isolated ligand may become active in the coordinated ligand, although seldom do they appear with great intensity. Ambiguities may arise if the infrared spectrum of the solid complex is recorded, because the symmetry of a molecule in the crystal lattice may well be lower than that of the isolated molecule owing to distortions caused by adjacent molecules in the lattice, and the selection rules are further modified. If the molecule is a potential ligand then one cannot always be sure whether or not it is coordinated. Thus, an infrared forbidden vibration of the isolated sulphate anion appears at 973 cm^{-1} in $[Co(NH_3)_6]_2(SO_4)_3 \cdot 5H_2O$ (where the anion is not coordinated), and at 970 cm^{-1} in $[Co(NH_3)_5SO_4]Br$ (where it is). This complication could be avoided by studying the infrared spectrum of a complex in solution, although this is not always possible—the complex may be too insoluble or too labile, or the only suitable solvents may absorb in the region of interest.

9-2-3 Band splittings

Just as a lowered symmetry on coordination may cause the appearance of new bands, so it may cause the splitting of bands which are degenerate in the isolated ligand. So, the free sulphate anion shows a band at 1,104 cm^{-1} which is triply degenerate. In $[Co(NH_3)_6]_2(SO_4)_3 \cdot 5H_2O$ this appears as a broad double-headed peak with a separation of ca 20 cm^{-1}. The complex $[Co(NH_3)_5SO_4]Br$, in which the sulphate is coordinated, shows a much larger splitting, ca 90 cm^{-1}, with double-headed bands at ca 1,040 cm^{-1} and 1,130 cm^{-1}.

Again complications arise if solid-state spectra are recorded. Suppose we have a non-degenerate ligand vibration, and there are four ligands per unit cell. Then the four ligand vibrations couple together to give the four unit cell vibrations shown in Fig. 9-1 (which, for simplicity, shows a two-dimensional unit cell). It is the latter, rather than the former, which are observed in the spectrum. Of these four, two are infrared active and will give rise to two bands in the infrared spectrum. Such splittings could account for the double-headed nature of the 1,040 cm^{-1} and 1,130 cm^{-1} peaks in the spectrum of $[Co(NH_3)_5SO_4]Br$ and may, on occasion, be confused with genuine coordination-induced splittings. Again, this complication may be avoided by recording infrared spectra in solution.

Relatively little work has been done with Raman spectroscopy because many coordination compounds are coloured. With the advent of the new Raman–laser techniques more information will become available.

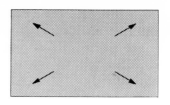

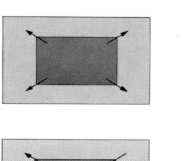

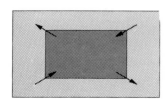

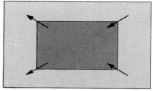

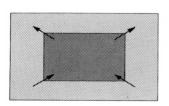

Fig. 9-1 Four independent ligand vibrations (top diagram) couple together to give four unit cell vibrations. The coupling between the modes of the individual vibrations is represented by the lines drawn between them. Of the four unit cell vibrations the upper two are Raman active and the lower two infrared active.

9-3 Spectroscopic methods unique to optically active molecules

If a weight at the end of a piece of string is set in motion so that it traverses a circular path this motion may be regarded as composed of two mutually perpendicular simple harmonic motions combined out of phase with each other by 90°. In the same way a single simple harmonic vibration of the weight may be regarded as an in-phase combination of two circular motions in opposite directions (Fig. 9-2). Thus, we always have a choice. A circular motion may be described as a combination of two simple harmonic motions and, similarly, a simple harmonic motion may be expressed in terms of two circular motions. This choice is analogous to those met elsewhere: between real and complex atomic (and molecular) orbitals, between linearly and circularly polarized light (with which we shall be concerned in this section), and it occurs in a.c. network theory. Which description is adopted is usually determined by that which leads to the simpler mathematics, even if it involves some initial conceptual difficulties. So, even though 'optically active compounds rotate the plane of

Fig. 9-2 A simple harmonic motion (centre) may be regarded as a sum of two circular motions. The motion represented takes place in the plane of the paper. The thickness of the lines represents time, rather like an oscilloscope trace on a tube with a persistent phosphor.

linearly polarized light', it is more convenient to discuss the phenomenon in terms of circularly polarized light. Fig. 9-3 shows how linearly polarized light may be regarded as compounded of two circularly polarized components.

Consider what happens when each of the circularly polarized components is propagated along the threefold axis of the optically active ion $[Coen_3]^{3+}$. From Fig. 9-4 it is evident that one of the circularly polarized components tends to pass along the 'backbone' of the ethylenediamine ligands whilst the other tends to cut it perpendicularly. This description is inaccurate in that the wavelength of visible or ultraviolet light (in which we shall be interested) is of the order of a thousand times greater than the molecular dimensions. Nevertheless, the vital point remains—the two circularly polarized components will encounter slightly different electron density distributions in passing through the $[Coen_3]^{3+}$ ion. As is

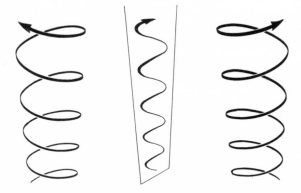

Fig. 9-3 Linearly polarized light (centre) regarded as a sum of two circularly polarized components. Fig. 9-2 may be regarded as a view of Fig. 9-3 along the axis of propagation, the thickness of the lines then indicating distance.

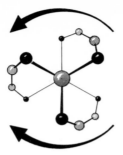

Fig. 9-4 Two circularly polarized beams of light passing through a molecule of $[Coen_3]^{3+}$, the threefold axis of the latter being coincident with the axis of propagation of the light. One circularly polarized beam (the top one) tends to 'cut' the backbone of an ethylenediamine molecule, the other to pass along it.

well known, the interaction between a light wave and electron density leads to a reduction in the velocity of propagation of the light wave—refractive indices are greater than unity—and the greater the electron density (roughly), the higher the refractive index and the slower the velocity of propagation. This means that we must expect one circularly polarized component to pass more rapidly through the $[Coen_3]^{3+}$ ion than the other; the faster might be that which tends to 'cut' the ligand backbone. Although this last statement is, in fact, not generally true, it correctly suggests that polarized light may enable one to determine the chirality of an optically active species. Because one circularly polarized component travels faster than the other, one of the helical 'springs' shown in Fig. 9-3 will be more extended than the other. This means that, after traversing the molecule, the two components will be slightly out of phase. Combining them (Fig. 9-5) leads to a rotation in the plane of polarization compared with the incident light, as observed. If a graph is plotted of the angle of rotation against wavelength (the angle of rotation being suitably corrected for path length and concentration of the optically active species) a curve of *optical rotatory dispersion* (O.R.D.) is obtained. At wavelengths for which the species is transparent (i.e. there is no electronic absorption) the O.R.D. curve is unexciting, varying relatively little with wavelength. It is only when absorption occurs that things begin to happen!

It is well known that the absorption of light by a molecule is frequently anisotropic. That is, a light wave incident on a molecule in one direction may excite an electronic transition, but light of the same wavelength, incident in another direction, may not be absorbed. In a region of absorption of light by an optically active species, we must expect plane-polarized light to be attenuated, but what of its circularly polarized components; are they attenuated equally? Since these follow slightly different 'paths' through a molecule (say, the $[Coen_3]^{3+}$ ion we referred to earlier) we would expect them to be absorbed to different extents. This prediction is confirmed by measurements made with circularly polarized light (it is possible to pass left and right circularly polarized light alternately through a solution of an optically active species and to compare their relative

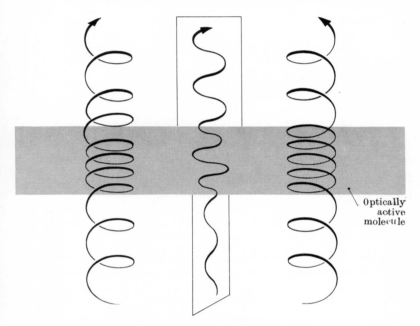

Optically
active
molecule

Fig. 9-5   The passage of a beam of linearly polarized light through an optically active molecule. Note the rotation of the plane of polarization and correlate this with the different behaviour of the two circularly polarized components within the molecule.

absorption). The difference in extinction coefficients between left (anticlockwise) and right (clockwise, viewed in the direction of propagation) circularly polarized light, $e_l - e_r$, is small but measurable and is termed the *circular dichroism* (C.D.). O.R.D., C.D., and related phenomena are collectively called the Cotton effect. A plot of C.D. against wavelength shows a maximum at the position of maximum absorption in an ordinary absorption curve. The O.R.D. plot behaves as the derivative of the C.D. curve, passing through a point of inflexion at the absorption maximum. These relationships are shown in Fig. 9-6. As shown in this figure, the curves for one species are the negative of those of its enantiomorph.

A complication arises, however. Although the $[Coen_3]^{3+}$ cation

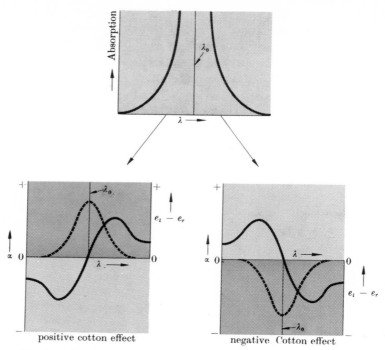

Fig. 9-6 Idealized diagrams of an electronic absorption band of an optically active species (top diagram) and the corresponding O.R.D. (solid line) and C.D. (broken line) plots for the two different 'hands' of the species.

is shown behaving as a left-handed screw in Fig. 9-4, the same molecule, when viewed in a perpendicular direction, behaves as a right-handed screw (Fig. 9-7)! This duality is not unique to this example but occurs for all optically active molecules.

When a molecule absorbs light and undergoes an electronic excitation this occurs through a displacement of electron density within the molecule. It turns out that the absolute configuration of a molecule can be related to the Cotton effect only if the direction of charge displacement is known. For an optically active molecule this displacement occurs along a helical path and, as we have seen, within a given molecule there are always both right- and left-handed

Fig. 9-7

helical paths available for displacement along a molecular backbone. This is made more complicated when we recognize that if the displacement is perpendicular to, say, a left-handed helical backbone, then the displacement itself has the character of a right-handed helix (Fig. 9-8)! Yet, only if we know something about the nature of the electronic transition can we hope to deduce molecular configuration from the Cotton effect. Evidently, it is best to study a compound with as few electronic transitions as possible for this will reduce the probability of error. It is for this reason that much more detailed work has been done with complexes like $[Coen_3]^{3+}$ than with those like $cis[Coen_2Cl_2]^+$. The former has the higher symmetry and, therefore, fewer absorption bands. If the same d–d transition can be observed in a series of closely related compounds then (remembering that in the crystal field model, at least, the ligands generate an electrostatic field but are not otherwise involved) if the absolute configuration of one of the members can be established so too can that of each of the others. In practice, it is usually possible to identify transitions by band intensity criteria and, as mentioned earlier (Section 2-4-10), the absolute configuration of $(+)$-$[Coen_3]^{3+}$ has been determined.

In d^6 complexes which, like $[Coen_3]^{3+}$, have D_3 symmetry there are two d–d transitions derived by reduction in symmetry from the $^1T_{1g} \leftarrow {}^1A_{1g}$ transition of an octahedral complex (Table 6-2). These transitions are to excited states of A_2 and E symmetry, and it has been suggested that the latter usually gives rise to the more intense C.D. band—it has the higher *rotational strength*. If the suggestion is correct and the transition to the E excited state has positive rotational strength, then the absolute molecular configuration is that shown in Figs. 9-4 and 9-7. However, the generality of this suggestion has recently been questioned (the splitting caused by the reduction in symmetry may be small and the two observed bands may originate, rather, in a Jahn–Teller splitting of the $^1T_{1g}$ excited state). Fortunately, this uncertainty does not affect the principal use of the Cotton effect, which is that of following the stereochemical

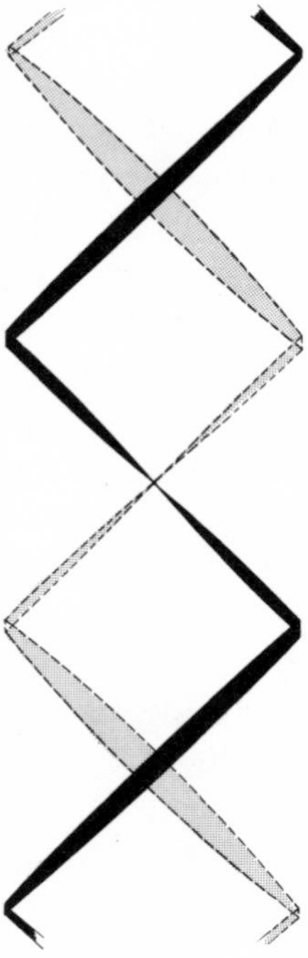

Fig. 9-8 A helical molecule (black, perspective is indicated by the line thickness) and a charge displacement perpendicular to it (dotted).

changes accompanying the reactions of optically active molecules.

Finally, it should be mentioned that the sign of an O.R.D. curve at any arbitrary point—like the sodium D-line wavelength—is composed of a superimposition of tail absorptions from all of the O.R.D. curves due to absorption bands in the molecule. The sign of the specific rotation at such a point is therefore an uncertain guide to molecular structure.

9-4   Nuclear spectroscopy

In this section we shall outline three methods which have been used to study the properties of nuclei in coordination compounds. None of the techniques is of universal application and they suffer from the disadvantage that the connection between the spectra obtained and the molecular bonding is seldom simple. This means that, although the spectra can be usefully used to obtain details of molecular structure, from the bonding viewpoint they are generally best used to compare two compounds rather than discuss either in isolation.

9-4-1   Nuclear magnetic resonance

We shall discuss in Section 11-1 the use of nuclear magnetic resonance (n.m.r.) spectroscopy in kinetic investigations. At this point it must be emphasized that spectra obtained at room temperature may be misleadingly simple because of exchange processes in which two (or more) species interconvert so rapidly that they give an averaged spectrum. In this section we give illustrative examples of the use of n.m.r. spectroscopy in coordination chemistry.

Structure determination. Complexes of WF_6, $[WF_6 \cdot L]$, exist in which the tungsten atom might be seven-coordinate. A low-resolution ^{19}F spectrum shows three lines of relative intensity $4:1:1$, which does not appear to be consistent with a seven-coordinate structure. The probable structure is $[WF_5 \cdot L]^+F^-$, in which the tungsten atom is octahedrally coordinated by six ligands, five of which are fluorines. The four coplanar fluorines give rise to the largest peak and the axial fluorine to one of the other peaks. The fluoride anion gives rise to the remaining peak. The fine structure of the peaks confirms this assignment as does the conductivity of the compounds in liquid sulphur dioxide (see Section 9-6).

Spin density distribution. It is not usually possible to observe the n.m.r. spectra of paramagnetic species because the lines are extremely broad. In particular cases, however, the spectra can be observed but cover a frequency range perhaps 50 times as great as that encountered with similar diamagnetic compounds. As we saw in Chapter 6, unpaired electrons, which, in crystal field theory, we would expect to be localized on a transition metal ion are, in fact, delocalized onto the ligands. (Main group elements rarely form paramagnetic coordination compounds.) If, in particular, the ligands are conjugated systems, the unpaired electron density will also be delocalized over the entire ligand. The additional shifts observed in the n.m.r. spectra of paramagnetic compounds are directly proportional to the unpaired electron densities on the nuclei giving rise to the various peaks. Unpaired electron spin densities may be either positive or negative according to whether the unpaired electron density is of α or β spin (spin densities usually alternate in sign along a conjugated system in a manner similar to the superexchange mechanism discussed at the end of Chapter 8). So, in a nickel(II) aminotropone-imineato complex the following unpaired electron spin densities have been calculated from the observed spectra.

$$\left[\; +0{\cdot}00073\rightarrow \;\; \text{(phenyl)}\;-\text{O}-\;\text{(ring)}\begin{array}{c}\text{Et}\\ |\\ \text{N}\\ \\ \text{N}\\ |\\ \text{Et}\end{array}\;\text{Ni}\;\right]_2$$

$-0{\cdot}00004\quad +0{\cdot}0020\quad +0{\cdot}040$

$-0{\cdot}022$

In this compound the shifts of the proton resonances were studied. The unpaired electron densities given above, however, are those at the corresponding carbon atoms. This is because there is a direct proportionality between them.

Chemical shifts.　^{59}Co resonances may be studied and it has been predicted (and roughly confirmed by experiment) that the chemical shift shown by octahedral cobalt(III) complexes should be inversely proportional to the energy separation between the $^1A_{1g}$ ground state and the lowest excited $^1T_{1g}$ state, a separation which may, of course, be observed spectroscopically. In Fig. 9-9 we give a plot of chemical shift against the wavelength of this transition (which is proportional to the inverse of the energy separation) for some octahedral Co(III) complexes. Studies on some compounds containing ^{55}Mn have yielded similar plots, but no correlation has been found for ^{195}Pt, probably because of the difficulty of interpreting the electronic spectra of the compounds.

9-4-2 Nuclear quadrupole resonance

Atoms which have nuclear spins greater than $\frac{1}{2}$ behave as if the distribution of charge within the nucleus is non-spherical. The nucleus does not behave as a dipole because the nuclear charge distribution remains centro-symmetric. It does, however, possess an electric quadrupole moment (CO_2, which is linear, is an example of a *molecule* which has an electric quadrupole moment). In an applied non-uniform electrostatic field the non-uniformly charged nucleus can take up at least two orientations (the number of orientations depends

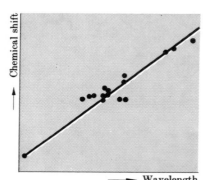

Fig. 9-9   The ^{59}Co chemical shifts shown by cobalt(III) complexes plotted against the wavelength of the corresponding $^1T_{1g} \leftarrow {}^1A_{1g}$ electronic transition.

on the magnitude of the nuclear quadrupole moment), one of which is more stable than the others. It is possible to excite the nucleus from a lower to an upper state by application of a suitable radio-frequency radiation. This is a classical description of the phenomenon, but the essentials are carried over into a quantum mechanical treatment. In practice, the non-uniform electrostatic field is generated by the local environment of the nucleus, in particular by the charge distribution about (but very close to) the nucleus. A more detailed discussion shows that any variation in field gradient at the nucleus is almost entirely due to unequal occupancy of the p orbitals of an atom.

The most studied of the nuclei which exhibit quadrupole resonance spectra are ^{35}Cl and ^{37}Cl. The method is inherently insensitive and the high concentrations of these isotopes in samples such as (solid) $K_2[PtCl_6]$ is a great advantage. The experimental data have usually been interpreted to give the percentage ionic character of a bond. This is because in Cl$^-$ all of the p orbitals are equally occupied whilst in Cl$_2$ the σ bond, if composed of p orbitals only, corresponds to one electron in the $p\sigma$ orbital of each chlorine atom, and so Cl$^-$

and Cl_2 differ in their resonance frequencies. Interpolation allows a value for the ionic character of a Cl—M bond to be determined from the chlorine frequency. Some correction may be applied to allow for the fact that a chlorine pure p orbital may not be involved in the M—Cl bond. In this way Table 9-1 was compiled.

When there are two non-equivalent chlorines in a unit cell of the solid these give rise to separate resonances which may be resolvable. In this way nuclear quadrupole resonances gives structural information. Both bromine and iodine, but not fluorine, may be studied by nuclear quadrupole resonance spectroscopy, as too may ^{14}N, ^{33}S, ^{63}Cu, ^{65}Cu, ^{75}As, ^{121}Sb, ^{123}Sn, and ^{201}Hg. A nuclear quadrupole

Table 9-1   Ionic character of the M—Cl bond in $[MCl_6]^{2-}$

Species	Ionic character of the M—Cl bond (%)
$[PtCl_6]^{2-}$	44
$[PdCl_6]^{2-}$	43
$[SnCl_6]^{2-}$	66
$[TeCl_6]^{2-}$	68
$[SeCl_6]^{2-}$	56

resonance spectrometer has recently become commercially available and is likely to lead to a considerable increase of interest in this technique.

9-4-3   Mössbauer spectroscopy

Just as there are ground and excited electronic states of an atom so too there exist both ground and excited states of nuclei. In decaying from an excited state a nucleus may emit γ-radiation (that is, light of a very short wavelength). If this γ-radiation falls upon another (identical) nucleus it may be absorbed, leaving the second nucleus in an excited state. The same nucleus in different chemical environments has slightly different energy levels, the environment-induced changes being so small that the Doppler shift of the γ-ray frequency introduced by moving the emitter either towards or away from the absorber can compensate for them. In Mössbauer spectroscopy the absorption of γ-rays by the sample is measured as a function of the velocity of the source (solid samples are used; the source may be moved by attaching it to the diaphragm of a loudspeaker driven by a suitable frequency generator). The effect has been observed for relatively few nuclei, of which ^{57}Fe and ^{119}Sn have been the most widely studied. The difference in absorption position between a sample and suitable standard is called the isomer (or chemical) shift (δ) and is usually expressed in units of either mm s^{-1} or cm s^{-1}. The chemical environment affects the nuclear energy levels through those electrons which are in orbitals which allow them to make contact with the nucleus. This means that only s electrons can directly affect isomer shifts since for all other orbitals the nucleus is contained in a nodal plane. Examples of isomer shifts (relative to a stainless-steel standard) of ^{57}Fe in some iron compounds are given in Table 9-2.

If the same nucleus has two different chemical environments in a compound, these will give rise to separate resonances. In this way it has been shown that the iron atoms in 'insoluble Berlin blue',

Table 9-2 Isomer shifts for some iron compounds at $-130°C$

Compound	Isomer shift (mm s^{-1})
High spin Fe(II)	$+0\cdot93$ to $+1\cdot01$
$K_4[Fe(CN)_6]$	$-0\cdot33$
High spin Fe(III)	$+0\cdot10$ to $+0\cdot16$
$K_3[Fe(CN)_6]$	$-0\cdot41$
K_2FeO_4	$-1\cdot20$

$Fe_4[Fe(CN)_6]_3$, which is formed by the reaction of ferric salts and ferrocyanide ions in aqueous solution, are not all equivalent but retain their distinct oxidation states.

Isomer shift data have also been used to conclude that the π-bonding ability of ligands decreases in the order

$$NO^+ > CO > CN^- > SO_3^{2-} > PPh_3 > NO_2^- > NH_3$$

A complication arises in that, if the resonant nucleus experiences a non-zero electrostatic field gradient, a quadrupole splitting of the resonance may be observed (cf. the previous section). In an octahedral environment, such as $[Fe(CN)_6]^{4-}$, there is no field gradient (the chlorine atoms we considered in the previous section were not in an octahedral environment although in an octahedral complex), but in $[Fe(CN)_6]^{2-}$ the extra electron in an e_g orbital has the effect of introducing a very temperature-dependent quadrupole splitting (it presumably operates through vibrational distortions of the octahedron). For $[Fe(CN)_5NO]^{2-}$, where there is a built-in asymmetry, the quadrupole splitting is almost temperature-independent.

9-5 Electron spin resonance spectroscopy

As was emphasized in Chapter 8, the energy level splittings caused by placing a paramagnetic ion in a magnetic field are small, and in order to give a complete account of them it is necessary to include all effects which give rise to comparable or larger splittings. This is particularly important in electron spin resonance spectroscopy, where transitions are induced (and observed) between pairs of these split energy levels.

Suppose we have a single crystal containing paramagnetic ions, held in a fixed orientation in the lattice. At any orientation of the crystal within an applied magnetic field there will, in general, be a splitting of the energy levels of the paramagnetic ion. If we now rotate the crystal (keeping the magnetic field constant) then the splittings will vary (unless the ion has perfectly octahedral symmetry). Consequently, the frequency at which resonance will occur varies with crystal orientation. This splitting may be thought of as represented by an ellipsoid, with a paramagnetic ion at the centre. As the ion is rotated, so the ellipsoid rotates with it, but at all points faithfully represents the relative splittings of the energy levels between which transitions are being observed. The ellipsoid is represented mathematically by a tensor and is referred to as a **g**-tensor, the splitting of the energy levels at any particular orientation being of the form $g\beta H$, β being the Bohr magneton and H the applied magnetic field, and it is the job of the theoretician to explain its properties in terms of a suitable model. A superimposed effect is often caused by the interaction of nuclear spins with the unpaired electron(s). Effectively, the crystal consists of several sets of equivalent ions, the sets being distinguished by virtue of the unique orientation of a nuclear spin (or of the effect of several nuclear spins) that each of them has. Each set gives rise to its own resonances and a many-line spectrum is observed.

The interpretation of an electron spin resonance (e.s.r.) spectrum may involve all the parameters introduced in our discussion of magnetic susceptibilities and so information may be obtained about them. Further, in a powdered sample, magnetic susceptibility measurements lead only to an average **g** value, whereas e.s.r. measurements can give the individual components of the **g**-tensor and so provide a more stringent test of the theory.* The individual components can also be derived, in suitable cases, from e.s.r. measurements on samples in solution.

There are snags, however. E.s.r. spectra can usually be observed only for ions which have spin-degenerate ground states in the absence of a magnetic field, i.e. for molecules with an odd number

---

* In Table 8-2 the g value for each Kramer's doublet is, for each doublet, equal to the separation between members of the doublet (shown in the $E_n(1)$ column) divided by βH. Thus for E_3(a) and E_3(b) $g = 2$ whilst for the other pairs $g = 0$ (more strictly, these are the values of $g_{\parallel}$).

of unpaired electrons, the observed spectra then consisting of transitions between members of this Kramer's doublet (Section 8-4). Further, there are often peak-broadening phenomena which can only be overcome by working at very low temperatures, perhaps as low as that of liquid helium. These are particularly severe when the ground state has another orbital level above it not very far (ca kT) removed in energy. Thus, it is very difficult to observe spectra of titanium(III) (d^1), for which the ground state is derived from the $^2T_{2g}$ octahedral state by application of spin–orbit coupling and low symmetry crystal field perturbations. Here the ground state is usually such that it has two orbital (four spin–orbital) states not far removed from it because of their common $^2T_{2g}$ parentage (as we saw in Section 8-7). Mangenese(II) (d^5), however, with its high spin $^6A_{1g}$ ground state, gives room temperature spectra. Another broadening mechanism may occur if the paramagnetic species is at all concentrated. For this reason, 'single crystal' data are usually obtained on a crystal of a diamagnetic compound, isomorphous with that under study, in which a very low concentration of the paramagnetic species is incorporated as an 'impurity'.

We mentioned earlier that e.s.r. spectra may show fine structure due to interaction between the inpaired electron(s) and nuclei with non-zero spin. These nuclei may be those of the paramagnetic ion (for example ^{55}Mn, with spin $\frac{5}{2}$, which has a 100% natural abundance) or those of the ligand. E.s.r. spectra of copper(II) complexes with nitrogen ligands show evidence for interactions of this sort and have been extensively studied. The best-known example, however, is that of the e.s.r. spectrum of the $[IrCl_6]^{2-}$ ion (this is a strong field complex of Ir(IV), which has a d^5 configuration), incorporated as an 'impurity' in a crystal of $Na_2[PtCl_6]6H_2O$. The fine structure observed (Fig. 9-10) can be interpreted in terms of interaction with the (^{35}Cl and ^{37}Cl) nuclei of the ligands.

Such observations provide excellent evidence for covalency in transition metal complexes, emphasizing the superiority of the molecular orbital method over the crystal field approach (it appears that the unpaired electron in $[IrCl_6]^{2-}$ spends about 5% of its time on each ligand).

This is a convenient point at which to bring together the various pieces of evidence indicating covalency in transition metal complex ions. They are:

   1. Ligand hyperfine splittings in e.s.r. spectra, discussed above.

   2. The percentage of ionic character in metal—chlorine bonds as measured by nuclear quadrupole resonance spectroscopy (Section 9-4-2).

3. Unpaired electron spin densities on ligand atoms as measured by n.m.r. spectroscopy (Section 9-4-1).

4. The superexchange mechanism of anitiferromagnetic coupling which allows the electrons on one atom to 'see' the spin of those on another and which operates through their mutual overlap with a ligand atom (Section 8-10).

5. The orbital reduction factor k which has to be introduced to allow for the effect of covalency on the magnetic properties of ions (Section 8-6).

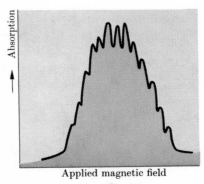

Fig. 9-10   The e.s.r. spectrum of a crystal of $Na_2[PtCl_6]6H_2O$ containing the isostructural compound $Na_2[IrCl_6]6H_2O$ as an impurity.

6. The reduction in spin–orbit coupling constants in a complex compared with the free ion (Section 8-3).

7. The reduction in electron repulsion energies (the nephelauxetic effect) in a complex compared with their values for the free ion (Sections 7-2 and 7-3).

8. Band intensities. Some spectral bands have intensities other than those which might be expected in terms of a purely ionic model. This evidence tends to be more speculative than the others listed above, and we have not discussed the matter in the text. There are three band intensity anomalies which may be taken to indicate covalency: (*i*) *d–d* electronic transitions are more intense when close to charge-transfer bands. This is indicative of mixing between the two transitions which implies covalency within the M—L bonds (Section 7-7); (*ii*) some metal–ligand stretching vibrations have much lower infrared intensities than would be expected for vibrating, non-overlapping, charged atoms (Section 9-2-2); and (*iii*) the optical

activity introduced into formally d–d electronic transitions by an optically active ligand may be greater than expected (Sections 2-4-10 and 9-3).

9-6 Molar conductivities

In water, equivalent ionic conductivities (the contribution of an ion to the equivalent conductance of a salt at infinite dilution) are about 60 ohm^{-1} at 20°C for each species (large inorganic ions give lower values, and H$^+$ and OH$^-$, for which chain conduction mechanisms are available, give higher values). As a first approximation, then, we would expect the contribution to the *molar* conductivity of an ion I$^{l\pm}$ to be about $60l$ ohm^{-1}. For ions M^{m+} and X^{n-} in the salt M$_n$X$_m$, the contributions will be $60m$ ohm^{-1} (from M^{m+}) and $60n$ ohm^{-1} (from X^{n-}). Multiplying by the number of ions of each sort and adding leads us to the conclusion that a salt M$_n$X$_m$ will have a molar conductivity of about $120nm$ ohm^{-1} at 20°C. So, CoCl$_3$·5NH$_3$ has a molar conductance of 261 ohm^{-1} and we may conclude that it is [Co(NH$_3$)$_5$Cl]Cl$_2$, with $nm = 2$. Similarly, CoCl$_3$·5NH$_3$·H$_2$O has a molar conductance of 390 ohm^{-1} and so is [Co(NH$_3$)$_5$H$_2$O]Cl$_3$, with $nm = 3$.

Water is a coordinating solvent and, particularly for labile complexes, is best avoided for conductivity measurements. Nitrobenzene and nitromethane are commonly used alternatives although solubility problems sometimes arise. The usual procedure is to measure the conductivity at a concentration of *ca* 10^{-4} molar and (assuming a molecular weight) to compare the value with that obtained for similar complexes of known ion type (1:1, 1:2 etc.). A rather better method is to make measurements over a range of concentrations and to plot $(\lambda_0 - \lambda_e(c))$, where $\lambda_e(c)$ is the equivalent conductivity at concentration c and λ_0 is the equivalent conductivity at infinite dilution, against $\sqrt{c}$. Again, this plot is compared with those obtained for similar species in the same solvent. The equivalent weight of the complex is needed for this method and this may be obtained by choosing a suitable counter-ion for the complex species. The potassium ion is a suitable cation and the perchlorate a suitable anion. Neither of them is often involved in coordination and so, assuming that this is the case for the complex under study, the equivalent weight of the complex may be obtained from its empirical formula.

9-7 Conclusion

In this chapter we have briefly reviewed some of the more important methods of studying coordination compounds. The detailed interpretation of the experimental results is rather difficult, and, for the phenomena of optical activity and nuclear quadrupole resonance spectroscopy, for example, the theory of the method has only been worked out incompletely. We have, therefore, confined discussion to the qualitative level, considering it important that the student should have a pictorial idea of the phenomena considered. In this way he is both made aware of which technique is likely to be of use in tackling a particular problem and of some of the difficulties associated with it.

Problems

9-1   A compound of empirical formula $Fe(acac)_2Cl$ is formed by refluxing together appropriate quantities of $[Fe(acac)_3]$ and $FeCl_3$ in chloroform and might, for example, be a five-coordinate species or an octahedral binuclear complex with bridging chlorine atoms. Which of the methods discussed in this chapter might be expected to provide information on its structure (which is not, at present, known)?

9-2   Discuss the statement 'Ligand field theory explains experimental data better than does crystal field theory only because it has more adjustable parameters.'

9-3   Discuss the use of infrared spectroscopy as a method of determining the stereochemistry of a coordination complex.

9-4   Explain what is meant by the 'Cotton effect.' What information may a study of the effect provide?

9-5   Describe in detail the evidence for covalency in coordination compounds.

9-6   Outline the ways in which a study of nuclear energy levels can provide chemical information.

10 Thermodynamic and related aspects of crystal fields

10-1 Introduction

One of the earliest applications of crystal field theory was to use it to explain irregularities observed in thermodynamic and related properties of a series of transition metal complexes as the transition metal was varied. These applications of the theory are usually dealt with in one of the early chapters of a book such as this; we have deferred their consideration in order to be able to draw upon the concepts introduced in Chapters 5 and 6.

10-2 Ionic radii

The crystals of simple salts such as NaCl and ZnS have lattices which are often regarded as ionic. That this approximation is plausible is indicated by, amongst other things, the fact that it is possible to ascribe ionic radii to the component ions and to use the additivity of these radii to predict interionic distances.* Crystal field theory similarly assumes that the forces between a transition metal cation and the surrounding ligands are purely electrostatic. The theory suggests, therefore, that it should be possible to obtain values for the ionic radii of transition metal ions from crystallographic data.

How might these radii be expected to vary from one ion to the next? If we neglect crystal field effects, the essential difference between pairs of ions such as Ti^{3+} and V^{3+}, V^{3+} and Cr^{3+}, and so on, is that the second member has an extra positive charge on its nucleus and an extra, compensating, d electron. As a first approximation, therefore, we might expect no change in ionic radii. Recognizing the incomplete screening of the additional positive charge by the additional electron, however, a small decrease in ionic radius seems more probable. These qualitative ideas find support in the gradual

---

* It is not generally recognized that although the ionic radius approach is reasonably self-consistent the radii discussed may not correspond to physical reality. For example, in the KCl crystal the minimum of electron density along the K–Cl axis is ca 1·45 Å from the potassium and 1·70 Å from the chlorine, compared with ionic radii of 1·33 Å and 1·81 Å respectively. However, the (presumably) more accurate radius of 1·70 Å for Cl^- is not constant but varies from compound to compound and so the additivity is lost.

decrease in ionic radius exhibited by successive trivalent ions in the lanthanide series—the so-called 'lanthanide contraction'. This is shown in Fig. 10-1 together with the metal–ligand separation in halides of the first transition series. By plotting metal–ligand separation we avoid making an assumption about the ionic radius of the halide ion. We have omitted values for copper(II) compounds from this diagram. These complexes are usually highly distorted, so that Cu—X distances both greater and smaller than the values predicted by interpolation of the data for adjacent ions have been reported. The smooth curves which we anticipated do not appear in

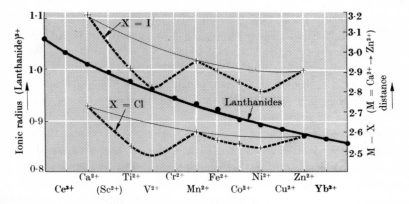

Fig. 10-1   The lanthanide contraction and metal–halogen distances for divalent first-row transition and related metal ions. The dotted lines indicate the probable values for the M–X distances corrected for crystal field effects.

Fig. 10-1. There is a simple explanation of this which becomes evident when we include crystal field effects. In the absence of a crystal field all of the metal d orbitals are degenerate and, therefore, effectively equally occupied. Application of an octahedral crystal field removes the degeneracy, so that the t_{2g} set is preferentially filled. This means that the d electrons are preferentially placed in orbitals which do not screen the ligands from the increased (attractive) nuclear charge as we go from one metal ion to the next. When an electron is placed in an e_g orbital, however, it has an enhanced screening effect, because these orbitals are concentrated along the metal–ligand axes. For a d^5 (high spin) configuration all of the d orbitals are equally occupied and the screening is the same as it would have been in the absence of a crystal field. It follows that the additional screening of an electron in an e_g orbital compensates for the deficiencies in the screening of one and a half electrons in the t_{2g} orbitals. We therefore expect the deviation of ionic radii from that given by the simple picture to be in the order:

$$t_{2g}^6 > t_{2g}^5 > t_{2g}^6 e_g > t_{2g}^4 > t_{2g}^3 \simeq t_{2g}^6 e_g^2 > t_{2g}^2 \simeq t_{2g}^5 e_g^2 > t_{2g}^6 e_g^3 \simeq t_{2g}^3 e_g$$
$$> t_{2g}^1 \simeq t_2^4 e_g^2 > t_{2g}^3 e_g^2 = t_{2g}^6 e_g^4 = 0$$

Remembering that all the examples given in Fig. 10-1 are high spin, it will be seen that this series is followed quite well. The only exception appears to be d^7 (h.s.) cobalt(II) for X $=$ I$^-$. However, as we have already recognized (Section 5-5), this ion has the configuration $t_{2g}^{24/5} e_g^{11/5}$ in the weak field limit (I$^-$ is a very weak field ligand) which, together with d^2 (h.s.), $t_{2g}^{9/5} e_g^{1/5}$, should be placed with the configurations $t_{2g}^6 e_g^3$ and $t_{2g}^3 e_g$ in the above series. In practice, high spin cobalt(II) complexes have configurations intermediate between $t_{2g}^{24/5} e_g^{11/5}$ and $t_{2g}^5 e_g^2$ and so occupy variable positions in the series. This leads us to predict that, when data are available for the vanadium(II)—iodide bond length, that for titanium(II)—iodide will be found to be similarly out of line.

10-3 Heats of ligation

We introduced crystal field theory in Chapter 5 by considering a free, gaseous, ion and then placing it in an octahedral crystal field. The heat released in this hypothetical process is known as the *heat of ligation* (the ligands are similarly assumed to originate as free, gaseous, molecules). Values of the heat of ligation may be obtained from experimental data on reactions in solution by the use of suitable energy cycles. The heat of ligation is conveniently broken down into several parts. Thus, within a purely electrostatic model, the most important term is the stabilization resulting from the attraction between the ligand and transition metal ion. A destabilization results from the electrostatic repulsion between the ligands themselves—the effect of this term is to cause a decrease in the increments of energy liberated as additional ligands are added to the central atom. Because the energy released when two point charges of opposite sign are brought together from infinity depends inversely upon their final separation, we would expect the major, stabilizing, term to be modulated by the changes in ionic radius discussed in the previous section. There is, however, another term which changes from one transition metal ion to another, as the following hypothetical sequence demonstrates. Form an octahedral complex ion from its infinitely separated components, so that the final metal–ligand distance is that observed in the complex. Energy will be liberated, most of which is lost from the molecule. Suppose that sufficient is retained for the split d orbitals each to be equally populated (that is, the electron distribution is identical with that in the free ion). At this state in the process the energy lost will differ from one transition-metal ion to another only by virtue of a) their different effective nuclear charges (a d electron, even if fully delocalized in the set of d orbitals, does not exactly offset a unit increase in the nuclear charge) and b) the different metal–ligand distances. Of these, the former would be expected to vary smoothly along the series. Now, let the d electrons in the complex assume their ground-state configuration. An additional increment of energy will be liberated if, in the ground state, the d orbitals are not equally occupied. This

Table 10-1   Crystal field stabilization energies for weak field octahedral complexes

d^n configuration	Crystal field configuration	Crystal field stabilization energy
d^0		0
d^1	t_{2g}^1	$-\frac{2}{5}\Delta$
d^2	$\left\{\begin{array}{l} t_{2g}^2 \\ t_{2g}^{9/5}e_g^{1/5} \end{array}\right.$	$-\frac{4}{5}\Delta$ $-\frac{3}{5}\Delta$
d^3	t_{2g}^3	$-\frac{6}{5}\Delta$
d^4	$t_{2g}^3 e_g$	$-\frac{3}{5}\Delta$
d^5	$t_{2g}^3 e_g^2$	0
d^6	$t_{2g}^4 e_g^2$	$-\frac{2}{5}\Delta$
d^7	$\left\{\begin{array}{l} t_{2g}^5 e_g^2 \\ t_{2g}^{24/5}e_g^{11/5} \end{array}\right.$	$-\frac{4}{5}\Delta$ $-\frac{3}{5}\Delta$
d^8	$t_{2g}^6 e_g^2$	$-\frac{6}{5}\Delta$
d^9	$t_{2g}^6 e_g^3$	$-\frac{3}{5}\Delta$
d^{10}	$t_{2g}^6 e_g^4$	0

energy, the so-called 'crystal field stabilization energy', will be different for different metal ions. It is a simple matter to calculate crystal field stabilization energies for they depend only on the electron configuration and the magnitude of the crystal field splitting, Δ. An electron confined to the t_{2g} set contributes a stabilization of $-\frac{2}{5}\Delta$, one confined to the e_g set contributes a destabilization of $\frac{3}{5}\Delta$ (see Fig. 5-10). Crystal field stabilization energies for weak field octahedral complexes are listed in Table 10-1. A similar table can be constructed for strong field complexes but an additional destabilizing term, allowing for the pairing energy of two d electrons, would have to be included. The presence of this term makes the interpretation of the experimental data more difficult, and we confine our discussion to weak field complexes. In Fig. 10-2 we show the variation of heats of ligation with transition metal for the case where the ligand is water—that is, Fig. 10-2 shows heats of hydration. The data are most complete for this ligand, but the available data for other ligands indicate a similar behaviour. The deviations from a curve drawn through the data for calcium(II), manganese(II) and zinc(II) are in good agreement with the crystal field stabilization energies given in Table 10-1. Indeed, if one 'corrects' for the crystal field stabilization energies, using this table and the spectroscopic value of Δ, then the points fall on an almost straight line. For vanadium(II) and cobalt(II) two points are shown, corresponding to stabilizations of $-\frac{3}{5}\Delta$ and $-\frac{4}{5}\Delta$. The curve passes between these limits. This relationship between experimental and 'corrected' values of the heats of ligation has led to the suggestion that it may be used as a method

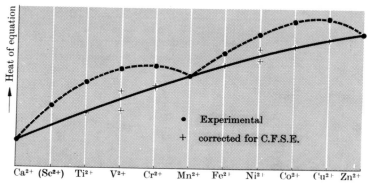

Fig. 10-2   Heats of hydration of first-row transition metal ions.

for obtaining approximate values of Δ. However, our discussion suggests that the agreement that is found with spectroscopic values of Δ is somewhat fortuitous, for the ionic radius effect must be superimposed on the crystal field stabilization contributions in Fig. 10-2. Further, we have made several assumptions in our discussion. In particular, we have overlooked the fact that, when the randomized arrangement of d electrons changes to the ground-state arrangement, there is an increase in the effective charge 'seen' on the cation by the ligands—the number of e_g electrons screening the nucleus decreases. Accordingly, there will be a change in the electrostatic energy. This emphasizes the interrelationship between effects which we have discussed separately. However, since the contributions to the total energy arising from the variation in metal–ligand distances and the crystal field stabilizations act in the same direction (compare the inequalities given in Section 10-1 with the relative magnitude of stabilization energies in Table 10-1), the essential point is that the seemingly rather erratic nature of the experimental data in Fig. 10-2 may be understood in terms of simple crystal field theory.

10-4   Lattice energies

In the previous section we discussed an isolated octahedral complex ion. Ionic lattices, in which the structure consists of interconnected octahedra, tetrahedra or other geometrical arrangements of ligands, when regarded as coordination compounds, may be similarly treated. Here, the lattice energy replaces the heat of ligation as the experimental quantity under discussion. A complication arises when the members of a series of compounds which one wishes to study are not isomorphous, that is, they crystallize with different structures (possibly in part due to the irregularities in ionic radii). Detailed

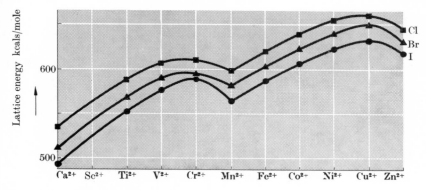

Fig. 10-3   Lattice energies of the dihalides of transition metal and related elements.

consideration of this particular case indicates that the differences in lattice energy caused by this are fairly small and may be neglected as a first approximation. In this way the data shown in Fig. 10-3 were compiled. The now-familiar pattern is repeated; its interpretation closely follows that of the previous section and again provides good qualitative support for the simple crystal field theory.

10-5   Site preference energies

We have seen that the crystal field stabilization energy is a relatively small component of the total energy involved in the formation of a complex in the gas phase—compare the 'corrections' in Fig. 10-2 with the total energy involved, as indicated by the scale of the ordinate. In a more realistic situation, when, say, the hexaquonickel(II) cation is converted into trisethylenediaminenickel(II), there will be a change in crystal field stabilization energy because water and ethylenediamine exert rather different crystal fields (the complexes are green and purple, respectively). However, the major energetic change is due to the difference in other features of the two complexes, notably the difference in electrostatic attraction between Ni^{2+} and a water and an ethylenediamine molecule (there are also entropy and heat terms which favour the formation of the ethylenediamine complex—these were discussed in Section 4-5). Unless it is certain that these changes are zero, or at least very small, any argument based on crystal field stabilization energies alone must be regarded with suspicion. If they lead to predictions which agree with experiment, this may be because the changes of crystal field stabilization energy parallel the major energy changes rather than because the crystal field stabilization energy is the determining factor.

Table 10-2   Crystal field stabilization energies for tetrahedral complexes and comparison with high spin octahedral complexes

d-electron configuration	Tetrahedral field configuration	Crystal field stabilization energies Tetrahedral field		Octahedral field	(Octahedral) site preference energy
d^0		0		0	0
d^1	e^1	$-\frac{3}{5}\Delta_{tet.}$	$= -\frac{4}{15}\Delta_{oct.}$	$-\frac{6}{15}\Delta_{oct.}$	$\frac{2}{15}\Delta_{oct.}$
d^2	e^2	$-\frac{6}{5}\Delta_{tet.}$	$= -\frac{8}{15}\Delta_{oct.}$	$-\frac{12}{15}\Delta_{oct.}$	$\frac{4}{15}\Delta_{oct.}$
d^3	$e^2 t_2^1$	$-\frac{4}{5}\Delta_{tet.}$	$= -\frac{16}{45}\Delta_{oct.}$	$-\frac{54}{45}\Delta_{oct.}$	$\frac{38}{45}\Delta_{oct.}$
d^4	$e^2 t_2^2$	$-\frac{2}{5}\Delta_{tet.}$	$= -\frac{8}{45}\Delta_{oct.}$	$-\frac{27}{45}\Delta_{oct.}$	$\frac{19}{45}\Delta_{oct.}$
d^5	$e^2 t_2^3$	0		0	0
d^6	$e^3 t_2^3$	$-\frac{3}{5}\Delta_{tet.}$	$= -\frac{4}{15}\Delta_{oct.}$	$-\frac{6}{15}\Delta_{oct.}$	$\frac{2}{15}\Delta_{oct.}$
d^7	$e^4 t_2^3$	$-\frac{6}{5}\Delta_{tet.}$	$= -\frac{8}{15}\Delta_{oct.}$	$-\frac{12}{15}\Delta_{oct.}$	$\frac{4}{15}\Delta_{oct.}$
d^8	$e^4 t_2^4$	$-\frac{4}{5}\Delta_{tet.}$	$= -\frac{16}{45}\Delta_{oct.}$	$-\frac{54}{45}\Delta_{oct.}$	$\frac{38}{45}\Delta_{oct.}$
d^9	$e^4 t_2^5$	$-\frac{2}{5}\Delta_{tet.}$	$= -\frac{8}{45}\Delta_{oct.}$	$-\frac{27}{45}\Delta_{oct.}$	$\frac{19}{45}\Delta_{oct.}$
d^{10}	$e^4 t_2^6$	0		0	0

An exception to this is when one compares a series of related ions, for which all energy factors other than crystal field stabilization energies would be expected to vary smoothly and slowly along the series. In this case, the *differences* between members of the series may be largely determined by crystal field stabilization energies.

An example of this sort of use of crystal field stabilization energies is the following. Just as we obtained a table of stabilization energies for weak field octahedral complexes, so we can obtain one for tetrahedral complexes. A simplified version is given in Table 10-2 in terms of $\Delta_{tet.}$ and, remembering that $\Delta_{tet.} \simeq \frac{4}{9}\Delta_{oct.}$, also in terms of $\Delta_{oct.}$. The corresponding values for weak field octahedral complexes are also included. It can be seen that the octahedral stabilization energies are invariably greater than the corresponding values for tetrahedral complexes, unless both are zero. The difference—the (octahedral) site preference energy—is given in the final column of Table 10-2. For d^3 and d^8 ions it is particularly large. This has led to the suggestion that it is the cause of the relative rarity of tetrahedral complexes of chromium(III) (d^3) and nickel(II) (d^8). Since this suggestion was first made many tetrahedral complexes of nickel(II) have been prepared (the simplest to make is $[NiCl_4]^{2-}$, which is formed when $NiCl_2$ is added to molten $NaCl$) and examples of tetrahedral chromium(III) complexes have been claimed.

To put this suggestion into perspective, let us consider the complexes $[Cr(H_2O)_6]^{3+}$ and $[Cr(H_2O)_4]^{3+}$. The heat of hydration for the former is approximately 1,410 kcal mol^{-1} and its crystal field stabilization energy 84 kcal mol^{-1}, calculated using the spectroscopic value of Δ. Assuming that 1,410/6 kcal mol^{-1} is the energy of a $Cr—H_2O$ bond, the difference in heats of hydration of the two species is 470 kcal mol^{-1}. To this must be added the crystal field stabilization contribution of $\frac{38}{45} \times \frac{5}{6} \times 84 = 71$ kcal mol^{-1}, to give a total heat of hydration of $[Cr(H_2O)_4]^{3+}$ to $[Cr(H_2O)_6]^{3+}$ of 541 kcal mol^{-1}. Of this, approximately 13% is the contribution from the crystal field stabilization term. This is a crude, order-of-magnitude, calculation, but it indicates that, whilst the crystal field stabilization term is not negligible, it is by no means the dominant factor in determining the relative stabilities of the two species (note that we have neglected the entropy term, which is also of importance). However, such data may be used to explain why, for example, cobalt(II) forms tetrahedral complexes more readily than does nickel(II).

Another use of site preference energies is their application to the spinels. Spinel itself is a mineral of composition $MgAl_2O_4$ and may be considered the progenor of a class of 'mixed oxides' of composition $M^{2+}M_2^{3+}O_4^{2-}$ which are referred to as 'the spinels'. The oxide anions are arranged in a cubic close-packed lattice. Like all close-packed lattices, there are two sorts of hole between the close-packed atoms. These are 'tetrahedral' and 'octahedral' holes, so called because they occur between four and six anions which have these geometrical arrangements, respectively. There are twice as many tetrahedral holes as there are octahedral holes, and there is one of the latter for each anion. The holes are large enough to be filled by cations. In MgO, for example, each octahedral hole in a cubic close-packed arrangement of oxide anions is filled by a magnesium cation to give a sodium chloride lattice. One might reasonably expect a similar arrangement in the spinels, with the divalent cations occupying octahedral holes, for these are larger than the tetrahedral holes. In fact, the structure is not as simple as this. There are two main classes of spinels. In 'normal' spinels, the divalent cations are in tetrahedral holes. As is evident from what has been said, they occupy one in eight of the available tetrahedral holes. The trivalent cations occupy one-half of the available octahedral holes. In the 'inverted' spinels the divalent cations *are* in octahedral holes, having changed places with one-half of the trivalent ions. So, spinels with $M^{3+} = Cr^{3+}$ are normal and most of those with $M^{2+} = Ni^{2+}$ are inverted. Similarly, Fe_3O_4 ($Fe^{2+}Fe_2^{3+}O_4^{2-}$) is inverted, but Mn_3O_4 and Co_3O_4 are normal. The problem is to decide what determines the structure that is adopted.

Table 10-3

M^{2+} High spin configuration	Octahedral site preference energy	M^{3+} High spin configuration	Octahedral site preference energy		Difference in site preference energies	Predicted spinel type
$d^1,\ d^6$	$\frac{2}{5}\Delta(M^{2+})$	$d^0,\ d^5$	0	0	$\frac{2}{5}\Delta(M^{2+})$	Inverted
$d^2,\ d^7$	$\frac{4}{15}\Delta(M^{2+})$	$d^1,\ d^6$	$\frac{2}{15}\Delta(M^{3+})$	$\simeq \frac{1}{5}\Delta(M^{2+})$	$\frac{1}{15}\Delta(M^{2+})$	Inverted
$d^3,\ d^8$	$\frac{38}{45}\Delta(M^{2+})$	$d^2,\ d^7$	$\frac{4}{15}\Delta(M^{3+})$	$\simeq \frac{2}{5}\Delta(M^{2+})$	$\frac{4}{9}\Delta(M^{2+})$	Inverted
$d^4,\ d^9$	$\frac{19}{45}\Delta(M^{2+})$	$d^3,\ d^8$	$\frac{38}{45}\Delta(M^{3+})$	$\simeq \frac{19}{15}\Delta(M^{2+})$	$\frac{38}{45}\Delta(M^{2+})$	Normal
$d^5,\ d^{10}$	0	$d^4,\ d^9$	$\frac{19}{45}\Delta(M^{3+})$	$\simeq \frac{19}{30}\Delta(M^{2+})$	$\frac{19}{30}\Delta(M^{2+})$	Normal

First, we must consider the large cation–anion attraction terms. This is more difficult than for an isolated complex ion, for these terms, together with the cation–cation and anion–anion repulsion terms, must be summed over the whole lattice to give the Madelung constants for normal and inverted spinels. Such calculations have been made and indicate that the two structures have very similar energies. It is therefore reasonable that site preference energies should play an important part in determining which structure is adopted. It is at once understandable that both Cr^{3+} and Ni^{2+} should be located in octahedral holes, and their spinels be normal and inverted respectively.

The essential difference between normal and inverted spinels is the interchange of M^{2+} and half of the M^{3+} between octahedral and tetrahedral sites. If site preference energies are the only important factor, the spinel will be inverted if the octahedral site preference energy of M^{2+} is greater than that of M^{3+}. Consider spinels like Fe_3O_4, where M^{2+} and M^{3+} are ions of the same element differing only in charge. As a (crude) approximation, we will set $\Delta_{oct.}(M^{3+}) = \frac{3}{2}\Delta_{oct.}(M^{2+})$. Using Table 10-2, we derive the data in Table 10-3, in which we also predict the type of spinel lattice adopted. It will be remembered that Mn_3O_4(Mn^{2+} is d^5) is normal and Fe_3O_4(Fe^{2+} is d^6) is inverted, as predicted. Co_3O_4(Co^{2+} is d^7) is normal, but is predicted to be inverted. However, the energy difference between the two forms for d^2 and d^7 is only $\frac{1}{15}\Delta_{oct.}(M^{2+})$, so that the prediction that these configurations will give rise to inverted spinels is hardly to be regarded as reliable. For Co_3O_4 and other cases which do not follow the simple predictions, more detailed analysis leads to agreement with experiment. It will be noted that we have had to assume high spin configurations throughout this discussion. The presence of low spin configurations would introduce the complication of pairing energies.

10-6   Conclusions

In this chapter we have used chemical intuition and some rather crude approximations to make predictions based on crystal field theory. Although no one piece of evidence is really definitive, taken together they provide strong support for the simple crystal field approach. It should be emphasized that crystal field stabilization energies must be used with great care and with due regard to their limitations.

Problems

10-1   Explain carefully what is meant by 'Crystal field stabilization energy'. How would you measure it for an octahedral complex of vanadium(III)? Under what conditions does it become of energetic importance?

10-2   Write an essay on the structure of Fe_3O_4 (Section 8-10 should be consulted).

10-3   Give a detailed explanation of the lattice energy data given in Fig. 10-3.

10-4   The ionic radii of the lanthanides show no sign of a crystal field effect whilst those of ions of the first transition series do (Fig. 10-1). Discuss the factors responsible for this difference.

10-5   Given that $e^2/r \sim 330$ kcal mol^{-1} for $r = 1$ Å, calculate the approximate energetic consequences of the variation of interatomic separation shown for ions of the first transition series in Fig. 10-1. Compare your results with the data in Fig. 10-2. (It may be helpful to re-read Section 6-5.)

10-6   Give an account of the factors influencing the stereochemistry of complexes of (a) a main group element, and (b) a transition element. (Chapters 4, 6 and 7 contain relevant material.)

11 Reaction kinetics of coordination compounds

11-1 Introduction

We have already encountered the distinction between inert and labile complexes. A convenient dividing line may be drawn by defining inert complexes as those for which reactions may be studied by classical techniques, i.e. where $t_{1/2}$ values are greater than about one minute at 25°C for concentrations of ca 0·1 M. Labile complexes are not so readily studied and less is known about the kinetics of their reactions.

Reactions of inert complexes are usually studied by mixing solutions of the reactants and monitoring either the appearance of a product species or disappearance of a reactant by some suitable technique. It is difficult to mix two solutions completely in less than a millisecond (and only then in some sort of flow system) and this limits the extent to which technical ingenuity may be used to apply classical techniques to fast reactions.

Some further extension is possible by working at low temperatures with very dilute solutions, but for very fast reactions quite different methods must be used. The simplest has already been mentioned (Section 4-3): if a stepwise equilibrium constant is known, together with the rate of either the forward or backward reaction, then the other rate may be determined. Other methods study an equilibrium and we shall give two examples. Suppose that a complex containing coordinated trimethylamine is dissolved in trimethylamine and its proton magnetic resonance spectrum studied. If the coordinated trimethylamine exchanges with the solvent slowly, then two resonances will be observed (provided that complicating features are absent), one due to coordinated and the other due to free trimethylamine. If the exchange is rapid only one resonance will be observed. In favourable cases, if the temperature of the sample is varied, both cases will be observed (when it will be found that the position of the single resonance is a concentration, i.e. peak area weighted, average of those of the two) as will be the intermediate region, in which broad peaks occur. From such measurements one may obtain the rate of exchange at the temperature for which intermediate behaviour is observed. Strictly speaking, the terms 'slow' and 'rapid' in this example are relative to the n.m.r. time-scale and this depends on the energy separation between the peaks due to coordinated and solvent trimethylamine. If the complex is paramagnetic, additional line-broadening and shifts occur. These may be analysed to give rate data but are somewhat ambiguous, since it is the slower of two processes which is measured. These are the exchange process in which we are interested, and that of a change in the nuclear spin state of the protons of the coordinated ligand. Measurements with a different but similar ligand may establish which process is the slower, but often one has to be content with being able only to put a limit on the rate of the exchange process.

A most important approach to the study of fast reactions involves relaxation phenomena. The position of dynamic equilibrium in a system depends not only on reactant concentrations but also on such quantities as temperature and pressure and even electric field gradient (if present). If one of these is suddenly changed the position of equilibrium will also change and, with sensitive instruments, this change may be detected. The speed with which the new equilibrium is reached depends on reaction rates which may thus be measured. In this way Eigen and his co-workers have determined unimolecular rate constants greater than 10^9 s^{-1}, which is approaching the limit for diffusion-controlled reactions.

11-2   Electron-transfer reactions

The simplest class of reaction of coordination compounds which has been studied is that of *electron-transfer reactions*. Suppose that a solution of potassium ferrocyanide is mixed with one of potassium ferricyanide, then, if a $[Fe(CN)_6]^{4-}$ anion loses an electron and a $[Fe(CN)_6]^{3-}$ anion gains one, a chemical reaction has occurred, although there is no change in the composition of the mixture. If one of the atoms in one of the complex ions is labelled in some way—with ^{14}C, for example—then the reaction may be studied. In this particular case the reaction is fast, the second-order rate constant being *ca* 10^5 at 25°C. This rate is much greater than those of reactions involving ligand exchange of either species, so a simple electron-transfer mechanism is indicated. Because there is no net chemical reaction there is no heat change associated with the electron transfer.

The Fe—C bond in $[Fe(CN)_6]^{3-}$ is slightly shorter than that in $[Fe(CN)_6]^{4-}$, so, if an electron were to be transferred between the anions in their ground-state equilibrium configurations, by the Franck–Condon principle, the product $[Fe(CN)_6]^{3-}$ would be expanded and the $[Fe(CN)_6]^{4-}$ compressed relative to these configurations. That is, the products would be of higher energy than the reactants, contradicting the requirement of zero heat change. It follows that an electron-exchange reaction will only occur between precisely matched molecules which are vibrationally excited (although it should be noted that transfer would not occur between $[Fe(CN)_6]^{4-}$ and $[Fe(CN)_6]^{3-}$ anions, which are, respectively, compressed and expanded into each other's equilibrium geometry). It is not essential that two matched anions are in contact at the instant of electron transfer—the electron lost is not the same as the one gained and so such electron-exchange reactions are often referred to as occurring by a *tunnelling* or *outer sphere* mechanism.

However, it is reasonable to expect that electron transfer will occur most readily when the two reacting species are relatively close together. That this is so is indicated by the observation that outer-sphere electron-transfer reactions are more rapid for complexes containing ligands such as *o*-phenanthroline and the cyanide anion than for corresponding complexes with ligands such as H_2O or NH_3. That is, a ligand over which a 'metal' electron may be extensively delocalized (cf. Chapter 6) significantly reduces the magnitude of the barrier to electron transfer (one may draw an analogy with a current flowing through a piece of resistance wire; replacing part of the resistance wire by a piece of copper wire increases the current).

In the example discussed above, the electron configuration of the iron atom in the $[Fe(CN)_6]^{4-}$ anion is t_{2g}^6 and that in the $[Fe(CN)_6]^{3-}$ anion is t_{2g}^5. Removal of an 'iron' electron from $[Fe(CN)_6]^{4-}$ leaves a t_{2g}^5 configuration and addition of one to $[Fe(CN)_6]^{3-}$ gives a t_{2g}^6 configuration. It is not always as simple as this. Consider an electron-transfer reaction between a molecule of a cobalt(III) complex and one of cobalt(II), both octahedrally coordinated. Cobalt(III) complexes are usually low spin and cobalt(II) are high spin, so the electron configuration of the cobalt atoms will be: cobalt(III) t_{2g}^6, cobalt(II) $t_{2g}^5 e_g^2$. After transfer of an electron from cobalt(II) to cobalt(III) these configurations will presumably become $t_{2g}^6 e_g$ and $t_{2g}^5 e_g$ (cobalt(II) and cobalt(III), respectively). However, these are not the ground-state configurations of the ions. That is, after the electron-transfer reaction both complexes will be electronically excited (this excess of energy will rapidly be lost either by radiation or, more probably, it will be converted into thermal energy). Because this electronic energy contributes to the activation energy of the process, the rate of electron-transfer reactions between cobalt(II) and cobalt(III) complexes is much slower than that between the $[Fe(CN)_6]^{3-}$ and $[Fe(CN)_6]^{4-}$ anions. The reader may find it helpful to reconsider the use of charcoal in the preparation of cobalt(III) complexes (Section 3-2-3) in the light of the above discussion.

So far we have discussed electron-transfer reactions in which only the formal valence states of the metal ions involved changed. There is another class, in which concomitant electron transfer and ligand transfer occur. Such reactions require a more intimate contact between the two reacting molecules in a *bridge* or *inner sphere* mechanism.

Reactions of the type:

$$Cr(II) + Co(III) \rightarrow Cr(III) + Co(II)$$

have been extensively studied, notably by Taube and his co-workers. Cobalt(III) and chromium(III) form inert complexes whilst the corresponding divalent ions give labile complexes. This means that if a ligand is transferred from cobalt(III) to chromium(III) in the reaction it will be possible to show that this transfer has occurred. Consider the reaction:

$$[Co(NH_3)_5Cl]^{2+} + [Cr(H_2O)^6]^{2+} \rightarrow [Co(NH_3)_5H_2O]^{2+} + [Cr(H_2O)_5Cl]^{2+}$$

The reaction is carried out in water and the final cobalt(II) product is actually $[Co(H_2O)_6]^{2+}$, but this is immaterial to our discussion.

It was found that if the $[Co(NH_3)_5Cl]^{2+}$ contained labelled chlorine (^{36}Cl) all of the activity appeared in the $[Cr(H_2O)_5Cl]^{2+}$ product, even though free non-labelled chloride ions were present in solution. This observation indicates an intimate contact between the reacting species, a Cl^- ion being transferred from cobalt(III) to chromium(II) and an electron migrating in the opposite direction. It therefore seems likely that the activated complex is something like:

Similar transfer of the ligand X from $[Co(NH_3)_5X]^{n+}$ to chromium(II) occurs for $X = Cl^-$, Br^-, N_3^-, acetate$^-$, SO_4^{2-}, and PO_4^{3-}. This structure for the activated complex is supported by the observation that for $X = NCS^-$ (the complex having a Co—N bond) the initial product is $[Cr(H_2O)_5SCN]^{2+}$, with a Cr—S bond, which subsequently rearranges to $[Cr(H_2O)_5NCS]^{2+}$ (with a Cr—N bond).

Strong supporting evidence for the suggested mechanism comes from the observation of fairly stable intermediate species in some inner sphere electron-transfer reactions. For example, reaction between vanadium(II) and vanadyl (VO^{2+}) complexes, to form vanadium(III) species, rapidly gives a brown intermediate, believed to contain a V—O—V bridge which, relatively slowly, gives the final product. In some cases there is evidence that there are two or even three bridges in the intermediate (for example, in some inner sphere electron transfer reactions between chromium(II) and chromium(III) complexes containing the azide anion as ligand).

11-3   Mechanisms of ligand substitution reactions

The other reactions which we shall consider involve the replacement of a ligand. That is, they are of the general type:

$$[ML_nX] + Y \rightarrow [ML_nY] + X$$

where the ligand Y replaces the ligand X. Several mechanisms may be involved in these processes and these we shall now consider.

The first possible mechanism is:

$$[ML_nX] \xrightarrow[k_1]{\text{slow}} [ML_n] + X$$

followed by

$$[ML_n] + Y \xrightarrow{\text{fast}} [ML_nY]$$

In this mechanism the M—X bond is first broken, to give a complex of lower coordination number. Subsequent addition of Y gives the final product. The rate-determining step is the first, so that the rate of disappearance of $[ML_nX]$ is proportional to the concentration of $[ML_nX]$. As the overall reaction is one of *nucleophilic substitution* by the ligand X and the rate-determining step is *unimolecular*, this is usually referred to as the S_N1 mechanism.

The energy required to break the M—X bond in the rate-determining step must come from somewhere, and we may conveniently distinguish two sources. The first is the internal vibrational energy of $[ML_nX]$ itself which could momentarily become largely concentrated in an extension of the M—X bond. Secondly, the collisions between the complex ion and the solvent molecules which surround it could lead to the breaking of the M—X bond. The solvent most commonly used is water, which is itself a good ligand and so it might well coordinate in place of the expelled ligand. This leads us to recognize that, kinetically, it would be very difficult to distinguish between the mechanism given above and an alternative:

$$[ML_nX] + H_2O \xrightarrow[k_1]{\text{slow}} [ML_nH_2O] + X$$

followed by

$$[ML_nH_2O] + Y \xrightarrow{\text{fast}} [ML_nY] + H_2O$$

This is because the first mechanism leads to a rate law:*

$$\frac{d[ML_nY]}{dt} = k_1[ML_nX]$$

whilst the second gives:

$$\frac{d[ML_nY]}{dt} = k_1[ML_nX][H_2O]$$

However, the concentration of water present is essentially constant (*ca* 55·5 M) and so the second rate reduces to:

$$\frac{d[ML_nY]}{dt} = k_1'[ML_nX], \qquad \text{where } k_1' = k_1[H_2O]$$

Another basic mechanism is a simple bimolecular one:

$$[ML_nX] + Y \xrightarrow[k_1]{\text{slow}} [ML_nXY]$$

followed by

$$[ML_nXY] \xrightarrow{\text{fast}} [ML_nY] + X$$

which leads to a rate expression:

$$\frac{d[ML_nY]}{dt} = k_1[ML_nX][Y]$$

In this mechanism the coordination number of M is increased in forming the activated complex. The rate of disappearance of $[ML_nX]$ is proportional to the concentrations of both $[ML_nX]$ and Y, so this mechanism is usually referred to as the S_N2 mechanism (*s*ubstitution, *n*ucleophilic, *bi*molecular). However, there are some complicating features which must be discussed. First, it is possible that there is a pre-equilibrium of the type:

$$[ML_nX] + Y \underset{k_{-1}}{\overset{k_1}{\rightleftharpoons}} [ML_nX]Y$$

In the species $[ML_nX]Y$, $[ML_nX]$ and Y are associated with each other but Y has not entered into direct coordination with M. This is particularly important when $[ML_nX]$ carries a net positive charge and Y is an anion, for then $[ML_nX]Y$ is simply an ion pair. If the complex $[ML_nX]Y$ gives the final product by a unimolecular reaction:

$$[ML_nX]Y \xrightarrow[k_2]{\text{slow}} [ML_nY] + X$$

* In this chapter, as in Chapter 4, we shall use square brackets to indicate both complex species and their concentration.

then the rate of reaction is dependent on the concentration of $[ML_nX]Y$ which, in turn, depends on the concentrations of $[ML_nX]$ and Y. Thus, although the rate-determining step involves a unimolecular reaction, a second-order rate law is followed, the rate expression being:

$$\frac{d[ML_nY]}{dt} = \frac{k_1 k_2 [ML_nX][Y]}{k_{-1} + k_2} = k[ML_nX][Y] \qquad \text{where } k = \frac{k_1 k_2}{k_{-1} + k_2}$$

Strong experimental evidence for the kinetic importance of ion pairs (and ion triplets) has come from studies made in non-aqueous solvents such as acetone, methanol, dimethyl sulphoxide, and dimethylformamide. Because, in general, such solvents have lower dielectric constants than water, ionic aggregation in them would be expected to be more extensive. Although quite a variety of rate laws appear to be followed they are usually interpretable in terms of a basic mechanism involving an ion pair equilibrium such as that given above and have led to values for the ion pair equilibrium constants, k_{-1}/k_1, in good agreement with those obtained from non-kinetic measurements on the same solutions. One other important result of kinetic measurements in non-aqueous solvents is that, to date, they have provided no evidence at all for the existence of a simple bimolecular rate-determining step in substitution reactions of octahedral complexes.

A second complicating feature of what are apparently $S_N 2$ reactions may be found when Y is OH$^-$. The kinetics of substitution reactions of cobalt(III) ammine complexes have been extensively studied and it has become apparent that their rate is almost always first-order in the cobaltammine and independent of the concentration of the entering ligand. This is explained by the intermediate formation of an aquo-cobaltammine complex, giving pseudo-first-order kinetics, as discussed above (we shall discuss this topic in more detail in Section 11-5-2). Hydroxide ion reacts much more rapidly than other ligands (by a factor of the order of 10^6) and the rate follows a second-order law, depending on both the ammine and hydroxyl concentrations. For example, in the reaction:

$$[Co(NH_3)_5Cl]^{2+} + OH^- \rightarrow [Co(NH_3)_5OH]^{2+} + Cl^-$$

the observed rate law is:

$$-\frac{d[Co(NH_3)_5Cl]}{dt} = k[Co(NH_3)_5Cl][OH]$$

(for simplicity, we shall usually omit charges from rate expressions).

It is believed that this is another example of a unimolecular rate-determining step giving rise to second-order kinetics because of a pre-equilibrium. In the example given above, it is believed that the species $[Co(NH_3)_4(NH_2)Cl]^+$ is formed by proton abstraction by the hydroxyl anion:

$$[Co(NH_3)_5Cl]^{2+} + OH^- \underset{k_{-1}}{\overset{k_1}{\rightleftharpoons}} [Co(NH_3)_4(NH_2)Cl]^+ + H_2O$$

Suppose the rate-determining step involves the expulsion of a chloride ion from this amide complex followed by rapid addition of water. That is:

$$[Co(NH_3)_4(NH_2)Cl]^+ \overset{slow}{\underset{k_2}{\longrightarrow}} [Co(NH_3)_4(NH_2)]^{2+} + Cl^-$$

followed by

$$[Co(NH_3)_4(NH_2)]^{2+} + H_2O \overset{fast}{\longrightarrow} [Co(NH_3)_5OH]^{2+}$$

it follows that the rate law would be:

$$\frac{d[Co(NH_3)_5OH]}{dt} = \frac{k_1k_2[Co(NH_3)_5Cl][OH]}{k_{-1}[H_2O]^2 + k_2[H_2O]}$$

$$= \frac{k_1k_2[Co(NH_3)_5Cl][OH]}{k'_{-1} + k'_2}$$

with $k'_{-1} = k_{-1}[H_2O]^2$ and $k'_2 = k_2[H_2O]$. This, then, explains the observed rate law, with the observed rate constant, k, equal to:

$$\frac{k_1k_2}{k'_{-1} + k'_2}$$

We have separated the last two steps in the mechanism, but it would be difficult to distinguish between this sequence and

$$[Co(NH_3)_4(NH_2)Cl]^+ + H_2O \overset{slow}{\longrightarrow} [Co(NH_3)_5OH]^{2+} + Cl^-$$

The essential correctness of this explanation of the accelerated rates obtained when OH^- is the nucleophile is indicated by the observation that if there is no N—H bond in the cobalt complex the observed rate is independent of the concentration of the hydroxyl anion.

The postulated intermediate in the above sequence,

$$[Co(NH_3)_4(NH_2)Cl]^+,$$

is related to the starting complex by the loss of a proton from the latter. That is, the intermediate is the conjugate base of the starting material and so the mechanism is referred to as 'the S_N1CB mechanism'.

11-4 The substitution reactions of square planar complexes

The majority of work with square planar complexes has been concerned with those formed by platinum(II), although complexes of gold(III), rhodium(I), and iridium(I) have also received attention; the reaction of square planar complexes of nickel(II) and palladium(II) appear to resemble those of platinum(II) but have rate constants that are larger by a factor of ca 10^6, and so are less readily studied. One might expect that an S_N2 substitution mechanism would be favoured for square planar complexes since there is probably no large steric constraint opposing the bonding of the incoming ligand whilst the outgoing ligand is still attached. This expectation is fulfilled in practice. For example, the rates constants of the reactions:

$$[PtCl_4]^{2-} + H_2O \rightarrow [Pt(H_2O)Cl_3]^- + Cl^-$$

$$[Pt(NH_3)Cl_3]^- + H_2O \rightarrow [Pt(NH_3)(H_2O)Cl_2] + Cl^-$$

$$[Pt(NH_3)_2Cl_2] + H_2O \rightarrow [Pt(NH_3)_2(H_2O)Cl]^+ + Cl^-$$

$$[Pt(NH_3)_3Cl]^+ + H_2O \rightarrow [Pt(NH_3)_3(H_2O)]^{2+} + Cl^-$$

are very similar (the $t_{1/2}$, with 0·1 molar reactants, for the first three reactions at 25° are all ca 300 min, that for the fourth is ca 700 min). It is difficult to understand this in terms of other than an S_N2 mechanism, for a consideration of the formal charges on the various species suggests that the rates should drop rapidly in the above series if the reactions were of the S_N1 type. For an S_N2 mechanism, however, this factor, which will make it more difficult for a chloride ion to be expelled, will make it easier for a water molecule to become attached, thus leading to a relatively small variation in the rate constants. It should be remembered that the fact that a second-order rate law is followed is not, of itself, sufficient to establish that the rate-determining step involves an S_N2 mechanism. In fact, the rate law most generally observed for substitution reactions of platinum(II) complexes for the reaction:

$$[PtL_3X] + Y \rightarrow [PtL_3Y] + X$$

is:

$$-\frac{d[PtL_3X]}{dt} = k'[PtL_3X] + k''[PtL_3X][Y]$$

Here, for simplicity, we have represented the ligands not involved in the substitution by L_3; however, they need not all be identical.

Of the two terms in the rate expression the second, $k''[PtL_3X][Y]$, corresponds to the S_N2 mechanism which we have been discussing. The first indicates the existence of an alternative reaction pathway, one that we have also discussed:

$$[PtL_3X] + H_2O \xrightarrow[k_1]{\text{slow}} [PtL_3H_2O] + X$$

$$[PtL_3H_2O] + Y \xrightarrow{\text{fast}} [PtL_3Y] + H_2O$$

so that $k'[PtL_3X] = k_1[PtL_3X][H_2O]$. Here we have assumed that water is the solvent, as is commonly the case. This explanation of the first term finds support in the observation that this term only appears when the solvent for the reaction is itself a good ligand.

We have already discussed the application of the *trans* effect in the preparation of complexes of platinum(II) (Section 3-2-6). Because the *trans* effect is kinetic—that is, it is a generalization of the relative rates of the various alternative substitution reactions— explanations of the effect which do not take account of the S_N2 nature of the processes involved must be to some extent incomplete. There are two extreme points of view which regard the *trans* effect as a consequence of the effect of the *trans*-directing ligand on (a) the σ-electron distribution, or (b) the π-electron distribution of the molecule. So, the most strongly *trans*-directing ligands are those which probably form the strongest π bonds with the platinum ion (PR_3, CO, C_2H_4, CN^-). This suggests that these ligands remove π-electron density both from the metal atom and the *trans* ligand, making it easier for the incoming group to insert where the electron density is depleted. The σ effect is believed to operate through the polarization of the electron density along the *trans*-directing ligand–metal–*trans*-ligand axis, and to be of importance for ligands with relatively low *trans* labilizing power (H_2O, OH^-, NH_3). For such ligands the rates at which they substitute in Pt(II) complexes resembles the order of their *trans* effect:

Rate constants	$H_2O \simeq OH^- < Cl^- < Br^- < NH_3 < I^-$
trans effect	$H_2O < OH^- < NH_3 < Cl^- < Br^- < I^-$

Unfortunately the activated complex is almost certainly of low symmetry and in this situation a rigorous distinction between σ and π bonding cannot be made. It therefore appears that until a more detailed picture of the activated complex is obtained the true origin of the *trans* effect will remain somewhat obscure.

Reference is made sometimes to a 'static' *trans* effect (or '*trans* influence') which is distinguished from the 'kinetic' *trans* effect which we have discussed. The 'static' effect refers to the fact that bond lengths, vibrational frequencies, and some n.m.r. resonances seem to be sensitive to the ligand *trans* to the one which is being studied. Surprisingly, the results often run counter to the kinetic effect.

Ligands which exert a strong kinetic *trans* effect often seem to have a small *trans* influence. That is they do *not* seem to weaken the *trans* bond. The explanation for this probably lies in the difference between kinetic and thermodynamic stabilities.

11-5 The substitution reactions of octahedral complexes

A great deal of work has been done on this subject and it is impossible to survey it completely in this book. We shall therefore confine our discussion to two topics which have been studied in some detail.

11-5-1 The reactions of aquo ions

The number of water molecules bonded to metal cations in aqueous solution is known in only a few cases. Thus, $[Be(H_2O)_4]^{2+}$, $[Mg(H_2O)_6]^{2+}$, $[Al(H_2O)_6]^{3+}$, $[Cr(H_2O)_6]^{3+}$, and $[Rh(H_2O)_6]^{3+}$ are well established, but it is not known for certain whether the potassium ion exists as $[K(H_2O)_4]^+$ or $[K(H_2O)_6]^+$ (some evidence indicates the former) or whether the trivalent lanthanide ions are $[M(H_2O)_9]^{3+}$ (they have this coordination in some crystal structures). It is convenient at this point to include ions in our discussion whether they are octahedrally coordinated or not, and later or return to the transition metal species, which are almost certainly six-coordinate. Despite the uncertainty in coordination number of the species involved, it has been established that the rate constants for reactions in which coordinated water exchanges with the bulk solvent are usually rather large (in the majority of cases which have been studied the first-order rate constants are between 10^6 and 10^{10} s^{-1}). A survey of the experimental data shows (*i*) that for a given formal charge, larger ions exchange more rapidly than smaller. Thus the rate constants vary: $Cs^+ > Rb^+ > K^+ > Na^+ > Li^+$ (all $\simeq 10^9$); $Ba^{2+} > Sr^{2+} > Ca^{2+} \gg Mg^{2+} > Be^{2+}$ and so on; (*ii*) it is usually true that for a given ionic size an increase in formal charge is associated with a decrease in reaction rate; (*iii*) for the first-row divalent transition metal cations the rates are in the order $Cu^{2+} \simeq Cr^{2+} \gg Mn^{2+} > Fe^{2+} > Co^{2+} > Ni^{2+} > V^{2+}$, the range being from 10^2 (for V^{2+}) to 4×10^8 s^{-1} (for Cr^{2+} and Cu^{2+}); (*iv*) the slowest exchange occurs with Rh^{3+} and Cr^{3+}, both of which have $t_{1/2}$s measured in days, while the slowest of the others (which are nonetheless quite fast) have rate constants: Al^{3+} ($\simeq 1$), Be^{2+} and V^{2+} (10^2), Ga^{3+} (10^3), Ni^{2+} (10^4), and Mg^{2+} (10^5 s^{-1}).

It is almost invariably found that, in aqueous solution, substitution of a ligand by another proceeds through the intermediate formation of an aquo complex (exceptions are found in platinum(II) chemistry, where, it will be recalled, a direct substitution may occur).

It is therefore of interest to study the replacement of coordinated water in some detail. The mechanism generally involved seems to be:

$$[ML_5(H_2O)] \underset{k_{-1}}{\overset{k_1}{\rightleftharpoons}} [ML_5] + H_2O$$

$$[ML_5] + Y \xrightarrow{k_2} [ML_5Y]$$

where the five ligands not involved in the reaction are collectively denoted L_5. It is readily shown, asuming a steady-state concentration of $[ML_5]$, that the rate of formation of $[ML_5Y]$ is:

$$\frac{d[ML_5Y]}{dt} = \frac{k_1 k_2 [ML_5(H_2O)][Y]}{k_{-1}[H_2O] + k_2[Y]}$$

$$= \frac{k_1 k_2 [ML_5(H_2O)][Y]}{k'_{-1} + k_2[Y]}$$

where $k'_{-1} = k_{-1}[H_2O]$.

If $k_2 \simeq k'_{-1}$ the kinetic behaviour may be complicated (although if [Y] is made very small simple second-order behaviour will be found), and if [Y] is large the rate law will be first-order. If $k_2 \gg k'_{-1}$ a simple first-order rate will be observed whilst if $k_2 \ll k'_{-1}$ the rate will be second-order. The reaction of $[Co(CN)_5H_2O]^{2-}$ with N_3^- or SCN^- is probably a case where $k_2 \simeq k'_{-1}$ and the reactions of $[M(H_2O)_6]^{2+}$, where M is one of the first-row transition metal ions, with anions are cases where, usually, $k_2 \ll k'_{-1}$.

11-5-2   The hydrolysis of cobalt(III) ammine complexes

As we have already mentioned, substitution reactions commonly involve an aquo intermediate if the reaction is carried out in water. We have just discussed some aspects of the reaction of these intermediates; in this section we consider their formation in the particular case of cobalt(III) ammine complexes. The rate of hydrolysis of $[CoL_5X]$:

$$[CoL_5X] + H_2O \rightarrow [CoL_5(H_2O)] + X$$

is pH-dependent, the rate law commonly observed being:

$$\frac{-d[CoL_5X]}{dt} = k_A[CoL_5X] + k_B[CoL_5X][OH^-]$$

If $k_A > k_B[OH^-]$ the first term will be the more important, but if $k_B[OH^-] > k_A$ the second will be. Now, k_B is commonly about $10^6 k_A$, so remembering that at pH = 8, $[OH^-] = 10^{-6}$, it follows that the first term will dominate at pH below about 8 and the second term will be the more important at higher pH. k_A and k_B are referred to as the acid and base hydrolysis rate constants, respectively—hence the choice of suffixes.

The term $k_A[CoL_5X]$ could mean that the rate-determining step is the breaking of a Co—X bond to give a five-coordinate intermediate. However, as we have pointed out, it is difficult to distinguish this from an S_N2 mechanism involving simultaneous addition of water and loss of X. One method of distinguishing is to compare the hydrolysis rates (under similar experimental conditions) of analogous complexes of two closely related ligands, one of which is more bulky than the other. For example, the hydrolysis of a chloride ion in a series of complexes trans-[Co(alkyl-substituted ethylenediamine)$_2$Cl$_2$]$^+$ has been studied. If the rate-determining step corresponds to an increase in coordination number of the metal, the complex containing the larger ligand would be expected to hydrolyse more slowly. Conversely, it would be the more readily hydrolysed if the coordination number of the cobalt in the activated complex is less than six. It was found that, in general, increasing size corresponded to increasing rate of hydrolysis, indicating an S_N1 mechanism (the few exceptions to this generalization can be explained).

It is possible to obtain from the variation of rate with applied pressure a value for the volume of activation. This should be positive for an S_N1 mechanism and negative for an S_N2. The observed volume of activation is positive, but is smaller than predicted for a pure S_N1 mechanism.

These and other data seem to be explicable in terms of a mechanism which is intermediate between S_N1 and S_N2 but which is closer to the former. The two extremes are distinguished in that a water molecule is not involved in the rate-determining step of an S_N1 mechanism but is fully involved in an S_N2. Evidently, a continuous range of intermediate exists in which the incoming water molecule contributes to some extent in the rate-determining step. Indeed, many workers distinguish between limiting S_N1 and S_N2 mechanisms—S_N1(lim.) and S_N2(lim.), reserving the simpler designations for reactions that are predominantly S_N1 or S_N2.

The recognition that pure S_N1 and S_N2 (that is, S_N1(lim.) and S_N2(lim.)) mechanisms are seldom, if ever, encountered has led Langford and Gray to introduce a new classification scheme for ligand substitution reactions. A reaction in which the intermediate formed in the rate-determining step has a lower coordination number than the starting material is kinetically a dissociation reaction and is termed D. Similarly, if the coordination number is increased in the intermediate the reaction is one of association and is termed A. If the reaction is one in which the coordination number does not change, but proceeds by the interchange of ligands between the inner (first) and outer (second) coordination spheres (with no kinetically detectable intermediate), it is termed I.

Evidently, an A mechanism is that which we have called S_N2(lim.) and a D mechanism that which we have called S_N1(lim.). I mechanisms are those in which the reaction rate is sensitive to the nature of both the entering and leaving groups. A subdivision of the I class is possible on the basis of this sensitivity. Consider a series of reactions, all of which are of I type:

$$[ML_nX] + Y \rightarrow [ML_nY] + X$$

in which X and Y are varied. If the rates of reaction are more sensitive to variations in Y than to change of X then the rates tend to be *a*ssociation-controlled and are labelled I_a. On the other system of nomenclature these would be labelled S_N2. Similarly if, in the above series, the rates depend more on X than on Y then they tend to be *d*issociation-controlled and are labelled I_d. Langford and Gray also include in this class those reactions for which the rate dependence on X and Y is similar, so that it corresponds to both what we have called S_N1 and to some reactions which have been recognized as intermediate between S_N1 and S_N2 but which have been designated as the latter.

The Langford–Gray nomenclature is being increasingly used and might well become the accepted classification scheme for ligand substitution reactions.

We now return to our consideration of the hydrolysis reactions of cobalt(III) ammine complexes.

The base hydrolysis term in the rate expression, $k_B[CoL_5X][OH^-]$, could indicate either a genuine S_N2 rate determining step or a S_N1CB mechanism. Of these two possibilities, the evidence is strongly in favour of the latter, although there is no reason why the two should not occur simultaneously with the S_N1CB process being by far the more important.

The evidence in support of the S_N1CB mechanism rests largely on the unique character of the hydroxyl anion. In aqueous solution there are few cases where another substituting anion appears in a rate expression and so a unique mechanism involving the hydroxyl ion is indicated. Supporting evidence comes from the fact that exchange of the protons in $[Co(NH_3)_5Cl]^{2+}$, for example, with those of the solvent water are several orders of magnitude faster than the rate of base hydrolysis. Similarly, the failure of complexes without such protons—dipyridyl complexes, for example—to undergo rapid base hydrolysis supports the S_N1CB mechanism.

11-6 The relative rates of substitution reactions of transition metal complexes

It is found that inert and labile transition metal complexes are associated with quite specific d-orbital occupancies. So, inert complexes are formed by ions with the configurations t_{2g}^3, t_{2g}^4, t_{2g}^5, and t_{2g}^6. Labile complexes are those in which the metal ion has electron configurations in which the e_g orbitals are occupied by one or more electrons, together with those with the configurations t_{2g}^1 and t_{2g}^2.

We recall the discussion of Section 10-4 and note that, provided that their reactions are mechanistically similar and that other energies vary smoothly along the series, the differences in kinetic behaviour associated with different d-electron configurations may be explicable in terms of crystal field stabilization energies. That is, in going from the ground state of the reactants to the activated complex, the contribution made by the change in crystal field stabilization energy to the potential 'hill' may be of importance. To test this theory we have to know the detailed geometry of the activated complex, not only its shape but also the metal–ligand bond lengths (for these may not be the same as in the ground-state complex), so that the crystal field stabilization energy of the activated complex may be calculated. Unfortunately our ignorance of the activated complex is profound. Calculations have been carried out assuming idealized geometries for activated complexes in which the metal ion is seven- or five-coordinate and give reasonable agreement with experiment. It is predicted that t_{2g}^1, t_{2g}^2, and $t_{2g}^3 e_g^2$ ions will always react rapidly (that is, they do not lose crystal field stabilization energy in forming the activated complex). For t_{2g}^3, t_{2g}^4, t_{2g}^5, and t_{2g}^6 configurations a loss of crystal field stabilization energy in forming the activated complex predicts, as observed, relatively slow reaction. For other configurations, the predictions usually depend on the geometry assumed for the activated complex.

Problems

11-1   Distinguish between the order and molecularity of a reaction. Explain carefully ways in which *pseudo*-first-order and *pseudo*-second-order kinetics may arise in inorganic substitution reactions.

11-2   Show that the mutual *trans* influence of the ligands indicated in the square planar complex of platinum(II) given in the diagram must operate, largely, through the p_x (σ-effect) and/or d_{zx}(π-effect) orbitals of the platinum. Using Table 6-2 show that the picture becomes less clear for five-coordinate complexes which might be a reasonable approximation to the transition state involved in the kinetic *trans* effect.

Appendix 1
Some aspects of
group theory

Fig. A1 shows a square planar complex. This figure also shows those symmetry operations by which the complex can be transformed to a configuration indistinguishable from that shown. In Table A1, these 16 operations are listed across the top. Each number in the table is known as a character and the whole table is called a character table. This group of 16 symmetry operations is called the '$\mathbf{D_{4h}}$' group, and the character table is 'the $\mathbf{D_{4h}}$ character table'. Down the left-hand side are listed some of the symmetry symbols used in the text (in Table 6-2, for example). Each symmetry symbol is associated with a unique row of characters—no two rows are identical, although careful inspection will reveal that the characters block into four 5×5 squares, the characters within one square being very simply related to the corresponding characters within another. This fundamental building unit of the $\mathbf{D_{4h}}$ character table is, in fact, the character table of the $\mathbf{D_4}$ group (which has only the E, $2C_4$, C_2, $2C_2'$, and $2C''$ operations of the $\mathbf{D_{4h}}$ group). In Table A1 any one character corresponds to a symmetry symbol (its row) and to a symmetry operation (its column). The character has the property of telling us how something which carries its particular symmetry symbol behaves under its particular symmetry operation. So, something of A_{2u} symmetry is multiplied by 1 (i.e. turned into itself) by a C_4 rotation or C_2 rotation. However, it will be multiplied by -1 (i.e. turned into itself with all signs reversed) by the C_2' and C_2'' rotations. The p_z orbital shown in Fig. A2 has A_{2u} symmetry and the reader should check that it behaves as we have described under these operations. Those symmetry symbols which, for the 'leave alone' operation (E), have characters of 2, describe the behaviour of *two* interdependent things simultaneously. The number 0, for these species, means that neither of the things is turned into itself by the symmetry operation—the two are interchanged in some way. The number -2 means that each is changed into itself with signs reversed. So, p_x and p_y (Fig. A2) together have E_u symmetry. The reader should show that the $\mathbf{D_{4h}}$ character table gives an accurate description of their behaviour under the symmetry operations.

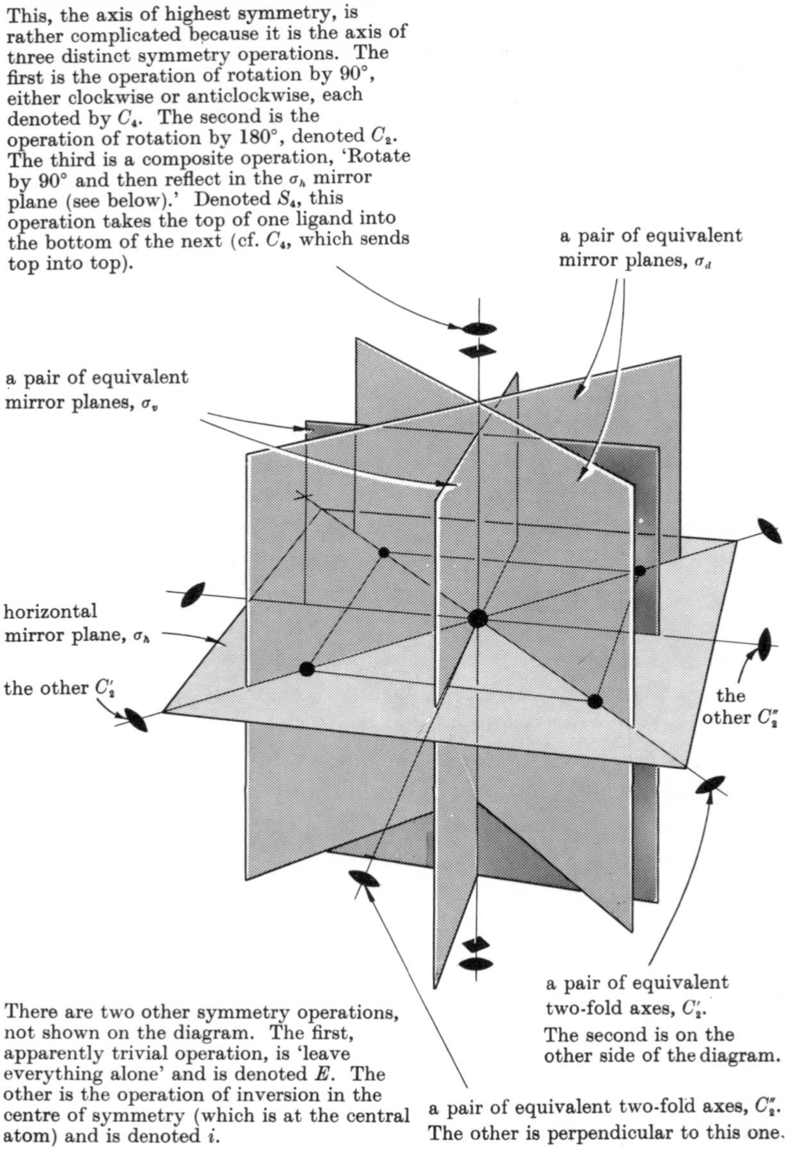

This, the axis of highest symmetry, is rather complicated because it is the axis of three distinct symmetry operations. The first is the operation of rotation by 90°, either clockwise or anticlockwise, each denoted by C_4. The second is the operation of rotation by 180°, denoted C_2. The third is a composite operation, 'Rotate by 90° and then reflect in the σ_h mirror plane (see below).' Denoted S_4, this operation takes the top of one ligand into the bottom of the next (cf. C_4, which sends top into top).

a pair of equivalent mirror planes, σ_d

a pair of equivalent mirror planes, σ_v

horizontal mirror plane, σ_h

the other C_2'

the other C_2''

a pair of equivalent two-fold axes, C_2'. The second is on the other side of the diagram.

There are two other symmetry operations, not shown on the diagram. The first, apparently trivial operation, is 'leave everything alone' and is denoted E. The other is the operation of inversion in the centre of symmetry (which is at the central atom) and is denoted i.

a pair of equivalent two-fold axes, C_2''. The other is perpendicular to this one.

Fig. A1

The direct product of two symmetry species, say $A_{2g} \times B_{1g}$, is formed by multiplying together in turn their characters under each symmetry operation, thus:

	E	$2C_4$	C_2	$2C_2'$	$2C_2''$	i	$2S_4$	σ_h	$2\sigma_v$	$2\sigma_d$
A_{2g}	1	1	1	−1	−1	1	1	1	−1	−1
B_{1g}	1	−1	1	1	−1	1	−1	1	1	−1
$A_{2g} \times B_{1g}$	1	−1	1	−1	1	1	−1	1	−1	1

Table A1   The D$_{4h}$ character table

D$_{4h}$	E	2C$_4$	C$_2$	2C$_2'$	2C$_2''$	i	2S$_4$	σ_h	2σ_v	2σ_d
A$_{1g}$	1	1	1	1	1	1	1	1	1	1
A$_{2g}$	1	1	1	−1	−1	1	1	1	−1	−1
B$_{1g}$	1	−1	1	1	−1	1	−1	1	1	−1
B$_{2g}$	1	−1	1	−1	1	1	−1	1	−1	1
E$_g$	2	0	−2	0	0	2	0	−2	0	0
A$_{1u}$	1	1	1	1	1	−1	−1	−1	−1	−1
A$_{2u}$	1	1	1	−1	−1	−1	−1	−1	1	1
B$_{1u}$	1	−1	1	1	−1	−1	1	−1	−1	1
B$_{2u}$	1	−1	1	−1	1	−1	1	−1	1	−1
E$_u$	2	0	−2	0	0	−2	0	2	0	0

Comparison with Table A1 then shows that the set of characters produced is, in fact, that labelled B_{2g}. That is, $A_{2g} \times B_{1g} = B_{2g}$. For E-type symmetry species direct products are a bit more difficult. Consider $E_g \times E_u$:

	E	2C$_4$	C$_2$	2C$_2'$	2C$_2''$	i	2S$_4$	σ_h	2σ_v	2σ_d
E$_g$	2	0	−2	0	0	2	0	−2	0	0
E$_u$	2	0	−2	0	0	−2	0	2	0	0
E$_g \times$ E$_u$	4	0	4	0	0	−4	0	−4	0	0

This direct product does not correspond to a symmetry species in Table A1. It does, however, correspond to a sum of them. Consider the sum $A_{1u} + A_{2u} + B_{1u} + B_{2u}$:

	E	2C$_4$	C$_2$	2C$_2'$	2C$_2''$	i	2S$_4$	σ_h	2σ_v	2σ_d
A$_{1u}$	1	1	1	1	1	−1	−1	−1	−1	−1
A$_{2u}$	1	1	1	−1	−1	−1	−1	−1	1	1
B$_{1u}$	1	−1	1	1	−1	−1	1	−1	−1	1
B$_{2u}$	1	−1	1	−1	1	−1	1	−1	1	−1
A$_{1u}$ + A$_{2u}$ + B$_{1u}$ + B$_{2u}$	4	0	4	0	0	−4	0	−4	0	0

This is the same as that generated by $E_g \times E_u$, so $E_g \times E_u = A_{1u} + A_{2u} + B_{1u} + B_{2u}$ (note that the product of suffixes $g \times u$

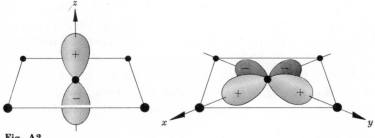

Fig. A2

gives u). What we have called 'symmetry species' are often called 'irreducible representations' (of the group of symmetry operations) so, 'the A_{2u} irreducible representation'. Similarly, one may meet statements like 'the p_z orbital of the central metal atom transforms as the A_{2u} irreducible representation'. The direct product $E_g \times E_u$ is an example of a 'reducible representation' which, as we have demonstrated, may be reduced to its irreducible components.

Table A2   The O character table

O	E	$8C_3$	$6C_2'$	$6C_4$	$3C_2$
A_1	1	1	1	1	1
A_2	1	1	-1	-1	1
E	2	-1	0	0	2
T_1	3	0	-1	1	-1
T_2	3	0	1	-1	-1

As we have seen, orbitals may be characterized by symmetry labels. In a similar way, if we are interested in an integral such as

$$\int \psi_1 \psi_2 \, d\tau,$$

an overlap integral, we can discuss its symmetry properties (in particular, whether it is zero or not) by considering the direct product of the symmetry species of the two orbitals concerned. In this particular case this leads to the well-known result that 'only orbitals of the same symmetry species have non-zero overlap integrals'. So, in those places in the text where we have used direct products, it is because, really, we are interested in products of orbitals (as in Section 5-5 where we want to know the symmetry species of the product wavefunctions of the t_{2g}^2 configuration). Similarly, in Section 7-7 we are interested in integrals which give the intensities of spectral bands. These integrals involve products of wavefunctions and, again, the use of direct products permits a simple discussion.

Finally, in Table A2 we give the character table for the octahedral group O. The reader should use it to check that Table 5-3 is correct. The full octahedral group, which has symmetry species with g and u suffixes, is denoted O_h and is four times as large as that of O. The two are related in that the character table for the group O appears in that of the group O_h in the same way as we noted above that the character table of the group $\mathbf{D_{4h}}$ is 'built up' of one a quarter its size.

Appendix 2
The equivalence of d_{z^2} and $d_{x^2-y^2}$ in an octahedral ligand field

In Section 5-3 it was noted that the action of a C_3 rotation operation converted $d_{x^2-y^2}$ into $d_{y^2-z^2}$ and d_{z^2} into d_{x^2} (or, for a C_3 rotation in the opposite sense, into $d_{z^2-x^2}$ and d_{y^2}). In order to see how the 'new' orbitals are related to $d_{x^2-y^2}$ and d_{z^2}, we must first recognize that the d_{z^2} orbital is more correctly written as $d_{(1/\sqrt 3)(2z^2-x^2-y^2)}$ (this gives it the central annulus which the label d_{z^2} does not). Working with the labels alone (this is a perfectly valid simplification) we have:

$$y^2 - z^2 = -\tfrac{1}{2}(x^2 - y^2) - \frac{\sqrt 3}{2} \cdot \frac{1}{\sqrt 3}(2z^2 - x^2 - y^2)$$

and

$$\frac{1}{\sqrt 3}(2x^2 - y^2 - z^2) = \frac{\sqrt 3}{2}(x^2 - y^2) - \frac{1}{2} \cdot \frac{1}{\sqrt 3}(2z^2 - x^2 - y^2)$$

That is:

$$d_{y^2-z^2} = -\tfrac{1}{2}d_{x^2-y^2} - \frac{\sqrt 3}{2}d_{z^2}$$

and

$$d_{x^2} = \frac{\sqrt 3}{2}d_{x^2-y^2} - \tfrac{1}{2}d_{z^2}$$

In other words the 'new' orbitals are simply linear combinations of the old. The reader should check that this is also true of $d_{z^2-x^2}$ and d_{y^2} (he has only to change two of the signs in the right-hand-side expressions given above).

A final word for the reader of Appendix 4 who has returned to this Appendix in search of a character of -1. When $d_{x^2-y^2}$ is rotated into $d_{y^2-z^2}$ its contribution to the latter is $-\tfrac{1}{2}$. Similarly d_{z^2} contributes $-\tfrac{1}{2}$ to d_{x^2}. The required character is the sum of these $(-\tfrac{1}{2} - \tfrac{1}{2} = -1)$. As the reader should have discovered, the same result is obtained if rotation into $d_{z^2-x^2}$ and d_{y^2} is considered.

Appendix 3
The Russell–Saunders
coupling scheme

Let us consider a free atom or ion in which several electrons occupy
but do not fill a set of orbitals (which need not all be degenerate).
There are several ways in which the electrons may be distributed,
some of which are of lower energy than others. For example, the electron–electron repulsion energy will be least when the electrons occupy
spatially well-separated orbitals. Similarly, when the electrons are
arranged so that all unpaired electrons have parallel spins, the
exchange stabilization is a maximum.

If we are to discuss the energetics of free atoms or ions we have to
separate the possible electron arrangements into sets, the members
of each set all being degenerate. There are two schemes commonly
adopted for this. The first, which we shall discuss, is the Russell–
Saunders coupling scheme. The second, the j–j coupling scheme,
is used when an interaction which we shall neglect, spin–orbit coupling, is large. It is of much less common applicability than the
Russell–Saunders scheme.

In the Russell–Saunders coupling scheme, the orbital motions
of the electrons are coupled together as are their spins. Within the
simplified scheme discussed here (neglect of spin–orbit coupling)
there is no coupling between these two sets. For any particular
arrangement of the electrons within the orbitals the coupling between
the orbital motions gives rise to a resultant; similarly the spins
couple to give a resultant, the resultants simply being vector sums
of the individual orbital and spin motions. It turns out that it is
possible to measure not only the magnitude of the resultants, but also
something about their orientation in space. For each atom or ion
there is at any particular instant an axis—let us call it the
z-axis—along which the z-components of the orbital and spin
resultants have well-defined values (unless something happens,
absorption or emission of radiation, for example, which changes
them). Not any z-component can exist, however. If the largest
component is M_z, then the others are $(M_z - 1)$, $(M_z - 2) \ldots$,
$(M_z - 2M_z)$. That is, the components run from M_z to $-M_z$, a total
of $(2M_z + 1)$ values in all. Each resultant will correspond to a

particular arrangement of electrons in the orbitals and, for resultants related in the way we have just described, the arrangements will also be related. Note that if we wish to hold the z-axis fixed in space we have to apply some fixed axial perturbation, an electric or magnetic field, for example.

So far we have not specified the nature of the vectors. They represent angular momenta (there is more on this topic in Chapter 8) and one talks about the 'orbital and spin angular momenta', their magnitudes and z-components. The quantization of orbital angular momentum, introduced arbitrarily in the Bohr theory of atomic structure, appears in present-day quantum mechanics in the way that we have just discussed. The various z-components of orbital and spin angular momenta are (within our approximation) energetically unimportant. The energy of a particular arrangement is determined solely by the absolute magnitude of the orbital and spin angular momenta, and is independent of their z-components. The reason that we have introduced the z-components is the following. For each of the $(2L + 1)$ z-components of an orbital angular momentum vector and for each of the $(2S + 1)$ z-components of a spin angular momentum vector there is an individual orbital or spin wavefunction. Since a complete wavefunction contains both orbital and spin parts and any of the orbital functions may be combined with any of the spin functions, $(2L + 1)(2S + 1)$ distinct combinations exist. All of these wavefunctions are degenerate. It is the removal of this degeneracy by such things as a crystal or magnetic field which is discussed in detail in Chapters 5 and 8. An individual energy level of a free atom or ion could be characterized fairly well by specifying the numerical quantities $(2L + 1)$ or $(2S + 1)$—they are both integers—or, alternatively, and more simply, by specifying L and S. L is always an integer but S may not be, so a combination of the two alternatives is used. L and $(2S + 1)$ are specified. Rather than quoting L as a number it is replaced by a letter: $L = 0$ is indicated by S, $L = 1$ by P, $L = 2$ by D, $L = 3$ by F, $L = 4$ by G, $L = 5$ by H, $L = 6$ by I, and so on. (The parallel with orbitals should be evident; for example, there are five d orbitals; similarly, a D label indicates $(2 \cdot 2 + 1) = 5$-fold orbital degeneracy.) The value of $(2S + 1)$ is given as a number, written as a pre-superscript to the L symbol. Thus ^1S, ^3P, ^1D, ^4F, etc. When verbally referred to they are not called 'one, two . . . ' but 'singlet, doublet, triplet, quartet, quintet . . . .' Hence ^2D is 'doublet dee'. One talks of a ^2D 'state' (or 'term'). When one has, say, two electrons distributed within a set of three (degenerate) p orbitals, this is referred to as a p^2 (pee two) configuration. Such a configuration will usually give rise to several terms. The p^2 configuration gives rise to ^1D, ^3P, and ^1S terms. There is a simple check which can be applied to a list of terms stated as arising from a given configuration. Consider the p^2 configuration. The first of the two electrons can be fed into the set of three orbitals in any one of six ways (allowing for spin) and the second in any one of five (it can only go into the same orbital as the first electron with opposite spin). Recognizing that we have counted each arrangement twice ($\uparrow\downarrow$ is the same as $\downarrow\uparrow$), the number of distinct arrangements (and therefore, wavefunctions) is $6{\cdot}5/2 = 15$. Now, the ^1D, ^3P, and ^1S terms correspond to 5, 9, and 1 wavefunctions respectively, again a total of 15.

It is not necessary that the reader should be able to work out the terms arising from a given configuration and so we do not give the method here. It is, however, very simply done and is discussed in almost all elementary texts on quantum mechanics. The job of working out the wavefunctions of the terms is more difficult; that of evaluating the relative energies of the terms is rather hard work. It is for this reason that we simply quote these data in the text on the few occasions that they are needed.

Finally, a word about spin–orbit coupling. Its effect is to cause relatively small energy differences between functions which we have so far regarded as degenerate. These splittings may be observed spectroscopically and values of spin–orbit coupling constants thus obtained (Section 8-3).

Appendix 4
Ligand group orbitals

When we have two similar atomic orbitals, ψ_1 and ψ_2 say, the former on atom 1 and the latter on atom 2, symmetry demands that the electron density at a given point in ψ_1 is equal to the electron density at the corresponding point in ψ_2. That is, $\psi_1^2 = \psi_2^2$ at these points. It follows that $\psi_1 = \pm\psi_2$. In other words, ψ_1 and ψ_2 may be either in-phase or out-of-phase with each other (this breaks down if the separation between the two orbitals is large, because the velocity of light is not infinite). If ψ_1 and ψ_2 combine to form a molecular orbital, φ say, then an analogous argument shows that φ may either have the form $(\varphi_1 + \varphi_2)$ or $(\varphi_1 - \varphi_2)$, all other combinations leading to unequal electron densities on atoms 1 and 2. Normalizing (that is, multiplying by a factor so that the sum of squares of the coefficients multiplying ψ_1 and ψ_2 equals unity), but neglecting overlap between ψ_1 and ψ_2, gives the orbitals:

$$\varphi_1 = \frac{1}{\sqrt{2}}\,(\psi_1 + \psi_2)$$

$$\varphi_2 = \frac{1}{\sqrt{2}}\,(\psi_1 - \psi_2)$$

which, if atoms 1 and 2 are part of a larger, polyatomic, system, are called group orbitals.

In what follows we shall, for simplicity, assume:

1. That all orbitals labelled ψ are of σ-type with respect to a suitably placed metal ion (the meaning of this will become clear as we proceed), although the discussion has to be little modified to cover π- and δ-type interactions.

2. That all such orbitals have the same (positive) phase. That is, that $\varphi_1 = (1/\sqrt{2})(\psi_1 + \psi_2)$ is a combination of two orbitals of identical phase. Thus, in $\varphi_2 = (1/\sqrt{2})(\psi_1 - \psi_2)$, ψ_2 has the opposite phase to ψ_1 because of the minus sign, not because it is inherently of opposite phase.

What if we had four identical orbitals ψ_1, ψ_2, ψ_3, and ψ_4 on atoms arranged in the form of a square? Orbitals on the ligands of a square planar complex are an example of this situation. The simplest way of discussing this case is as follows. Label the orbitals cyclically

(Fig. A3) and consider the pairs ψ_1 and ψ_3, ψ_2 and ψ_4. We can treat each *trans* pair as if the other were not present and use the discussion above to obtain group orbitals for each pair. These are:

$$\varphi_1 = \frac{1}{\sqrt{2}} (\psi_1 + \psi_3)$$

$$\varphi_2 = \frac{1}{\sqrt{2}} (\psi_1 - \psi_3)$$

and

$$\varphi_3 = \frac{1}{\sqrt{2}} (\psi_2 + \psi_4)$$

$$\varphi_4 = \frac{1}{\sqrt{2}} (\psi_2 - \psi_4)$$

All that we have to do now is to form suitable combinations of φ_1, φ_2, φ_3, and φ_4 to obtain the ligand group orbitals that we are

Fig. A3

seeking. But how do we know which combinations to take? The answer is that the transformations of the final group orbitals must be described by the irreducible representations of the $\mathbf{D_{4h}}$ point group. If the language of the last sentence seems obscure, re-read Appendix 1.

This boils down to the requirement that any nodal planes contained in φ_1, φ_2, φ_3, and φ_4 must be compatible with each other for interaction to occur. For example, neither φ_1 nor φ_3 contains any nodal planes; because they are equivalent to each other, the correct combinations are:

$$\theta_1 = \frac{1}{\sqrt{2}} (\varphi_1 + \varphi_3)$$

$$\theta_2 = \frac{1}{\sqrt{2}} (\varphi_1 - \varphi_3)$$

However, φ_2 contains a nodal plane which passes through ψ_2 and ψ_4 and so φ_2 cannot combine with either φ_3 or φ_4 (Fig. A4). Similarly, φ_4 cannot combine with either φ_1 or φ_2. We are therefore forced to the conclusion that the ligand group orbitals of a square planar complex are:

$$\theta_1 = \frac{1}{\sqrt{2}} (\varphi_1 + \varphi_3) = \tfrac{1}{2}(\psi_1 + \psi_2 + \psi_3 + \psi_4) \qquad A_{1g}$$

$$\theta_2 = \frac{1}{\sqrt{2}} (\varphi_1 - \varphi_3) = \tfrac{1}{2}(\psi_1 - \psi_2 + \psi_3 - \psi_4) \qquad B_{1g}$$

$$\left.\begin{array}{l} \varphi_2 = \dfrac{1}{\sqrt{2}} (\psi_1 - \psi_3) \\[2.2ex] \varphi_4 = \dfrac{1}{\sqrt{2}} (\psi_2 - \psi_4) \end{array}\right\} \qquad E_u$$

The reader is urged to check that these orbitals have the symmetries indicated by using the $\mathbf{D_{4h}}$ character table in Appendix 1.

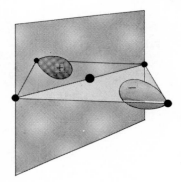

Fig. A4

Finally, we address ourselves to the problem of the ligand group orbitals appropriate to an octahedral complex ion. It is convenient to regard the octahedron as a synthesis of a square planar complex, with ligand orbitals ψ_1, ψ_2, ψ_3, and ψ_4, (which give rise to the four group orbitals listed above) and two additional ligands with orbitals ψ_5 and ψ_6 (which give rise to group orbitals $\varphi_5 = (1/\sqrt{2})(\psi_5 + \psi_6)$ and $\varphi_6 = (1/\sqrt{2})(\psi_5 - \psi_6)$). Applying our compatibility requirement we find that only θ_1 and φ_5, neither of which has a nodal plane, combine together. What are the correct combinations? It is a general rule that, for the type of ligand group orbital which we have considered, there is always a combination $(1/\sqrt{n})(\psi_1 + \psi_2 + \ldots + \psi_n)$, which has the symmetry given by the first row of the appropriate character table (this is always a row of ones—the so-called 'totally symmetric representation'). In the present case this means that one combination is $(1/\sqrt{6})(\psi_1 + \psi_2 + \psi_3 + \psi_4 + \psi_5 + \psi_6)$. As the reader should readily be able to show, this is simply $\sqrt{\tfrac{2}{3}}\,\theta_1 + \sqrt{\tfrac{1}{3}}\varphi_5$.

It follows that the orthogonal combination of θ_1 and φ_5 is $\sqrt{\frac{1}{3}}\,\theta_1 - \sqrt{\frac{2}{3}}\,\varphi_5$ (a combination of wavefunctions $(C_1\psi_1 + C_2\psi_2)$ is always orthogonal to $(C_2\psi_1 - C_1\psi_2)$ provided that ψ_1 and ψ_2 are, separately, orthogonal and normalized). Written in detail, this orthogonal combination is:

$$\frac{1}{\sqrt{12}}\,(\psi_1 + \psi_2 + \psi_3 + \psi_4 - 2\psi_5 - 2\psi_6)$$

In summary, the σ ligand group orbitals of an octahedral complex ion are:

$$\sqrt{\frac{2}{3}}\,\theta_1 + \frac{1}{\sqrt{3}}\,\varphi_5 = \frac{1}{\sqrt{6}}\,(\psi_1 + \psi_2 + \psi_3 + \psi_4 + \psi_5 + \psi_6) \qquad A_{1g}$$

$$\left.\begin{array}{c} \dfrac{1}{\sqrt{3}}\,\theta_1 - \sqrt{\dfrac{2}{3}}\,\varphi_5 = \dfrac{1}{\sqrt{12}}\,(\psi_1 + \psi_2 + \psi_3 + \psi_4 - 2\psi_5 - 2\psi_6) \\[4mm] \theta_2 = \dfrac{1}{2}\,(\psi_1 - \psi_2 + \psi_3 - \psi_4) \end{array}\right\} \quad E_g$$

$$\left.\begin{array}{c} \varphi_2 = \dfrac{1}{\sqrt{2}}\,(\psi_1 - \psi_3) \\[4mm] \varphi_4 = \dfrac{1}{\sqrt{2}}\,(\psi_2 - \psi_4) \\[4mm] \varphi_6 = \dfrac{1}{\sqrt{2}}\,(\psi_5 - \psi_6) \end{array}\right\} \quad T_{1u}$$

Again, the reader should check the transformation of these combinations by using the O character table given in Appendix 1 (he will have to drop the g and u suffixes). The only point of real difficulty is the transformation of the two E_g orbitals under the C_3 rotation operations, where the character is -1. This is, in fact, the same problem as that discussed in Appendix 2, to which the reader should refer.

Appendix 5
Tanabe–Sugano
diagrams

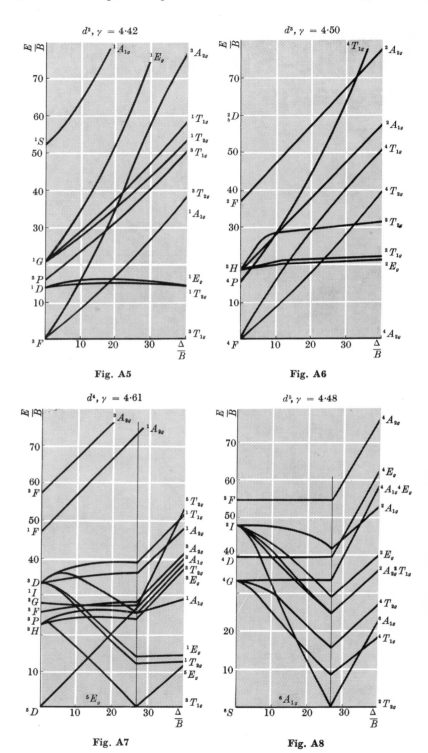

Fig. A5

Fig. A6

Fig. A7

Fig. A8

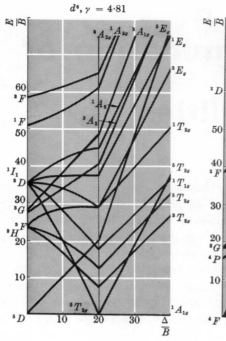

Fig. A9

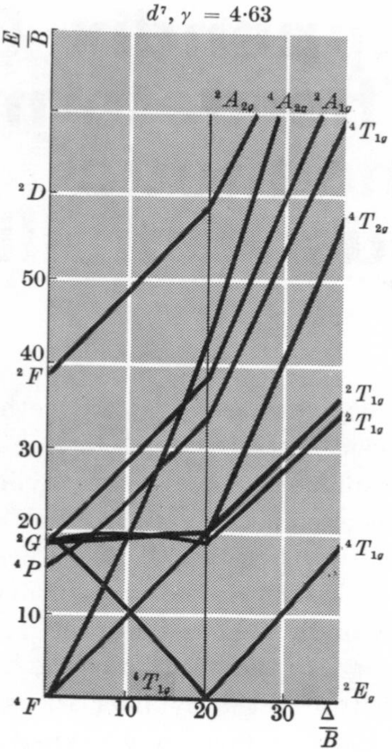

Fig. A10

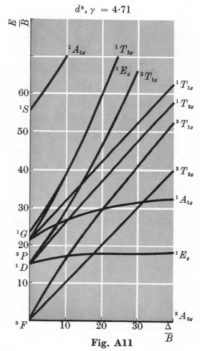

Fig. A11

Appendix 6
The determination of magnetic susceptibilities

We shall discuss the Gouy method for the determination of magnetic susceptibilities, the technique employed by the vast majority of coordination chemists. A cylinder of the complex under study is suspended between the poles of a magnet. The bottom of the cylinder is halfway between the two poles and on the inter-pole axis (Fig. A12). It is thus at the position of maximum field intensity. Ideally, this maximum field is constant within a small volume, so that small changes in the position of the bottom of the cylinder can be ignored. The top of the cylinder is, essentially, out of the magnetic field. In this way the cylinder experiences the full magnetic-field gradient, the observable quantity being an apparent change in weight of the sample when it is placed within the magnetic field (either by switching on an electromagnet or bringing up a permanent magnet). Paramagnetic materials are usually attracted into the magnetic field (an apparent weight increase), the only exception being when the inherent diamagnetism of the sample swamps its paramagnetism.

Experimentally, the sample is either a finely ground solid or a solution contained within a silica or Perspex (Lucite) tube. The sample length is usually from 5–10 cm and its diameter 2–10 mm. It is suspended from the beam of a balance in a suitable draught-proof enclosure. More complicated arrangements are used to study magnetic behaviour over a temperature range. The sample tube is filled to the same height for all measurements and, for solids, must be uniformly filled.

A compound with several unpaired electrons per molecule would be expected to show a greater paramagnetic effect than a compound with only one unpaired electron per molecule (assuming we studied the same number of molecules of each). That is, the quantity:

$$\frac{\text{weight increase in the field}}{\text{weight taken/molecular weight}} = \frac{\Delta w}{w/\mathrm{M}}$$

would be expected to be larger for the former. This quantity is proportional to the molar magnetic susceptibility of the compound:

$$\chi_M = \frac{\gamma \Delta w \cdot M}{w}$$

The constant of proportionality varies from apparatus to apparatus— the more powerful the magnet used, the greater Δw. Hence γ is called the 'tube calibration constant'; an explicit formula for it is given later. One slight alteration has to be made to the above formula: the sample tube is diamagnetic and will lose weight in

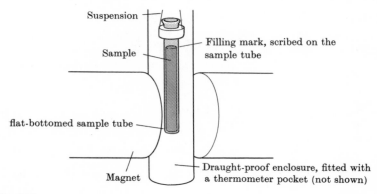

Suspension

Filling mark, scribed on the sample tube

Sample

flat-bottomed sample tube

Magnet

Draught-proof enclosure, fitted with a thermometer pocket (not shown)

Fig. A12

the field. The actual magnitude of this correction is determined by a trial run with the tube empty, when the weight drops by δ. δ (in milligrammes) must be added to the values obtained for Δw in the other measurements so as to make Δw more positive (or less negative). The corrected expression for χ_M is, then:

$$\chi_M = \frac{\gamma(\Delta w + \delta)M}{w}$$

It is convenient to measure Δw and δ in milligrammes and w in grammes. This, and multiplying γ by 10^3 (so that it is of the order of magnitude of unity), leads to the modified relationship:

$$10^6 \chi_M = \frac{\gamma(\Delta w + \delta)M}{w}$$

Note that this formula refers to the whole molecule. If we wish to find out how many unpaired electrons there are on the nickel ion in $NiSO_4 \cdot 7H_2O$ we must allow for the opposing diamagnetic effects arising from all the paired electrons present in the molecule. These effects are almost exactly additive and are listed for some of the more common chemical species in the following table.

Diamagnetic corrections $(g\text{-}atom^{-1})$
all values $\times 10^{-6}$ (Pascal's constants)

Li^+	1·0	F^-	9·1	H	2·93
Na^+	6·8	Cl^-	23·4	C	6·00
K^+	14·9	CN^-	13·0	N	1·54
NH_4^+	13·3	CNS^-	31·0	O	4·61
Fe^{2+}	12·8	SO_4^{2-}	40·1	S	15·0
Co^{2+}	12·8	CO_3^{2-}	29·5	P	26.3
Ni^{2+}	12·8	OH^-	12·0		

To make the correction one sums the appropriate values. For example, for $NiSO_4 \cdot 7H_2O$ the corrections are:

Ni^{2+} 12·8

SO_4^{2-} 40·1

$7H_2O = \underline{73\cdot3}\ [= 7 \times (2 \times 2\cdot93 + 4\cdot61)]$

$\underline{126\cdot2 \times 10^{-6}}$

The above figure (D, say) is then added to χ_M and the results is χ'_M, the susceptibility corrected for diamagnetism (denoted by the '). Hence:

$$\chi'_M = \chi_M + D$$

The diamagnetic corrections can be more elaborate than indicated above, but in practice, and particularly when a complicated ligand is involved, it is best to measure the diamagnetic correction, either directly on the ligand (using Pascal's constants for the remainder of the coordination compound) or by measuring the susceptibility of an analogous, but diamagnetic, complex.

$\mu_{eff.}$ is obtained from χ_M using a relationship derived in Chapter 8:

$$\mu_{eff.} = \sqrt{\frac{3R}{N^2\beta^2}}\sqrt{\chi'_M T} = 2\cdot83\sqrt{\chi'_M T}$$

$\mu_{eff.}$ can now be discussed by whichever approach is deemed appropriate. For example, if the 'spin only' formula is used, $\mu_{eff.} = \sqrt{(n(n+2))}$, then:

$$n(n+2) = 8\cdot07T\left[\frac{\gamma(\Delta w + \delta)\cdot M \times 10^{-6}}{w} + D\right]$$

Since $n = 0, 1, 2, 3, \ldots$, the left-hand side of this equation equals $0, 3, 8, 15 \ldots$

All that remains is to determine γ. There are two ways in which this can be done. The first, simplest and generally used, is to calibrate the apparatus using a standard. For $CuSO_4 \cdot 5H_2O$, for example, $\chi_M = 1{,}478 \times 10^{-6}$, although it is advisable to calibrate with several standards and take the average γ obtained. Alternatively, γ may be obtained from measurements on the tube and magnet, as follows.

The cylindrical sample used may be considered to consist of a stack of circular plates, each of thickness δs and area A. Across each plate, the magnitude of the magnetic field changes by δH. The force on the plate, δF, is produced by the interaction of the applied magnetic field with the magnetic moment induced within the sample. The latter is proportional to the applied magnetic field. The force on the plate is proportional to

(a) The applied magnetic field, H.

(b) The volume of the plate, $A \, \delta s$.

(c) The field gradient across the plate, $\delta H / \delta s$.

That is:

$$\delta F \propto H A \, \delta s \cdot \frac{\delta H}{\delta s}$$

In the limit:

$$\mathrm{d}F = \kappa A H \, \mathrm{d}H$$

where, provided we chose our units correctly, the constant of proportionality, κ, is the volume susceptibility of the substance under study. Integrating,

$$F = \tfrac{1}{2}\kappa A H^2 + \text{const.}$$

$F = 0$ at the upper edge of the sample (where $H = H_0$)

$$\therefore \quad F = \tfrac{1}{2}\kappa A (H^2 - H_0^2)$$

Since $F = \Delta w g$ (F in dynes) this may be rewritten:

$$\Delta w g = \tfrac{1}{2}\kappa A (H^2 - H_0^2)$$

If H_0 is negligible:

$$\Delta w g = \tfrac{1}{2}\kappa A H^2$$

$$\therefore \quad \kappa = \frac{2\Delta w g}{A H^2}$$

We now re-express this equation in terms of χ $(= \kappa/\rho)$ where ρ is the density of the substance and χ is the gram susceptibility:

$$\chi = \frac{2\Delta wg}{AH^2}\cdot\frac{1}{\rho} = \frac{2\Delta wg \cdot Al}{AH^2 w} \quad \text{where the length of the sample} = l$$

$$\therefore \quad \chi = \frac{2\Delta wgl}{wH^2}$$

Multiplying by the molecular weight of the substance M gives χ_M, the molar susceptibility:

$$\chi \cdot M = \chi_M = \frac{2gl}{H^2}\cdot\frac{\Delta wM}{w}$$

Comparison with the expression given earlier, remembering the factor 10^3, gives $\gamma = (2gl/H^2)\cdot 10^3$.

Further reading

Chapter 1

Werner centennial (Advances in chemistry series), American Chemical Society, Washington, 1967 (Articles 1 to 6 inclusive and, possibly, 7 also).

Chapter 2

Werner centennial (Advances in chemistry series), American Chemical Society, Washington, 1967 (Articles 11, 16, 20, 31, 36 and 37).

Chapter 3

Good sources are *Inorganic syntheses*, McGraw-Hill, New York, 1939 onwards (volumes have been published irregularly); W. G. PALMER *Experimental inorganic chemistry*, Cambridge, 1954; and G. BRAUER'S *Handbook of preparative inorganic chemistry* (2 vols), Academic Press, New York, 1965 (English translation). Article 36 of the *Werner centennial* volume (see the further reading references of chapters 1 or 2) contains a useful review of some methods applicable to multidentate ligands. Articles 17 and 18 are also relevant.

Chapter 4

A book by A. E. MARTELL and M. CALVIN, *Chemistry of the metal chelate compounds*, Prentice-Hall, Englewood Cliffs N.J., 1952, is easy to read. Much more difficult but more detailed is F. J. C. ROSSOTTI and H. ROSSOTTI, *The determination of stability constants*, McGraw-Hill, New York, 1961. The student will also find it helpful to read Article 19 of the *Werner centennial* volume (see the further reading references of chapters 1 or 2).

Chapter 5

Much of the material contained in this chapter is considered from a slightly different angle in Chapter 7 of B. N. FIGGIS, *Introduction to ligand fields*, Interscience, New York, 1966. However, the next step is really to become much more mathematical. Complementary accounts will be found in J. N. MURRELL, S. F. A. KETTLE and J. M. TEDDER, *Valence theory*, Wiley, London, 1965, Chapter 13, and T. M. DUNN, D. S. McCLURE and R. G. PEARSON, *Crystal-field theory*, Harper and Row and John Weatherhill, New York and Tokyo, 1965. Following these, the student will probably be able to tackle a book by C. J. BALLHAUSEN, *Introduction to ligand-field theory*, McGraw-Hill, 1962.

Chapter 6

All of the references given for chapter 5 contain sections on ligand field theory.

Chapter 7

All of the references given for chapter 5 contain sections on spectra. In addition, there is an excellent review by D. S. McCLURE in *Solid state physics*, 1959, **9**, 400. A. B. P. LEVER, in article 29 of the *Werner centennial* volume (see references for chapters 1 and 2), discusses the calculation of Δ (i.e. $10Dq$) values.

Chapter 8

There are few easy-to-read-articles on magnetism available and the author finds that he does best if he reads the corresponding sections of different accounts in parallel. The books by DUNN *et al.*, FIGGIS and BALLHAUSEN (see the further reading references for chapter 5) all discuss magnetism. A recent book, A. EARNSHAW, *Introduction to magnetochemistry*, Academic Press, London, 1968, should be mentioned, as should a review by B. J. FIGGIS and J. LEWIS in *Progress in inorganic chemistry*, 1964, **6**, 37.

Chapter 9

Few detailed accounts of the spectroscopic methods discussed in this chapter make easy reading. Perhaps the best advice that can be given the student is both to read the accounts of any method in which he is interested mentioned below and also to use them as a source of other references. He should read each article until he is lost and then pass on to the next (on the same subject!). After going round and round the whole set several times he should begin to see the light. Useful 'starter' articles are to be found in the *Werner centennial* volume (see the further reading for chapters 1 or 2), articles 24, 25, 26, and 27, and in H. A. O. HILL and P. DAY, *Physical methods in advanced inorganic chemistry*, Interscience, New York, 1968. Most review journals of inorganic or coordination chemistry will be found to have articles on several of the topics discussed in this chapter.

Chapter 10

The books by DUNN *et al.* and FIGGIS are recommended (see the further reading section of chapter 5), particularly the latter (however, there appears to be an error in Table 5-10 of the book by Figgis which leads this author to some conclusions at variance with ours).

Chapter 11

The Langford–Grey nomenclature is detailed in their book, *Ligand substitution processes*, Benjamin, New York, 1965. Other books which deserve mention are A. G. SYKES, *Kinetics of inorganic reactions*,

Pergamon, Oxford, 1966; J. O. EDWARDS, *Inorganic reaction mechanisms*, Benjamin, New York, 1964. Two important, more advanced, works are both titled *Mechanisms of inorganic reactions*, the first by F. BASOLO and R. G. PEARSON, Wiley, New York, 1967, and the second an American Chemical Society publication, 1965, R. F. GOULD (editor). A recent review is by McAuley and Hill in *Quarterly reviews* (of the London Chemical Society), 1969, page 18.

Index